The Judge

THE JUDGE

THE LIFE & OPINIONS OF ALABAMA'S FRANK M. JOHNSON, JR.

▲

By Frank Sikora

Introduction by
Hon. William J. Brennan

The Black Belt Press
Montgomery

The Black Belt Press
P.O. Box 551
Montgomery, AL 36101

Printed in the United States of America.

LIBRARY OF CONGRESS CATALOGING-IN-PUBLICATION DATA

Sikora, Frank, 1936-
    The Judge: the life & opinions of Alabama's
            Frank M. Johnson, Jr.
    / by Frank Sikora : introduction by William J. Brennan.
    p. cm.
    Includes index.
    ISBN 0-9622815-9-X : $32.50
1. Johnson, Frank Minis, 1918– . 2. Judges—Alabama—Biogra-
    phy. 3. Civil Rights—Alabama—Cases. 4. Civil Rights—
    United States—History. I. Title.
KF373.J55S55 1992
347.73'14'092—dc20
[B]
[347.30714092]
[B]   92-19155
                    CIP

All photographs are courtesy of the Johnson Family
and the *Birmingham News*.

Book design and composition by Randall Williams
Copyediting and indexing by George Littleton

To Millie,
with love forever.

CONTENTS

Preface

THE Civil Rights Movement that erupted in the South during the 1950s and 1960s was the most important domestic event in America since the Civil War. While much of the history of that movement was recorded in the streets of cities like Birmingham, Atlanta, Selma, and Montgomery, an equally dramatic and more far-reaching set of events was unfolding in federal courtrooms in some of these same Southern cities.

Dr. Martin Luther King, Jr., led the black drive for civil rights, but the changes he sought came in legal opinions issued by federal judges. Foremost of these was Frank Minis Johnson, Jr., of Montgomery, Alabama, who presided over some of the most emotional hearings and trials of the rights movement . . . hearings brimming with dramatic and poignant testimony from the black people who cried out for the freedoms that are the legacy of all Americans. The black petition for full freedom began in Montgomery in Johnson's court, and it would end in this city, also before Judge Johnson. Somewhat ironically, Montgomery, which had been the "Cradle of the Confederacy" prior to the Civil War, became the "Soul of the Civil Rights Movement" in 1955, the year Johnson became a federal judge.

This work covers many of the notable cases: the Montgomery Bus Boycott, the Freedom Riders, school desegregation, the Selma-to-Montgomery march, and the Ku Klux Klan conspiracy case in the night-rider slaying of Viola Liuzzo.

While many of his civil rights decisions angered most white Alabamians as well as other white Southerners, the judge never allowed public opinion to sway his resolve to issue opinions that were anchored in the Constitution and its statutes. During that tumultuous time Johnson was often threatened and he was besieged with hate mail and harassing telephone calls. When his mother's home was bombed in 1967, it was obviously a mistake — the bomber or bombers believed the judge lived there.

An Alabama lawyer once remarked that whenever he saw Judge Johnson, he immediately thought of Abraham Lincoln. It is an accurate comparison, one shared by many who know of Johnson. Indeed, it can be said that what Lincoln was to the Civil War, Johnson was to the Civil Rights Movement. Lincoln freed the slaves; Johnson forged a trail to bring the last measure of full freedom to the grandchildren of those slaves. President Lyndon Johnson once remarked, "I wouldn't have to be president, if my name was *Frank* Johnson."

Like Lincoln, Judge Johnson was from the hill country, not of Kentucky, but Northwest Alabama. More precisely, Winston County, Alabama. He was tall and rangy, and spoke with that twang that is common to that part of the state, a section that, during the upheaval of the Civil War, stood staunchly loyal to Lincoln and the United States.

When Johnson was named to the federal judgeship in Montgomery in November 1955, he almost immediately became a man viewed with some awe, as though destined to be legend. His crisp, no-nonsense courtroom manner became the stuff of which folklore is made: Lawyers were cautious talking to him; news reporters approached him with great trepidation. There was an aura of frontier justice about the man; it was often said that when Johnson looked at you, it was though he was aiming down the barrel of a rifle. He was a tough judge. Yet, he was always fair, and his even-handed manner of handling cases was sometimes seasoned with a dash of humor and compassion.

The interviews that form the basis of this book began in August 1976 and ended in January of 1989. Johnson didn't like tape recorders, so yellow legal pads were used to take notes. The interviews will always be among my most cherished memories: The judge would sit at his desk, lean back in the swivel chair, awaiting the first question. When it was asked, he would pause, open the desk door, take out a pack of Levi Garrett chewing tobacco, study for a moment, take the chaw, then slowly drawl, "Well . . ." And then he'd start to talk about civil rights, or human rights, or voting, or George Wallace, or the Ku Klux Klan, or Martin Luther King. Sometimes as he pondered a question, he would stand, walk to the window and gaze out.

Much of the book is almost autobiographical, direct quotes from Johnson as best I could record them. In 1989, he read the quotes for accuracy and made numerous changes, adding much material in some sections and deleting from other areas. He did not read the open narrative for accuracy and any errors are the fault of the author.

There are many people I wish to thank for helping in the preparation of this work. They include, first and foremost, my wife, Millie, and our children and other family members.

Also, Sue Cronkite of Dothan, who helped edit the original version; Pauline Jackson of Montgomery who typed it; Johnson's niece, Roseanna Whiteside, of Birmingham, and her husband, David; Tom Scarritt, Clarke Stallworth, Charlotte Painter, Melvis McKay, Veronica Pike Kennedy, Jeff Hansen, Scottie Vickery, Carolyn Angel, Lori Chandler, Haywood Paravicini, Nathan Turner Jr., Waylon Smithey, Oliver Roosevelt, Al Fox, Jerry Ayres, Richard Jaffe,Walter Bryant, John Henley, Tom Bailey, Jim Lunsford, Jo Strong and Jean Self, all of Birmingham; Dr. Bob McClung of Pell City; Gillis Morgan, Auburn; Dr. Jack Kirschenfeld, Cindy Cox, George Littleton and Randall Williams, Montgomery.

Much credit is due Mrs. Dorothy Perry, who served as the judge's secretary. She never lost her sense of humor or her patience during thirteen years of telephone calls, setting up appointments, and providing background material.

I also want to thank all the people who worked in the office of the United States Clerk in Montgomery, especially MarieThurman, Jane Gordon, Thomas Caver, Ridge Lint, Hunter Slaton and Robert L. Duncan, Jr. And the help of court reporter Glynn Henderson was invaluable.

A number of Judge Johnson's clerks were also of help,

among them Syd Fuller, Deborah Ellis, Lane Heard and Neil McKittrick.

Finally, the book would have fallen short had it not been for the help of the judge's wife, Ruth Johnson. And it would not have been written at all had not Judge Johnson himself provided so much time with the author. He was not only the interviewee, but also the counselor.

America needed Johnson during the 1950s and 1960s, just as surely as the nation needed Lincoln in 1861. The sad thing about Johnson's story, indeed the sad thing for America, is that he was never elevated to the Supreme Court. But even there, it is not likely he could have done more than he had already accomplished as a federal district judge in Montgomery.

Frank Sikora
Birmingham, Ala.

Introduction

By Justice William J. Brennan, Jr. (retired)

FRANK Johnson is a remarkable man and a remarkable judge. He was born and raised in the segregated South, and he remains to this day a loyal son of Alabama. Yet beginning with the first days of his tenure as a federal district judge in Montgomery, Judge Johnson issued a series of decisions that invoked federal authority to dismantle the system of official segregation and to require the overhaul of many state institutions and programs. These decisions, to put it mildly, were originally unpopular with many Alabamians. Indeed, Judge Johnson was subjected to ostracism by his community, vituperative abuse by press and politicians, innumerable death threats, and an attempt on his life that nearly killed his mother. Still, Judge Johnson decided the cases before him as he did, for the simple reason that the Constitution and laws of the United States required him to do so.

Frank Sikora's book admirably tells the story of Judge Johnson's courageous decisions. Deftly weaving the Judge's reflections on those times together with reports of the proceedings as they unfolded, Sikora situates Judge Johnson's decisions in a turbulent period of our history and offers the reader insight into the character of this outstanding jurist.

Judge Johnson's most notable decisions run the gamut of

civil rights issues and are inscribed in the defining events of an era. In May 1956, just six months after he became a federal judge, the case of *Browder* v. *Gayle* required Johnson to determine the constitutionality of a Montgomery ordinance requiring racially segregated seating on city buses — the ordinance whose enforcement was, at that moment, the focus of the Montgomery bus boycott that brought Martin Luther King to national prominence.

Two years later, Judge Johnson squared off against his law school acquaintance, Governor George Wallace, over Wallace's refusal to turn over voting records to federal authorities. The two did battle again in *Lee* v. *Macon County Board of Education*, when Wallace attempted to close down Tuskegee High School rather than comply with Judge Johnson's desegregation order. Judge Johnson was further called upon to adjudicate a dispute arising out of a vicious attack on the "Freedom Riders" in Montgomery. And in 1965, Judge Johnson was required to decide whether, and under what conditions, the famous Selma to Montgomery march could take place; later that year he presided over the criminal trial of four Klansmen who had shot and killed a participant in the march. Judge Johnson's decisions in each of these cases are all the more remarkable, considering that each concerned highly charged political events.

As Frank Sikora points out in this book, several of Judge Johnson's later decisions, while less visible to national observers, may have been equally important in enforcing federal constitutional rights. Four such decisions come to mind.

In *Wyatt* v. *Stickney* (1971), Judge Johnson ruled that the Alabama institutions housing the mentally ill and mentally retarded had failed to satisfy constitutional requirements. Similarly, he held in *James* v. *Wallace* (1974) that Alabama's prison system violated the constitutional guarantee against cruel and unusual punishment. The conditions of both mental institutions and prisons were, by any standard, truly hideous. Although Judge Johnson's decisions in *Wyatt* and particularly in *James* were much-criticized within Alabama as judicial overreaching, the fact of the matter is that the state had for years ignored its duty to maintain adequate facilities for those civilly committed or convicted of crime, and it would have continued to do so had

Judge Johnson not ordered the state to live up to constitutional requirements.

A third important case decided by Judge Johnson concerned racially discriminatory hiring by the Alabama state government. In *United States* v. *Frazer* (1970), the Judge ruled that the state had unlawfully discriminated in its hiring of support staff. He extended this ruling in *NAACP* v. *Allen* (1972) to the Alabama State Troopers. The latter ruling was particularly controversial, not just because the State Troopers had been the symbol of white power during earlier civil rights struggles, but also because Johnson adopted an explicit quota, ordering that at least one black be appointed for each white until the Troopers were 25% black. After fourteen years of state footdragging and further court proceedings, the Supreme Court approved this remedy in 1986. Judge Johnson's insistence that the state live up to the demands of the Constitution in hiring and promoting official employees served as a powerful symbol of the new order taking hold in the South.

The fourth opinion I want to mention is Judge Johnson's dissent in *Frontiero* v. *Laird* (1972). The issue in that case was whether the Army had unconstitutionally discriminated against a woman army lieutenant by refusing to pay certain spousal benefits unless she could prove that her husband was actually dependent upon her. (The Army simply presumed that a soldier's wife was dependent upon her husband.) Two members of a three-judge panel upheld this rule. Judge Johnson's dissenting opinion was soon vindicated, however, when the Supreme Court agreed with him that the Army's rule was unconstitutional. Johnson's position is particularly remarkable, since it was not until the year before that the Supreme Court found gender discrimination to raise any significant constitutional problem whatsoever.

Frank Sikora's rich account of the proceedings in which Judge Johnson reached these decisions shows a judge who is firm, always in control of his courtroom, and unwilling to condone attorneys who have failed to prepare or who employ improper tactics. Perhaps the greatest testimony to his courtroom manner is that even those who have not prevailed before him have still acknowledged that they received a fair hearing conducted by a superb judge. Frank Johnson is also a savvy judge: While firmly committed to constitutional principle, he is aware that the strength of a decision is its enforceability. This principled yet realistic attitude toward the judicial process, I think, was absolutely essential in a time and place where the powerful seemed disdainful of the law.

ð   ð   ð

In most of the cases considered in this book, Judge Johnson was charged with interpreting and enforcing general provisions of the Constitution that were drafted long ago and have sometimes proved difficult to apply to circumstances that the Framers could never have anticipated. But for Judge Johnson, as for myself, this difficulty is not a weakness of the Constitution, but precisely its genius. "The strength of the Constitution," Judge Johnson has said, "lies in its flexibility, in its need to change and respond to the special needs of society at a particular time.... What has made it endure is the American people's love of liberty, and the willingness of courts to uphold it — most of the time — regardless of the consequences."

These words, I think, express the greatness not just of the Constitution, but of Judge Johnson. I am proud to count Frank Johnson as my friend. I cannot imagine the state of our civil liberties without him. And I am delighted that Frank Sikora has seen fit to honor him with this book.

The Judge

Part I

'Walk together children...'

The Montgomery
Bus Boycott
1955

1

WEDNESDAY, MARCH 2, 1955, was balmy and spring-like in Montgomery; the magnolia trees were in bloom, and around the Alabama State Capitol building, jonquils lined the winding sidewalks. But the sun was hazed by gathering clouds that signalled rain or thundershowers by nightfall. That afternoon, as usual, black students from Booker T. Washington High School stood along the cobblestone streets downtown waiting to catch a bus home. Among them was Claudette Colvin, a sophomore, age fifteen, a slim girl standing five-foot-three and weighing about one hundred and fifteen pounds.

She boarded the Highland Avenue bus, made her way to the back, noting the seats for "Colored" were full. However, the last seat in the "White" section was vacant. She hesitated a moment, then suddenly sat down there. A short time later, a pregnant black woman named Hamilton followed and sat beside her.

It didn't take the driver, Robert Cleer, long to spot them in the rear view mirror. He ordered them to stand and let a white woman have the seat. In those days, Southern bus drivers had almost as much power as police officers. But on this day, the two blacks remained in the seat.

Angered, Cleer parked the bus and summoned police. Minutes later officers Paul Headley and T. J. Ward came aboard and made their way down the aisle. After some exchange of words, a black man stood and Mrs. Hamilton moved and took his seat in the "Colored" section. Miss Colvin, however, remained. The officers warned her that she was in violation of state and city codes which declared there was to be segregated seating ("It's the law," one of them said.)

Still, she didn't move. Then, according to the police report filed later, she "struggled and kicked and scratched" as they forcibly pulled her from the seat and removed her from the bus. Sobbing, she was handcuffed and taken to jail.

The incident had occurred near the heart of downtown, called Court Square. It was just down the street from the imposing Capitol where Jefferson Davis had been inaugurated president of the Confederacy. The square had once been the site of the county courthouse; a century earlier, it had been the city's main slave auction block.

Miss Colvin was booked, held in jail for a short time, then released on bond. She would later be tried in city court, found guilty and placed on probation, a ward of the state.

Her solitary protest on that bus had come nearly a century after a civil war and laws that were supposed to give black people full freedom. It would be the first salvo of what would become a legal-social revolution. The Thirteenth, Fourteenth and Fifteenth Amendments of the Constitution had ended slavery, given blacks citizenship and the right to vote. Yet, one decision by the Supreme Court of the United States effectively froze those laws and the rights they carried.

It was the 1896 case styled *Plessy vs. Ferguson* in which the court upheld the State of Louisiana's right to segregate its public transportation facilities. But far more sweeping was the doctrinal trend it carried — separate but equal.

That case allowed Southern politicians and Southern society to oppress blacks along every avenue of day-to-day life, restraining them as second-class citizens. "Separate but equal" became the misguided beacon for life in the South and would go unchallenged for more than half a century.

But Miss Colvin, the school girl, would contest it, and so would others after her. Her action was the beginning of what would become the most dramatic American story in the post-

Civil War century. This plaintive cry for full freedom was not unlike that which had sparked the War Between the States nearly a hundred years before. And the backlash against it would be much the same as the terror that flamed across the Southern states during Reconstruction.

At the time, it seemed unlikely that Miss Colvin's arrest could in any way be affected by Frank Minis Johnson, Jr., then thirty-six years old. Johnson was a resident of Jasper, a coalmining town in Walker County. He was also the United States Attorney for the Northern District of Alabama, with his main office in Birmingham. Montgomery

RIGHT, Claudette Colvin, in a photo taken when she was about 13. BELOW, Frank M. Johnson, Jr., in his Jasper law office soon after World War II, before his appointment as U.S. Attorney.

was in the Middle District, out of his territory. Johnson was a
tall, rangy man, standing six-foot-two and weighing a hundred
and eighty pounds. He had thick brown hair which sometimes
fell over his right forehead; the cheekbones were high, the jaw
firm; his nose was long and hawklike; his brown eyes were
narrow and piercing, glinting darkly when he was riled, twin-
kling when he found something amusing. There was something
of the frontier about the man. He liked country music and buck
dancing. He hated hunting, but loved to spend a cool spring
morning fishing.

Like most attorneys, he knew change was coming across
the land. The year before, in May of 1954, the U.S. Supreme
Court had decided in *Brown vs. Board of Education* that racial
segregation in the public school systems was unconstitutional.
It would only be a matter of time, he felt, before the effects of that
ruling would cut across the entire social, political and economic
fiber of the country.

Johnson hadn't heard the first thing about the arrest of the
black girl on the Montgomery bus. But fate would put Johnson
and Miss Colvin on a course that would ignite the start of
dramatic change to the Southern way of life.

On June 6, 1955, U.S. District Judge Charles Kennamer of
Montgomery, the lone judge in the state's Middle District, died
at the age of eighty-four. Almost from that instant rumors began
that Johnson would be considered to fill the vacancy. A few days
later he received a telephone call from the Republican party
chairman in Alabama, Claude Vardaman, who asked if he would
be interested in the job. Johnson said he would be.

JOHNSON

At that time I was a rather scarce item in Alabama —
a Republican. My family came from Winston County, in
the northwest section of the state, a county which had
historic ties with the GOP dating back to the Civil War.
We were what I call Lincoln Republicans. I had played a
small part in politics; I hadn't sought any elected office
myself. When Dwight Eisenhower ran for president in
1952, I had headed the Alabama Veterans for Ike and had
been a campaign worker for him. In the national conven-

tion in 1948, I had been a delegate.

When Ike was elected president, he chose me in 1953 to be the United States Attorney for Alabama's Northern District. I had not planned to make a career of federal service. I figured I'd be back in private practice in a few years. But when the judgeship came open, it put a different slant on my future. It was a lifetime appointment. Most lawyers desire, I think, to be a federal judge. I was no different.

On September 26, 1955, Eisenhower suffered a heart attack while in Colorado; things like naming federal judges took a back seat. Then, on a Saturday night in late October, Johnson received a telephone call at his home in Jasper, Alabama, about forty miles northwest of Birmingham. The caller was a reporter from the *Birmingham News*.

"Mr. Johnson," the reporter said, "we have an AP story out of Denver here that says President Eisenhower has named you the federal judge for the Middle District of Alabama. We want to know what your reaction is."

"I haven't heard a thing," Johnson said. "You guys know more than I do."

"It's an authentic story," the reporter said.

"Well, if it's true, then you can just say that I am very pleased," Johnson said.

The following Monday, the Justice Department called him to confirm the report. The job was his. He was asked when he could take over and he replied, "I'll go to Montgomery as soon as I can, but I still have one very important bank robbery case up in Anniston to be prosecuted."

On November 7, 1955, eight days after he had turned thirty-seven, Johnson and his wife, Ruth, and their son, Johnny, eight, whom they had adopted at infancy, drove to Montgomery for the ceremony inducting him as a federal judge.

A city of 123,000, Montgomery was the heart of the Alabama Black Belt, the old plantation section curving across the middle of the state from Georgia to Mississippi, an area where cotton was still king. In the autumn months, before the harvest was complete, the cotton looked like snow lying on the repos-

The Johnson family, in a photo taken about 1952. They named their adopted son James Curtis Johnson, but he was best known as Johnny.

ing, amber meadows. On the low horizon were narrow hard-wood thickets, aging fences and stately mansions which contrasted sharply with the shanties where the black tenants lived.

Most of those blacks, as well as those living in places like Selma, Union Springs, Marion and Tuskegee, could not vote, could not serve on juries, could not run for political office, could not get a Coca-Cola at a soda fountain and drink it there, had separate but unequal water fountains and restrooms at public places, and could not go to the same school with white children, not to mention that they had to ride in the back of public buses and stand while white people sat.

In Alabama and other Southern states, "separate but equal" was more than a malady in the education system: it was woven through the entire fabric of life, touching every aspect of society. Johnson was not sure the nation would ever really comprehend what it did to the black people who endured it all those years. Slavery might have ended nearly ninety years earlier, but in 1955 the black people living below the Mason-Dixon Line truly were not free....

JOHNSON

I took the oath of office at 10 a.m. that day. Ruth and Johnny stayed for lunch, then drove back to our home in Jasper. Until school was out and we could buy a home in Montgomery, I would stay with my parents who had lived in Montgomery since World War Two, and Ruth and Johnny would stay in Jasper.

There was concern among the local people about me being the new judge; the Montgomery newspapers referred to me as an outsider, "a foreigner" from the hill country of Northwest Alabama; even called me a Yankee.

It went back to my Winston County heritage. During the Civil War, Winston had refused to fight against the Union and had, in effect, "seceded" from the State of Alabama. Most of the men there and in Fayette County, including great-grandfather James Johnson, had fought for the Union. Only a few people in Winston had owned any slaves. When I was growing up in the 1920s and 1930s, I remember only about a dozen black families in the whole county, so the caste system that marked much of life in the South was not a part of my upbringing. I just never thought about it in terms of racial discrimination (even though the few black children who lived there were not able to send their children to the same school with whites).

He was still getting settled into the new job when the sputtering fuse lighted by Claudette Colvin's arrest ignited a powder keg of human discontent.

2

ON THURSDAY, DECEMBER 1, 1955, less than a month after Johnson had become a federal judge, there was another incident on a Montgomery city bus. A woman named Rosa Parks, forty-two, was arrested after she refused to stand and give her seat to a white man. It was the final straw as far as black people were concerned. Overnight the word crackled like electricity across the city that some action was imminent. By Saturday, December 3, leaflets were being circulated in Negro neighborhoods reading, "Don't ride the bus on Monday."

At churches that Sunday morning, ministers called from the pulpit for the people to unite and "walk in dignity rather than ride in shame ...." After generations of segregation, something in the soul and heart of black Southerners had stirred. As one minister told his people, "This is God's movement."

It would prove to be a brilliant strategy, using the churches and the religious approach, especially so in the Deep South where the church was such a part of life for black people. In its Sunday editions, *The Montgomery Advertiser* ran a front-page story headlined "Negro Groups Ready Boycott of City Lines." (Carried as an expose, the story actually helped spread the word of the action to those black people who might not have gone to church or otherwise heard the word).

The boycott was the brainchild of E. D. Nixon, a tall, muscular man who was head of the Sleeping Car Porters Union and an NAACP official. He had signed bond to get Mrs. Parks out of jail, after obtaining legal guidance from white attorney Clifford Durr. Durr and his wife, Virginia, had accompanied him to the police station that night. When Nixon told his wife about the plans to boycott, she skeptically replied, "Cold as it is?"

On Monday morning, December 5, the city editor of *The Advertiser,* Joe Azbell, drove to downtown before five-thirty a.m. to see if the boycott would develop. He chose Court Square as the likely place . . . also the place with historic ties.

A misting rain glazed the streets; the wind, raw and whistling, rattled signs and rustled the Christmas decorations. Across the street was the National Shirt Factory, the building from where, in 1861, the Provisional Confederate government had wired the orders to troops in South Carolina to open fire on Fort Sumter.

Azbell spotted a solitary black man walking toward him. The man stopped by a shed adorned with a sign printed in crude lettering: "Remember it is for our cause that you do not ride the buses today."

Finally, from around the corner, one of the yellow buses came, easing down the brick-and-stone cobbled street. It stopped. The door opened. Azbell watched in fascination as one of the pivotal moments in the fledgling Civil Rights Movement began to unfold. The black man stood tensely in the moist chill, staring at the white bus driver.

"You gonna get on?" the driver asked.

Silence.

Again: "You gonna get on?"

"I ain't gettin' on," the man shot back, "until Jim Crow gets off."

For a moment there was no reaction from the driver; then, suddenly, he tilted his head back, roaring with laughter. The bus lumbered off. Azbell would later lament that he failed to get the name of either man. As a gray, somber dawn broke, the story was the same: buses would roll to a halt, the door would open, clusters of Negro men and women, some clutching brown paper bags, would stand stoically in the wind. The buses would roll away empty.

Some of the Negroes took taxi cabs or caught rides with

people they knew. Most waited. Or walked. Then, around 7:30
a.m., the makeshift bus system devised by the newly formed
Montgomery Improvement Association — headed by the Reverend Martin Luther King, Jr., — swung into action.

That same day, in city court, Mrs. Parks was found guilty; it
was appealed to the state court system.

Johnson's view of the boycott was limited. He saw scores of
blacks walking as he drove to work in the mornings, huddled in
the chill, waiting for a ride. And he read newspaper accounts of
their rallies at the churches. The national press was already
taking note of the Reverend King, then only twenty-seven.

The judge told his wife that the issue was bound to come
before him, sooner or later. It didn't take a crystal ball to know
that. He would see his wife on weekends, driving to Jasper every
Friday night and staying until Sunday night. The Johnsons still
hadn't found a house in Montgomery.

As 1956 began, the boycott movement continued; the transit system, minus about thirty-thousand black riders each day,
slipped into a precarious financial position. White resistance
began to stiffen; King and about a hundred other black ministers were arrested for violating an Alabama anti-boycott law.
Mrs. Parks, meanwhile, went before Montgomery County Circuit Judge Eugene Carter and was found guilty. Said the judge:
"And the defendant, asked why this sentence should not be
pronounced upon her, says nothing." She was given fifty-six
days of hard labor.

But the sentence was put on hold because, on February
1,1956, attorneys for Claudette Colvin — the teenage girl arrested the year before — and other black women, came to the
federal building and filed suit challenging the state's segregation code which required separate seating on buses. The case
would be styled *Browder vs. Gayle*, after Mrs. Aurelia Browder,
a black woman made to stand on a bus, and W. A. Gayle,
Montgomery's mayor.

JOHNSON

That same day I wrote Judge Joseph Hutchenson,
the chief judge of the U. S. Fifth Circuit, telling him a state
law was being challenged which would require a panel of

three judges to hear it. He must have thought me brash; a few days later he wrote back, brusquely noting that "it doesn't take a three-judge panel to hear a matter of local law." I sat down and fired off another letter, telling him the State of Alabama's segregation laws were overriding the city's bus segregation ordinance.

Hutchenson shot back a tersely worded message which, in effect, said "I beg to differ with you about the state's role." He told me to hear the case alone.

Finally, after a third letter, one which ran three pages single-spaced, the judge relented, agreeing that it would take a three-judge panel. He named Appellate Judge Richard Rives of Montgomery and District Judge Seybourn Lynne of Birmingham to hear it with me.

Hutchenson seemed to take a dim view of all my requests; when I had written him seeking permission to hire a law clerk, he popped back a quick reply: "You haven't been out of law school long enough to need a law clerk."

When the bus boycott began, the Reverend King and others pointed out the abusive treatment they had been subjected to on the Montgomery buses.

There were cases of pregnant black women being forced to stand. Negroes were expected to have the exact change; if they didn't, irate drivers often told them to get off.

There was the incident where a young Negro woman boarded with two small children and, while she hurriedly rummaged through her purse for change, had placed the youngsters in the front seat. The driver ordered her to move them. She asked for a few seconds. In anger, he sent the bus forward, sending the woman off balance. Then, he braked to a sudden halt; it threw the children out of the seat and onto the floor. In humiliation, the woman picked them up and asked to be let off.

Blacks, after paying their fare, were often told to leave the front entrance and enter through the second door, located about halfway back. There were cases, they said, where the driver would hurry away before they could get to the second entry point, leaving them on the sidewalk, minus their money.

But Claudette Colvin had challenged the system and so had Rosa Parks. On their behalf, and others similarly situated, the case had come to the federal court. It was set to be heard May 11, 1956.

Several days before, Judge Lynne came to Montgomery to join Judge Rives and Judge Johnson in preparation for the hearing.

In the meantime, the city of Montgomery had filed suit in state court asking that segregation laws be declared in force (this after the Chicago-based firm that owned the local transit system said it wanted to end segregated seating).

Montgomery County Circuit Judge Walter B. Jones — whose father Thomas Goode Jones, had carried the white truce flag at Appomattox — quickly issued a ruling, saying segregation was the law in Montgomery. Rives, Lynne and Johnson were going to lunch that day (May 9) when they saw the headlines in the *Alabama Journal*.

In his ruling, Judge Jones had said, "Where in the United States Constitution is there one word, one sentence, one paragraph that says . . . the sovereign states cannot make reasonable rules pertaining to the separation of the races in public transportation?"

The three federal judges read the story with interest, then put it aside for lunch.

3

MAY 11, 1956, THE DAY OF THE HEARING.
It was a sparkling morning; the magnolia trees near the entrance of the federal building shimmered in the sunlight. Blacks began gathering in front before 8 a.m. Most were tall, spare men in dark suits, and women in their Sunday dresses.

Johnson was joined in his chambers by Judges Rives and Lynne. Rives, the senior judge, was a member of the U.S. Fifth Circuit Court of Appeals. A minute or so after 9 a.m. a U.S. marshal popped his head in the door and asked, "Ready, your honors?"

Rives nodded. "Let's go," he said, beckoning for Lynne and Johnson to follow to the courtroom. They took their seats behind the sturdy oak bench, which measured about twenty feet in length. Johnson sat on the left, nearest the witness stand; Lynne was on the right, and Rives in the middle. As they waited, some of the spectators were still filing in.

It wasn't that large of a courtroom, with room for about two hundred. Johnson saw people shooting hurried glances over the place. The walls were beige, the drapes a pale yellow; the windows were high, the carpeting a soft green. Behind the judges' bench was a clock with Roman numerals, set against a backing of blue draping adorned with silver stars.

Within the restraining rail, NAACP attorneys Fred Gray

and Charles Langford of Montgomery, and Charles Carter of
New York, watched the crowd fill the seats. Across from them,
Montgomery city attorney Walter Knabe, a short, slim man with
close-cropped sandy hair, studied his notes. Also defending the
City of Montgomery and State of Alabama were Truman Hobbs,
who years later would become a federal judge, and Alabama
Attorney General John Patterson, who would later be governor.
Rives read the complaint. Then he turned to Gray and said, "Call
your first witness." Aurelia Browder, a widow, was thirty-four, a
nurse's aide, the mother of four, and a student at Alabama State
University.

"Would you state your name, please?" Gray asked.

"Aurelia Browder."

"Where do you live, Miss Browder?"

"I live at Ten-twelve Highland Avenue."

"Prior to December fifth, did you live here in Montgomery?"

"Yes."

"And prior to that date did you ride the city buses?"

"Yes. Sometimes two or three times a day."

"Have you been riding the buses since December fifth?"

"No."

"Why did you stop riding them?"

"I had stopped riding because I wanted better treatment. I
knew if I would cooperate with my color, I would finally get it."

"Have you experienced any difficulty on the bus in connection with the seating arrangements?"

"Yes," she answered, nodding for emphasis. "Several times
I have."

"Will you please tell the court what happened?"

She replied, "April twenty-nine of last year and I was on the
Day Street bus. I got a transfer from Oak Park bus in front of
Price Drug Store. I was going to get off and go to the dry cleaner,
where I would get out on Court and Day. After I rode up by the
Alabama Gas Company the bus driver had three of us to get up
and stand and let a white man and a white lady sit down."

"When you say three of you, do you mean yourself and . . .
along with two other Negroes?"

"Myself and two other Negroes," she said. "I was sitting in

a seat and another lady beside me and the seat just across from me there was just one colored person in there. And he made all three of us get up because he said we was in the white section of the bus."

Gray nodded. "If you were permitted to sit any place you wanted on the bus, would you ride . . . would be willing to ride it again?"

"Yes, I would."

"That is all."

Rives glanced at Knabe. "You may cross examine."

The Montgomery city attorney, a soft-spoken sort, rose, paused for a moment while he scanned his notes, then moved forward slowly, rolling a pencil in his hands. "You say you stopped riding the buses about December the fifth, 1955, is that correct?"

"Yes sir."

"And I believe you said you stopped riding at that time . . . because you wanted better treatment, is that correct?"

"That is right."

Knabe strolled about, his eyes on the floor. "It is a fact, is it not, that at that time the Reverend King and several others so-called Improvement Association, I believe, made such a demand? Is that right?"

"No." She shook her head slightly.

"They did make some request, did they not?"

"I would not call it that."

"What would you call it then?"

"We, the Negroes," she said, clasping her hands tightly in her lap, "request the Reverend King, and he not over us."

Knabe shrugged. "You didn't understand my question. Did Negro King ask three certain things at that time, did he not? One was, you said, for more courteous treatment on the part of the bus drivers. That is correct, isn't it?"

"That is correct."

"And you then asked for seating first come, first served, didn't you?"

"Yes."

"And that . . . you said unless you were granted all three of them, you would not return to riding on the bus, is that correct?"

"Yes," she said.

"In other words," he continued, "you did not stop on account of segregation, but you stopped riding before the segregation issue was ever raised; that is correct, isn't it?"

"It is the segregation laws of Alabama that cause all of it," she announced.

"Just answer the question," he snapped. "Isn't it a fact that your mouthpiece put into—"

"No!" she cried. "He did not put it into us—"

"—is it not true," he persisted, his voice rising, "that he put into the newspaper a statement of his requests, and he specifically stated in that that the segregation statutes were not involved?" A puzzled frown knitted her forehead. "Do you know that?" he quizzed. "Didn't you read what he put in the papers?"

"Yes, I did."

"And that was in there, wasn't it?"

She stared at him a moment. "Yes."

"And also your attorney sitting there," and Knabe turned to gesture, "attorney Gray, also at the meeting . . . put out a statement that the segregation laws were in effect. That is correct, isn't it?"

"Yes."

"And you had the bus boycott on at the time. That is correct, isn't it?"

"That is correct."

Actually, Knabe's argument was a play on words: Blacks wanted better treatment, black drivers, and seating first-come, first-served: *i.e.*, meaning no segregation.

The next witness was Mrs. Susie McDonald, seventy-seven, who testified that she had lived all her life in Montgomery and had been a regular rider on the city buses until December 5.

"Why did you stop riding the buses?" Gray asked her.

"Well, I stopped because we were asking for it, but we didn't expect to get it, we didn't. We all had to stop, so I thought I would stop, too."

"Were you involved in some incident on the bus?"

"Only I had to get up and let some white people sit down," she said. "I was asked to move."

"You were asked to get up?" Gray asked slowly.

"The . . . yes, by the Cleveland Avenue bus driver. I don't know who they are. They asked me to move. I had to get up."

"That is all."

Rives glanced at Alabama Attorney General John Patterson: "Mr. Patterson?" he invited. "Cross examine?"

"No questions."

"Mr. Knabe?"

"Yes, sir." Knabe questioned the elderly witness about King's involvement in the boycott.

She shook her head. "I couldn't tell you much about that."

"Now, when you stopped riding the buses on December fifth, there was no agitation of any type among Negroes for a change in segregation laws, or an interpretation of them, was there?"

"Well, there wasn't any court orders, but we have been mistreated for some time."

"That is not the reason you stopped riding the buses?"

Langford rose. "Your honor, I think all these questions are irrelevant. It is not what the Negroes in Montgomery have done or will do, is not an issue in this case. The question is whether or not this particular person is one who has been injured in being subjected to segregation."

Rives shrugged. "You have alleged the people stopped riding the buses for a particular reason," he said, directing the words to Langford, "and if segregation laws were declared (unconstitutional) in the matter that they would commence. I overrule your objection."

Knabe shot a glance at Langford, then turned again to face Mrs. McDonald. "You stopped riding the buses prior to the time any reference was made to any change in the segregation laws, is that right?"

"I had to," she said. "I was sick. I couldn't go."

"You stopped riding because of ill health?" There was surprise in his voice.

"No, not altogether. I was often mistreated."

"You stopped at the time there was agitation among the Negroes to stop, didn't you?"

"I didn't follow the others," she replied firmly. "I reached my own judgment. I stopped because I thought it was right and because we were mistreated."

"But you stopped at the same time the others stopped, didn't you? And their grievance at that time said they wanted more courteous treatment. That was one of the main things, wasn't it?"

A long pause. "Yes, sir."

"And that had nothing whatsoever to do with segregation law issues, did it?"

There was the first murmur from the crowd, an uneasy ripple that flowed through the courtroom.

"That is what we asked for," Mrs. McDonald responded, appearing to be slightly confused. "We didn't want no social equality. We wanted what we asked for. We wanted recognition."

"I see," Knabe said, "in other words, you stopped . . . you did not want equality of any type, but you merely wanted recognition?"

"That's right."

"No further questions."

Gray was on his feet. "Mrs. McDonald . . . will you ride the buses if segregation is removed?"

"We object to the question," Knabe said.

Rives shook his head. "She has said she will. Overruled."

"That's all," said Gray.

Mary Louise Smith, nineteen, the third plaintiff, took the stand. Langford questioned her, receiving responses that she had, like the others, stopped riding the buses on December 5.

"Now, prior to that time, have you had anything happen to you in any way . . . or any incidents?"

"Yes."

"Please tell the court what . . . just what happened.

Her eyes lifted for a moment, studying the ceiling of the high room. "Well, this particular incident took place on Highland Avenue bus on October twenty-first, 1955. I was riding the bus and I was sitting on the bus side reserved for 'white and colored.' I was sitting behind the sign that said for 'colored.' At this particular moment a white lady got on the bus and she asked the bus driver to tell me to move out of my seat for her to sit there and he asked me to move three times. And I refused. So he got up and said he would call the cops. And he asked me to move." Her eyes narrowed; her voice became more intense. "And I told him . . . I told him, 'I am not going to move out of my seat. I am not going to move anywhere. I got the privilege to sit here like anybody else does.' So he say I was under arrest, and he took me to the station."

"You were arrested at that time?"

"Yes, sir, I was." She said it in such a way to reveal that she was still perplexed by the incident.

"What happened after that?" Langford asked.

"Well," she said, "they arrested me and they kept me in jail for about two hours or more longer, and then they charged me five dollars and cost of court."

"You were subsequently tried in city court?"

"Yes. And they fined me nine dollars."

"As I understand it," he said, moving closer to her, "the bus on which you were riding had a sign, 'white' on one side and 'colored' on the other?"

"Yes, sir," she replied quickly, nodding her head. She gestured. "The card said this side was for white, and an arrow pointed to the back for colored."

"That, in effect, was a segregated bus?"

"Yes."

"You are a Negro," he said, "and you were required to move from that seat to allow a white woman to sit down?"

"That's right."

"Had it not been for the rule . . . , no I'm sorry. I will ask you this: Do you know what you were convicted of at the time they took you from the bus?"

"We think the record will speak for that," Knabe said. "We object to that."

"I asked her if she knew," Langford said. "Do you know what you were convicted of?"

She glanced up at Rives. He nodded at her. "Just answer yes or no," he said.

"No," she said. "No, I don't know."

"Would you ride the buses again," Langford asked, "if the laws were changed?"

She nodded. "I would ride the city buses provided we had

no segregation on the buses . . . the city buses."

She watched warily as Knabe approached. "You say you were arrested back in October?"

"October twenty-first, 1955," she answered.

"Did you have a lawyer?"

"No."

He seemed surprised. "You didn't have a lawyer?"

"No," she repeated.

"You didn't appeal the case?"

"No, sir," she said, "I did not."

He examined his notes for a moment. "You were not interested at that time in the question of segregation, were you?"

She stared evenly at him. "I have always been interested, all of my life, because I have grown up in a period—"

"When did you first employ attorney Gray in this case?" he snapped, cutting her off.

Gray objected. "When she employed me has nothing to do with it."

"One of our contentions," the Montgomery city attorney said, his voice growing testy, "is that all this is one scheme and plan. These people have had the opportunity when this woman was in there to have tested everything they asked for today. And we are trying to find out if at that time she was in contact with him (Gray) and why it couldn't have gone in the usual course of procedure."

Shaking his head, Gray countered: "Your honors, whether or not she decided to exhaust the state judicial remedy under the federal code is a question of law and not a question of fact."

Rives sustained Gray's objection.

Knabe continued: "Now, you said on this incident you mentioned here, you said, 'he' said you are under arrest. Who is 'he'?"

"Policeman."

"Policeman? Of the city of Montgomery?"

"Yes."

"It wasn't the driver of the bus, was it?"

She shrugged. "Yes. He first tells me to get up and move."

Knabe scanned his notes, then: "Are you riding free at this time?"

"No. I'm not riding at all."

Again the surprise: "You are not riding any of the free buses that the churches are furnishing you?"

"We don't have no free buses."

"You mean you pay for the buses when you ride on them?" She seemed puzzled. "What bus?"

"Those station wagons," he said quickly, exasperation in his voice.

"No. We ride those free."

"Now, you are riding those free then, aren't you?"

"Yes, I am."

He nodded. "Now, you said you stopped riding on December fifth. Why did you happen to decide on that particular day?"

"Well, I think one person has been treated wrong and somebody else had been treated wrong." She paused, her eyes playing over the crowd. "I just feel like I want to cooperate and do what I can to help them."

"You say," Knabe pursued mildly, "that you feel you should cooperate. Who are you cooperating with?"

"With the colored people of Montgomery."

"Did you get together and agree to stop riding on December fifth?"

"No, we didn't get together. We just stopped ourselves."

"You must have had a meeting," he said. "Who gave you instructions to stop on December fifth? Did you just say to one another, 'I am going to stop riding' and everybody at one time stopped?"

A silence. Then: "They must have said because nobody went back on the bus."

"Now, somebody said, 'Let's stop on a certain day.' Who was that?"

"I really don't know."

"But that was at the time when you had your first negotiations with the bus company and with the city, wasn't it? That you stopped, is that correct? That was December fifth, that is the time you stopped riding the buses, wasn't it?"

"Yes."

"And at that time nothing was said about segregation, whatsoever, was there?"

"Something was said about segregation," she replied sharply."As long as I have been living I have known myself."

"Well, you didn't represent to anybody anything about segregation, did you, to any officials at all?"

"Well, I still—"

"Just answer the question," he instructed. "You, yourself, did not at any time say anything about segregation to any of the officials . . . the city officials, did you?"

"I did not say anything to them," she said.

"As a matter of fact," Knabe persisted, "Reverend King represented you, didn't he?"

"No. He didn't represent no one. We represented ourselves.We appointed him our leader."

"You appointed him as your leader—"

"Our leader," she corrected.

"But he did represent the colored people. He was the spokesman for the colored people?"

She nodded. "Yes . . . he and his assistants."

"That is all," he said, turning abruptly from her.

Gray rose. "Miss Smith, do you object to segregation?"

"Yes."

"Do the rest of the Negroes in the Montgomery section object to segregation, Miss Smith?"

"Yes, they do."

"We object," Knabe intoned.

"Overruled," Rives said, matter of factly. "Anything else of this witness?"

"No, your honor," Gray said.

"You may step down," the judge said. "Call your next witness, Mr. Gray."

4

IF THERE WAS TO BE a star witness in the boycott case, it had to be Claudette Colvin, then sixteen. The blue dress she wore accentuated the firm dark skin. She walked up to the witness stand timidly, her eyes darting over the three judges.

"Where do you live, Miss Colvin?" Gray asked.

"I live at 658 Dixie Drive," she replied.

"And you stopped riding the buses on December fifth?"

"Yes, sir."

"Before that date, did you experience any incident on a bus?"

"The bus . . . yes, sir."

"Tell us about it, please," he invited.

"It was on March second, 1955. I was on my way home from school. It was the Highland Avenue bus."

"Tell us about . . . tell the court what happened, please."

She nodded, speaking in a soft voice. "I rode the bus and it was turning in on Perry and Dexter Avenue, and me and some other school children . . . well, I sit on the seat on the left hand side," and she gestured briefly, "on the seat just above the emergency door, me and another girl beside me."

"You say another girl was sitting by you and another girl was sitting across from you: Do you mean those two girls were Negroes?"

"Yes, sir," she said. "And he drove on down to the next

27

block and by the time all the people get in there, he seen there were no more vacant seats . . . he asked us to get up and . . . and the big girl got up but I didn't. So he drove on down into the square and some more colored people boarded the bus. So Mrs. Hamilton, she got on the bus, and she sat down beside me . . . and that leaves the other seat vacant."

Gray raised a hand to halt her. "You mean that from across the aisle the other two girls had gotten up when the bus driver asked them to?"

"Yes, sir. So, he looked back through the window and saw us, and he was surprised to see we was sitting down, too. He asked her to get up, then. And he asked us both to get up. She (Mrs. Hamilton) said she was not going to get up and that she paid her fare and that she didn't feel like standing. So I told him I was not going to get up. So he said, 'If you are not going to get up I will get a policeman.' So he went somewhere and got a policeman."

As she related the event, her voice achieved a subdued intensity. "The first policeman came in and asked who it was. So he told the policeman who I was. 'Why are you not going to get up? It's against the law here.' So I told him that I didn't know that it was a law that a colored person had to get up and give a white person a seat when there were not any more vacant seats and colored people were standing up. And so he got off. And then two more policemen come on. He said, 'Who is it?' And he was very angry about it. He said that is not new that 'I had trouble with that thing before.' So then he said, 'Aren't you going to get up?' He didn't say anything to Mrs. Hamilton, just to me. He said, 'Aren't you going to get up?' I said, 'No.' He saw Mrs. Hamilton but was afraid to ask her to get up. He said, 'If any of you are not gentlemen enough to give a lady a seat, you should be put in jail yourself.' And so a Mr. Harris, he got up and gave her a seat and got off the bus. And so she (Mrs. Hamilton) taken his seat and so the policeman again asked me if I was going to get up. I said, 'No, sir,' and I was . . . I was crying then—"

"Oh, God!" a woman in the crowd wailed.

Miss Colvin continued: "I was very hurt because I didn't know that white people would act like that and I . . . I was crying." She shrugged. "And (the policeman) said, 'I will have to take you off.' So I didn't move, I didn't move at all. So I just acted like a big baby. So he kicked me—"

Again the wail from the woman in the audience.

"—and one got on one side of me and one got the other arm and they just drug me out. And so I was very pitiful." She paused, shaking her head slowly, looking out over the crowd. "It really hurt me to see that I have to give a person a seat, when all those colored people were standing and there were not any more vacant seats . . . I had never seen nothing like that. Well, they take me on down, they put me in a car and one of the motorcycle men, he says, 'I am sorry to have to take you down like this.' So they put handcuffs on me through the window . . . ."

There was a hush in the room; she sat there shaking her head slowly, blinking, studying the floor. Several seconds went by. Then Gray asked: "And where did they take you, Claudette?"

Her eyes lifted and there was a trace of a smile tugged at the corners of her mouth. "City Hall. And from there I went to jail."

"Did they mention anything to you about the juvenile court or . . . well, instead of jail?"

She nodded. "One of the policemen, yes, sir. And they put me in jail and lock me up."

"Thank you," said Gray. "That's all."

Knabe drummed the pencil on the desk for a second or two, studying his notes; then he rose and walked slowly in front of the bench.

He spoke somewhat hesitantly. "You have changed . . . that is, you and the other Negroes have changed your ideas since December fifth, have you not?"

"No, sir," she said, shaking her head. "We haven't changed our ideas. It has been in me ever since I was born."

"But the group stopped riding the buses for certain named things . . . that is correct, isn't it?"

"For what?"

"For certain things that Reverend King said were the things they objected to."

"No, sir. It was in the beginning when they arrested me, when they seen how dirty they treated the Negro girls here, that they had began to feel like that all the time, although some of us just didn't have the guts to stand up."

"Did you have a leader?" he asked.

She puzzled for a few seconds. "Did we have a leader? Our leaders is just we, ourselves. We are just a group of people."

"But somebody," he insisted, "spoke for the group."

"I don't know. We all spoke for ourselves."

"Did you select anyone to represent you?" he pressed. "Like the Reverend King?"

She turned her head to one side, thinking. "We did select . . . quite naturally we are not going to have any ignorant person to lead us and . . . we have to have someone who is strong enough to speak up . . . someone with intelligence enough . . . we have got to have someone who can stand up and who knows the law and who knows . . . it is quite natural that we are not going to get up there ourselves and some of them can't even read or write . . . but they knew they were being treated wrong."

Knabe folded his arms. "Is the Reverend King the one you selected?"

"We didn't elect him," she said.

"You said you selected somebody who was better informed to represent you," he reminded her. "Now who did you select?"

"Well, I don't know anything about selections, but we all just got together—"

"But somebody spoke for your group," he snapped. "Now who was it?"

"I don't know," she said. "We all spoke for ourselves."

"Now just a minute ago I understood you to say that you selected somebody that knew the law better. Now . . . now who was that person?"

"Who knew the law better?" she asked, her eyes wide. "Now a lot of people know the laws better. Now, are you trying to say that Reverend King is the leader of the whole thing?"

Knabe rubbed his head in a gesture of exasperation. Then, with exaggerated patience, he said: "I am merely asking if Reverend King was one of the leaders who represented your group at that time, and expressed to the city commission what the Negroes wanted."

"Probably," she said slowly, "he was one of them who went to the city commission, but I don't know."

"You don't know at all then?"

She shrugged. "I don't know nothing."

"Now, was attorney Gray here one of those whom you felt knew the laws?"

She gazed at him, then shifted her eyes to Gray. "Yes, quite naturally . . . he is a lawyer."

"Did you know at that time," Knabe said, his voice rising,"that he sustained that the state law didn't apply at all in the city of Montgomery?"

She shook her head, perhaps confused by his question. "I go to school myself and I know there is a lot of law, state law, national law and local law."

The attorney at one point asked the judges to instruct her to be more direct in her answers, and Rives said: "If you know the answers, just answer 'yes' or 'no'; don't make speeches."

For the next several minutes she replied curtly with either one or the other. Then Knabe asked: "Why did you stop riding on December the fifth?"

"Because," she said, her eyes narrowing, "we were treated wrong, dirty and nasty."

That comment drew murmurs of agreement from the crowd and a warning look from Rives. The girl returned to her seat.

Montgomery Mayor W.A. Gayle, one of the defendants, was called as a hostile witness by the plaintiffs. Langford questioned him.

"Mayor Gayle, what instructions, if any, have you given to the city police with respect to enforcing segregation?"

"We have told them to enforce all laws and ordinances that are on the books."

"I am talking about policemen now, with respect to segregation in the buses," the attorney said.

"That is one of the laws," the mayor said, "and I believe in segregation and I believe in enforcing the city ordinance concerning it."

Langford nodded. "One further question, Mayor Gayle. I think you have answered it, but I want to make it clear for the record. Your instructions with respect to enforcing segregation laws, is to arrest persons who violate its operation now and in the future, is that correct?"

"That is right," the mayor said, nodding to reinforce it."That is the law and that is the way we enforce the laws."

"Your witness," the attorney said, turning to Knabe, who rose and moved forward.

"Mayor, did you, prior to the time of entering suit with this suit, have conferences with the various leaders . . . Negro leaders, including Reverend King?"

"Yes."

"And at that time did they make certain requests and state that those were the reasons for which the bus boycott had been begun?"

"That is right."

"Did they at any time say that there was any complaint with reference to segregation?"

"Reverend King made the statement and there was no reference to segregation even on December the fifth," Gayle replied.

"Since the bus boycott there . . . has there been disorder in Montgomery due to racial conditions?"

"We are trying to hold it down as much as we can," the mayor said, "but there is danger of bloodshed or something like that unless we can strictly enforce the segregation laws."

Knabe paused for a moment, then returned to his seat. Rives watched him. "Any further questions?"

"Yes, sir, your honor," Langford said, popping up, and moving quickly around the table. "Mayor, how did you know there was going to be bloodshed if segregation laws were not enforced? Have you taken a survey, too?"

Gayle shrugged. "It is my responsibility to look after the welfare and comfort of the people and if I anticipate anything I try to avoid it before it gets here . . . we don't wait until it happens."

Langford raised both hands in a gesture of bewilderment. "Well, people have not been riding the buses for about six months now and nothing untoward has happened, has it?"

"Well . . . they had shooting in the buses, knocked the windows out, and beating up the colored women and quite a number of things like that," the mayor said. "Are you familiar with what has been going on in Montgomery?"

"I am afraid I am not."

"You mention the people not riding the buses," Gayle continued. "I can cite you in my own mother-in-law's cook, who was cut up and beat up on account of it."

"Now, mayor," Langford said, "it is my understanding . . . I may be wrong . . . but the bus company, on or about April twenty-fourth, issued instructions that there was going to be no segregation on the buses—"

"And we warned them to cancel that order, too," the mayor injected.

"During those days of April twenty-four or April twenty-five, when the bus company issued orders that there would be no segregation," Langford said, "was there any bloodshed or violence?"

"None that I know of."

"That's all."

Knabe rose, a hand lifted to indicate further questions. Rives nodded. "Mayor, you said there were some Negroes who were injured during the time of this bus boycott. Who injured these people? Was it white or colored people?"

"It was colored people."

"Is it true that they were Negroes who were causing bloodshed because they objected to other Negroes riding the buses?"

"That is right."

"From your experience, is it your opinion that there will be violence in the event that segregation is permitted . . . I mean,that non-segregation is permitted?"

"In my opinion it would."

"Do you think the violence would be severe?" Knabe asked.

"I don't know what it would be," the mayor said, "but it would be dangerous."

Langford bolted up from his chair. "Mayor, do you know how many incidents of shooting, beating and knifing have been introduced?"

"No." The answer was hesitant.

"Well, if I told you that only two Negroes said they had been molested," the attorney said, "would you accept that, Mayor Gayle? Only two out of the twenty-thousand or more Negroes in Montgomery?"

Gayle fixed a testy gaze on Langford. "Do you say we had

no bombings?" he demanded. "Do you say we had no bombings, either? The only one I know of is the one that happened to my mother-in-law's cook. The rest were routine . . . that happened as the enforcement of the law."

"Well, the fact of the matter is," Langford said briskly, "you don't know how many shootings that have been as interference of Negroes riding the buses, do you?"

"I know some have called me and said they wanted to get back on the buses but they were afraid of a 'goon squad' who would hurt them."

"But you don't know for sure how many incidents there have been?"

"Not for sure."

There were other witnesses who, like the mayor, felt that if segregation laws were not enforced, there would be a dangerous situation not only in Montgomery, but throughout Alabama. One of them was city commissioner Clyde Sellers who predicted, "If segregation barriers are lifted, violence will be the order of the day."

To which Judge Rives puzzled aloud: "Can you command one man to surrender his constitutional rights — if they are his constitutional rights — to prevent another man from committing a crime?"

The hearing ended late in the afternoon; it was with an air of uncertainty that both sides left the federal building.

5

F OR A CASE THAT THE history books would call a
landmark, it had occurred with incredible swiftness —
less than five hours, all told. And while it would take
several weeks to write and announce the opinion, the actual
decision took only ten minutes.

JOHNSON

Actually, none of us knew how the others felt at first.
During the hearing both Judge Rives and Judge Lynne
had made comments that they were not sure the Supreme Court had ended segregation in society with its
decision on schools (in *Brown*). I had not said the first
word during the hearing. I just sat there listening.

So we went into my chambers after it was over and
sat there for a few moments. Finally Judge Rives says to
me, "Well, Frank, you're the junior judge here. You vote
first. What do you think?"

It was tradition that the junior member of a panel
vote first so as not to be swayed by the senior judges.

"Judge," I said, after thinking it over for a moment or
two, "as far as I'm concerned, state-imposed segregation
on public facilities violates the Constitution. I'm going to
rule with the plaintiffs here."

And right away Judge Lynne shakes his head, no.

But he doesn't speak.

Instead, Judge Rives looks at me and nods. "You know, I feel the same way as you."

Judge Lynne continues shaking his head. "I don't reach it that way," he says. "The (Supreme) Court has already spoken on this issue in *Plessy*. It's the law and we're bound by it until it's changed."

He had a tenable position, too, because, as he said, the Supreme Court had ruled in *Plessy* that segregation was valid provided "whites and coloreds" had "separate but equal" facilities in public transportation.

But I told Judge Lynne that there was no way to reconcile the *Plessy* case in light of the more recent *Brown* decision. I couldn't reconcile it in my mind how, on the one hand, the Court could put the stamp of approval on segregation as in *Plessy*, while, on the other, mandating the desegregation of the races in public schools, to wit, the *Brown* case.

In the way it spelled out the *Brown* decision, the Supreme Court had confined the ruling to schools alone, not desegregation in other areas of public life. The wording applied to children and how segregation had a psychological impact on black children. But while it was narrowed to the school issue, it nonetheless set a doctrinal trend as far as Judge Rives and I were concerned. While it said nothing about transportation, it suggested that courts should now conclude that *Plessy* was no longer valid. Judge Lynne on the other hand, felt the Supreme Court had not intended *Brown* to be applied in other areas. And he was on sound legal ground, too, because he had a Supreme Court decision directly on point that backed him up.

As far as I was concerned, it wasn't a difficult case to decide. There were no conflicting constitutional questions at issue. The long and short of it was that there was a state law that said Negroes — simply because they were Negroes — had to ride in the back of a bus and had been extended to say they had to get up when white folks wanted their seat. Now (Montgomery County Circuit)

Judge Walter Jones had asked the question, "Where in the Constitution is there one word, one sentence, one paragraph" that says you couldn't segregate folks in public transportation? My question was, "Where in the Constitution is there anything that says you *can* segregate them?" It just isn't there. To the contrary, it specifically says you can't abridge the freedoms of the individual. The boycott case was a simple case of legal and human rights being denied.

The testimony of the four women — Miss Colvin and the others — merely reinforced that position. What was going to be unusual was the fact that our decision would, in effect, overturn a Supreme Court decision, namely the *Plessy* case of 1896. That was what made it a novel decision. A lower court had never done that before.

I point out for the record that my vote in favor of the plaintiffs in the case was not based on any personal feeling that segregation was wrong: it was based on the law, that the state imposing segregation violated my interpretation of the Constitution of the United States. It wasn't for a judge to decide on the morality question, but rather the law.

Actually, there had been another suit filed regarding segregation on buses. A black woman in Columbia, South Carolina, had filed it but it was not a class-action suit. It simply asked damages for her as an individual and in July, 1955, the Fourth Circuit Court of Appeals in Richmond had upheld her claim. But that case was not a pervasive precedent on the matter. It certainly didn't pave the way for the decision that Judge Rives and I made.

At that time, the issue of segregation on public facilities was not getting clear-cut decisions from the courts. The day after the Fourth Circuit ruled on the Columbia case, it also ruled that Prince Edward County, Virginia school system could continue racial segregation, using the puzzling argument that to enforce integration immediately was not consistent with the Supreme Court guide regarding "all deliberate speed."

Georgia Governor Marvin Griffith reflected the mood of the white South after the Supreme Court issued a ruling November 7, 1955 — the day Johnson was sworn in — which struck down segregation on the city-owned golf courses of Atlanta. Said the governor, "Any decision respecting segregation is designed . . . to force intermarriage (of the races). The state will get out of the park business before allowing a breakdown in segregation in the intimacy of the playground."

Johnson was sympathetic to the plight of blacks, but his vote was not based on emotion. He recognized, too, that the social customs of the South were going to be upended. But the pressure would be much greater on Judge Rives, because he was a native of Montgomery, a "hometown boy." Johnson was "the foreigner." The Montgomery decision was made public on June 5, 1956. It was a cloudy, cool day. The reporters had been told that the order was going to be released and they had gathered around the district clerk's office at the federal building.

Judge Rives was working on another case; Judge Lynne was back in Birmingham. Johnson had the order in his office and reread it a final time, then called in his first law clerk, Syd Fuller. As he handed him the order, Johnson said, "Well, Sydney, we're getting on this horse now. Let's ride it."

Fuller carried the opinion down to the office of the U.S. Clerk to have copies made. As he entered that office, news photographers in the hallways snapped his picture, getting the back of his head. "It was history," he would say later, "and they got the back of my head."

Some news accounts would say Rives and Johnson had stopped Southern tradition in its tracks. Johnson's own view was less cavalier: what he and Rives had done, he said, was correct a denial of full freedoms.

In part, the order read:

> We hold that the statutes and ordinances requiring segregation of the white and colored races on the motor buses of a common carrier of passengers in the city of Montgomery and its police jurisdiction . . . violates the due process and equal protection of the law . . . under the 14th Amendment of

the Constitution of the United States.

The 'separate but equal' doctrine set forth by the Supreme Court in 1896 in the case of *Plessy vs. Ferguson* can no longer be applied.

There is no rational basis upon which the 'separate but equal' doctrine can validly be applied to public transportation in the city of Montgomery. In their private affairs, in the conduct of their private business, it is clear that the people themselves have the liberty to select their own associates and the persons with whom they will do business, unimpaired by the 14th Amendment. Indeed, we think that such liberty is guaranteed by the due process clause of that Amendment. There is, however, a difference, a constitutional difference, between voluntary adherence to custom and the perpetuation and enforcement of that custom by law . . .

We cannot, in good conscience, perform our duty as judges by blindly following the precedent of *Plessy vs. Ferguson* of 'separate but equal'.

An opposing view was taken by Judge Lynne who wrote:

Only a profound philosophical disagreement with the majority that the 'separate but equal' doctrine can no longer be safely followed as a constitutional statement of the law would prompt this, my first dissent.

In issuing the opinion, Rives and Johnson said the injunction against segregation would not become effective for two weeks, to allow the city and state time to file an appeal.

Mayor Gayle said he didn't need two weeks; he had no comment for reporters other than to say the case would be appealed to the Supreme Court.

The Reverend King was pleased with the decision. But the boycott would continue, he said, pending the outcome at the Supreme Court.

In Alabama, white resistance to the Civil Rights Movement began even before the boycott itself.

In 1953, a year before the Supreme Court's *Brown* ruling, the Alabama Legislature, "that august body," Johnson called it, named a committee to "prepare any such legislation as may be required . . . to protect the citizens of this state" in the event of a court decision "which destroys the principle of separation of the races . . . ."

To be sure, Alabama's lawmakers had been very active before that. In 1947 they had passed a bill "empowering any motor transport company to provide separate ticket windows and waiting rooms for whites and coloreds" whether interstate or intrastate.

Even on buses operated by Greyhound or Trailways, blacks often suffered at Alabama terminals; while cities like Birmingham and Montgomery and others had dual waiting rooms, smaller towns did not, and blacks would have to wait sometimes for thirty minutes before the bus even resumed its journey.

In 1949, the Legislature had a bill which stated with dubious wisdom that "segregation is well established and favored by a large majority of both races as being a measure for preventing racial animosities and violence . . . ."

That same session also rapped Congressional probes of the violence caused "by hooded men in Alabama," and knocked President Truman's civil rights program which included an anti-lynching law.

It added that the effort by the Congress and the president to desegregate was not only "unwise" but also "unAmerican."

And to ice the posture of the state, when the Supreme Court ruling was handed down in 1954, the Alabama Legislature simply declared it to be "null and void."

Still, there had been some courageous voices in those times. One was Governor Jim Folsom who, in 1950, noted in a speech that "all men should have equal rights" and pointed out that Negroes made up thirty-five percent of the state's population, yet had not a single park where they could take their children. Further, he had said, even though many Negroes were qualified to vote, they had "maliciously been kept from exercising their right." The speech was given a cool reception. Then, the legislators responded by making Robert E. Lee's birthday a state holiday "reaffirming the belief in the principles of Southern Civilization." They also refused to approve a scholarship program for Negro nursing students, then authorized the stamping of "Heart of Dixie" on auto license plates.

Folsom was a man ahead of his time; he had proposed "one man-one vote," revenue sharing, and the abolition of the state poll tax, one of the measures used to discourage blacks from trying to become voters.

The impact of the bus boycott decision began bouncing across the South; in Delray Beach, Florida, the city council voted four-to-one to exclude a black neighborhood from the city.

In Birmingham, police commissioner Robert Lindberg confidently said "we don't anticipate or contemplate any change being made now or in the future as far as segregation on buses is concerned." But blacks were already preparing to test the issue there.

In Montgomery, a telephone heckling campaign against King and other Negro leaders intensified; white women, who drove to pick up their maids and return them home in the evening, were also victimized by such calls.

Judge Johnson and his wife began receiving prank phone calls and threatening letters. One of the letters received came from Bullock County, dated June 6, the day following the decision. It read: "If I had been in your shoes before I would have rulled (sic) as you did, I would rather have had my right arm cut off. I trust that you will get on your knees and pray to Almighty God to forgive you for the mistake that you have made."

A photographer from Savannah, Georgia, wrote: "If you ever show up in Savannah, don't expect our photographers for *The Evening Dispatch* to snap your best side."

JOHNSON

A day or two after the decision, I dropped by my parents' home and my mother was in the kitchen cooking supper. They had moved to Montgomery some years earlier. When she saw me she kind of nodded, kept on cutting carrots. Then she said, "Well, son, you got them on the buses, didn't you?"

I never got into debates with my mother; I just grinned, sat down beside her, took a bite of a carrot and waited.

"Well, I'll tell you one thing," she said. "You may

have gotten them on the buses, but you'll never get them into the schools. The people of this state just won't put up with it."

Mother wasn't a segregationist; never had much to say about racial matters other than the fact that all people should be treated equally. She was a tough woman; tough, I mean, in her convictions and the way she viewed the world around her. She was stating what she considered the reality of the situation — not what she considered right. I told her when the school situation developed — as it surely would — I would deal with it. So she didn't say anymore. Just kept working on the carrots, looking at me every once in a while.

6

ON NOVEMBER 13, 1956, the Supreme Court of the United States upheld the June 5 decision of Rives and Johnson which banned segregation on Montgomery city buses. The impact in the city was like an electric shock; blacks gathered again for a mass rally at Dexter Avenue Baptist Church where King, now clearly a leader of national import, cautioned them. "We'll have to wait and see," he said. The city's mayor had not yet received the notification. Meanwhile, the State of Alabama asked for a rehearing by the Supreme Court; it was denied. On December 20, more than a year after the arrest of Rosa Parks, a U.S. marshal served the city and state officials with the federal injunction prohibiting segregation on the buses. "I guess we'll have to abide by it," Mayor Gayle said dejectedly, "because it's the law."

That night, more than fifteen hundred blacks collected at the Holt Street Baptist Church for a rally; the inside was packed, and people were spilled out onto the street for more than a block in each direction; loudspeakers affixed to the front carried the sounds of the freedom songs and the spirituals wafting through the winter night air.

"We sang "Swing Low, Sweet Chariot" and "This Little Light of Mine, I'm Gonna Let It Shine," and a whole lot of others," said Georgia Gilmore, then in her thirties. "Weary feet and weary souls were lightened. It was such a night. We didn't have to walk no more. Even before Martin Luther King got up there and told us it was over, we knew it was over and we knew we had won."

Bernice Robertson, seven, and her sisters, Rosetta, nine, and Naomi, ten, felt that triumph, too, as they sang. For more than a year they had walked more than eight miles a day, twice a week, just to take piano lessons, she said. "We had walked because it was right and because it was wrong to get on the bus. And it wasn't easy, either . . . because sometimes white folks would go by and blow the horn or yell things at us, because they knew what we were a part of, what we were doing."

At that rally King announced that the boycott would end.

"We must not take this as a victory," he said, "but merely with dignity. When we go back to the buses, go back with a quiet pride. Don't push your way. Just sit where there is a vacant seat. If someone pushes you, don't push back. We must have the courage to refuse to hit . . . we must continue to resist segregation non-violently. This dynamic unity, this amazing self-respect will soon cause the oppressor to become ashamed." He also praised the efforts of some whites. "If there had not been some discipline among them, some sense of moral responsibility, some sensitivity from the white community, there would have been more violence. We must return to the buses and we must be courteous."

The next day King, Nixon, Mrs. Parks and others boarded the buses for the first time in three hundred and eighty-one days. Most whites stared straight ahead in stony silence; but some spoke or nodded; it was reported widely in the press that one white man remarked to Mrs. Parks and some of the others, "Looks like it'll be a nice day."

(It's interesting that Claudette Colvin was not in the group and rarely, if ever, rode a bus again in Montgomery. After her arrest and later appearance in the court hearing, she was more or less forgotten. Later she would tell a reporter that she would sometime attend the rallies at the churches. "I would sit in the back," she said, "and no one would even know I was there." She would, within a few years, leave Montgomery, going to New York as a domestic worker.)

JOHNSON

> I remember that evening Ruth and I went to a Christmas Party at a home in the neighborhood. My mother was at home caring for Johnny. So right in the middle of the party mother calls and says, "Son, I think you better come on home."
>
> So we hurried back there, it was just a block or so away, and saw a fire flickering in the front yard. Somebody had put up a crude little cross there. It didn't bother me and it didn't bother Ruth. She's from Winston County and doesn't scare that easily.
>
> People are always asking me what I thought when I saw that cross. I didn't think anything. I guess I was supposed to say something; perhaps strike a dramatic pose, point, and in a falsetto declare, "Oh, look at that cross burning."

A few days later, the FBI picked up two juveniles; they were charged with disturbing the peace. It was passed off as a prank. But elsewhere the discontent was measured in more menacing tones. Early on the morning of December 23, a shotgun blast riddled the King home. No one was hurt.

The events in Montgomery again made ripples around the South; in Birmingham, the Reverend Fred Shuttlesworth, president of the Alabama Christian Movement, asked the city commission to lift segregation and when he was refused, he told them, "We plan to ride the buses in an unsegregated fashion." On Christmas night, his parsonage at the Bethel Baptist Church was bombed; his wife and children suffered minor injuries.

The spectre of violence haunted Alabama; on December 28, there were two buses fired upon by snipers; later, that same day, a third bus was riddled with bullets. Two shots struck a black woman, Mrs. Rosa Jordan; she was carried sobbing from the vehicle with wounds in both legs.

As the new year dawned, Montgomery was bristling with racial tension. The homes of King and Abernathy were bombed, and two black churches were heavily damaged by explosions.

And a black truck driver, Willie Edwards, Jr., the father of two, was pulled over one night by four Klansmen, driven to a bridge on U.S. Highway 231 north of Montgomery, and forced to jump into the cold waters of the Alabama River. He was accused of making remarks to a white woman. (He was driving the truck that night as a substitute for the regular driver, also a black; later, it was determined the Klansmen had gotten the wrong man). Edwards' body was found three months later, lodged against a log in his native Lowndes County, fifty miles downriver.

There were distressing times for Aurelia Browder, one of the four plaintiffs in the bus boycott case. There were phone calls through the endless nights, she said: harassing, threatening, frightening. Her daughter, Manervia, nine, would always remember the lights burning in the front bedroom, as her mother sat up studying. One night the girl was awakened by the phone ringing; she ran through the hallway to answer. "Your house is gonna be blowed sky high!" a voice said. She became hysterical. Her mother grabbed the telephone, and told the caller, "Blow it up. I need a new house, anyway."

By early spring of 1957, tempers in Montgomery began to cool; the integration of the buses gradually became accepted — or, at least, tolerated — by whites. The first crack in the wall of segregation in the South had been made.

It was during the boycott that another racial situation brought national attention to Alabama. In Birmingham, U.S. District Judge Hobart Grooms issued an order requiring the University of Alabama at Tuscaloosa to admit a black, Authurine Lucy. There was such a venomous reaction that Judge Grooms, a stately gentleman with graying hair, would go to bed each night with a shotgun within easy reach. He later became ill and was hospitalized.

Miss Lucy, meanwhile, was chased about the campus by a virtual lynch mob; she was the target of stone-throwing and racial slurs. One night the campus broke out into rioting and a mob tried to get into the dormitory where she lived. She was later expelled.

JOHNSON

Years later, in 1970 or so, I went to a football game at Tuscaloosa and watched Wilbur Jackson, the first black to start in the Crimson Tide backfield, run for a sixty-yard touchdown. The people went wild. And I could only shake my head in amazement. All this cheering at a place where Authurine Lucy had been stoned and driven away because she was black. If she had been able to play football, she might have made it.

But as for segregation, it was an American problem, not just one unique to the South. I used to ride a train from Montgomery to Washington and I never noticed that much difference in the seating arrangements once we crossed the Mason-Dixon Line.

As long as there are people, there will be discrimination of some type. Prejudice doesn't depend entirely on race, it's not always a black-and-white issue. It can be just as vicious and hateful among different ethnic or religious groups.

This country's great social problem, however, was race; for decades we kept it buried under the sand, trying to hide the stench. But it finally came to the surface, and permeated the country. Even when the Supreme Court issued the *Brown* ruling, the leadership of the country failed to tackle the problem of racial discrimination head-on. The churches failed, the lawyers failed, even the President of the United States, Dwight Eisenhower, to some degree defaulted on leadership when it came to civil rights.

When the movement began in Alabama, and then spread across the South, he could have provided some leadership for the nation in the area of racial equality. He could have been more aggressive with the Congress, trying to push through legislation in the rights area. He could have even issued executive orders. But he did nothing. His only action in the civil rights field was at Little Rock, Arkansas, when he sent federal troops there to enforce a court order on desegregating Central High

School in September, 1957. And the only reason he did that was because he had no choice. Attorney General Herbert Brownell in a formal opinion had spelled out for him in detail what his duties were.

When John Kennedy was elected in 1960 and sworn in, there was almost an immediate and dramatic change. He was like electricity compared to Eisenhower. His inaugural address, I felt, put the nation on notice that there were changes that were long overdue.

Part II

'Trampling out the vintage'

Coming of age
in Winston County

TOP LEFT, James Wallace Johnson, the Judge's great-grandfather, was a Lincoln man who fought for the Union during the Civil War. TOP RIGHT, Bessie Treadaway Johnson, his grandmother. ABOVE, Young Frank Johnson Jr., with his mother, Alabama Long Johnson, and some of his brothers and sisters, in a photo taken in the mid-1920s.

7

WINSTON COUNTY, where Johnson was born, is made up of rugged, rocky hills, deep ravines and hardwood-lined ridges. Part of the coal-mining region of the northwest part of Alabama, it was never much good for farming. In the summers, the hot winds would blow in from Mississippi; in the winter, the days would often be dismal with endless rain. The land was tough and hard, and so were the people. His mother, Alabama Long, was born there in 1897, at a place called Delmar. His father, Frank Minis Johnson, Sr., was born in 1895 in nearby Fayette County. They were married just before America got into World War One.

Winston is a place unto itself, rarely in step with the rest of Alabama. Most of the people were descendants of Andrew Jackson's Tennessee Volunteers who came into Alabama to fight Indians in 1814. After defeating the Creeks, many decided to settle there.

When the Civil War erupted, Winston County folks got together for a town meeting at a place called Looney's Tavern. Patriotic sorts, they held the meeting on July 4, 1861. Now their logic was simple. If Alabama as a political entity could secede from the Union, then it was just as right and legal for Winston County, as a political entity, to be able to secede from Alabama. That's what it did, the residents calling themselves the "Free State of Winston." Their resolution read:

> *We think that our neighbors in the South made a mistake
> when they bolted ... however, we do not desire to see our
> neighbors in the South mistreated, and, therefore, we are not
> going to take up arms against them; but on the other hand, we
> are not going to shoot at the flag of our fathers, 'Old Glory,' the
> flag of Washington, Jefferson and Jackson. Therefore, we ask
> that the Confederacy on the one hand, and the Union on the
> other, leave us alone, unmolested, that we may work out our
> political and financial destiny here in the hills and mountains of
> Northwest Alabama.*

It wasn't long before Confederate troopers were coming
into Winston looking for men to fill their ranks. The hill people
ran and hid in the ravines and forests. Finally, they began to
make a choice, knowing they would be forced to fight for one
side or the other. More than five-hundred went to join the Union
Army; seventy decided to fight for the South.

What followed then, was an unusual political stronghold in
Alabama; while most of the state became Democratic after the
war,Winston kept that allegiance to Abraham Lincoln, the Republicans and to the United States.

Johnson's father and mother were Republicans; so was he.

JOHNSON

When Daddy went into the Army in 1918, he was
assigned to Camp Pike, Arkansas. Mother was carrying
me and on October 30, 1918, I was born. I am told she had
a rough time with me; was in labor for more than a day. So
the family sent a wire to my father and the Army gave him
an emergency leave of ten days.

When he arrived home I was already born and Daddy
went to see the doctor and asks how much he owes him.

The doctor says, "Well, I usually charge ten dollars
to deliver a baby. But since you're a soldier I'll only
charge you five."

Later on when I grew up, Daddy told me, "That was
the best five-dollar investment I ever made."

I was the first of seven children. Next came Wallace,
then Bill, Jean, Jimmy, Mary Ann, and finally, when I was

about seventeen, the baby of the family, Ellen Ruth. I had helped them all, helped take care of them, even changed some of their diapers. In a large family like that, your mama has to have help.

We were living in Haleyville, where my father had become the postmaster in 1921 after Republican Warren Harding won the presidency.

Daddy was politically inclined and would be elected probate judge and a member of the State Legislature. We lived next to the First Baptist Church where he was a deacon.

Mother was a quiet woman, not much for socializing; people who know us say I favored her. She was a woman of strong morals and stuck to her convictions.

One day on the way home from school, I saw people picking peas in Opie Gamble's field. They were "working on halves," meaning they got to keep half of what they picked and gave the other half to Opie. I figured it was a chance to get some good peas and maybe a little spending money. So I joined in there and commenced to picking peas. Several hours went by and my mother got to wondering where I was because I was usually punctual when it came to coming home in the afternoons. So she came out looking for me. When she saw me out there in Opie Gamble's field she told a friend, "Well, he may never amount to much, but he's going to work hard at it."

An average student in grade school, Johnson liked history and geography, but had little use for mathematics or science. At the time his career goal was to be a carpenter. Grandfather William Rufus Johnson had taught him the trade and he was adept with hammer and nails.

In 1933, he met Ruth Jenkins. He was fifteen at the time, a tenth grader. She was two years younger. She would later say that she first took note of him as he rode a horse to a place called Tuggles Pasture, to see an airplane land. She was a slim girl with dark hair and brown eyes. Ruth became his girl friend. Johnson was already a lanky fellow and, in keeping with growing up in the1930s, he began smoking cigarettes, preferring a brand called Home Run, about the strongest ones made. It was also about that time that he began driving cars.

One night during the summer of his junior year, he went to get Ruth and bring her to his home to have supper with his family. He was driving his father's brand-new Chevrolet. As he drove the car, Johnson popped a cigarette into his mouth and asked Ruth to strike a match. She did and held it over toward him. He leaned toward the flame and next thing he knew they were off the road and plowing down an incline. The car came to an abrupt halt against the embankment. Neither was hurt, but he was in deep trouble. Only two nights earlier he and a pal, Pert Dodd, were driving home from a double date. They were in a Model-T Ford truck. He lost control and tore up a rail fence, coming to rest on a wood pile. He said another car had forced him off the road. But it didn't matter. Two wrecks in one week was enough; Johnson's father began to see the wisdom of sending him to a military school. There was soldier's blood in the family, and the boy wanted to attend such a school. So he signed up to attend Gulf Coast Military Academy at Gulfport, Mississippi. He said goodbye to Ruth and went off to school. After graduation, he came home and gained admission to Birmingham-Southern College on a football scholarship. But as luck would have it, the college dropped football and Johnson dropped the college, signing up at Massey Business College in Birmingham.

JOHNSON

I learned to type and do bookkeeping, probably the best training I ever received. By then, (1937), I was nineteen and Ruth and I wanted to get married. She was eighteen, which, in Winston County, was more than a proper age to be married. My daddy had a little talk with me, wanted to make sure I was certain, and I said, "Daddy, I just don't think I can do any better." We got married on January 16, 1938. I wore a dark blue suit and Ruth had a blue suit, a little lighter shade than mine.

We drove to Birmingham. We were looking for a preacher that we admired from Winston County, who had retired and moved to Birmingham. After a while we stopped at a church and another preacher came to the door, said he didn't know the preacher we were looking for. But he said he'd be glad to marry us. By then it was getting late. So he performed the ceremony and some of his family members stood by as witnesses.

We later moved to Birmingham and had a small apartment. I had a job with an accounting firm. Well, the first thing they did was fire me. Said something about the low pay and the fact that since I was married I might be prone to steal from them. So Ruth and I packed our belongings, called my folks, and waited for a ride to Walker County, where we'd stay with my grandparents. While we waited on our ride, we invested our last few cents in a pack of peanuts and two Pepsi-Colas. We picked Pepsi because they had the biggest bottles.

So the Johnsons lived in Carbon Hill and he got a job with the WPA. His carpentry background came in handy; he was made a supervisor of a project to build outhouses for all the homes in that part of Alabama that didn't have indoor plumbing. The number was considerable. His work was sturdy, and some of the outhouses stood for years, monuments to the New Deal. But as rewarding as building outhouses can be, Johnson told Ruth he wanted something more out of life.

JOHNSON

I figured that when my time on this earth was up, I needed something more substantial on my headstone than the fact that I built outhouses. I had spent some of my boyhood days going to the courthouse where my father had been probate judge in Winston County; sometimes I'd go in and watch the criminal trials. Maybe it had always been in me to get into law, but that desire came to be realized in 1938. Ruth and I both enrolled at the University of Alabama in Tuscaloosa. She was in education; I majored in pre-law. I became a serious student then — Ruth had always been one — and we both took on extra work to help pay the expenses. She got a job helping professors grade papers and later worked part

ABOVE: College students Ruth and Frank Johnson at a ball at the University of Alabama prior to their entry into World War II.
RIGHT: Naval officer Ruth Johnson, in a photo snapped by Michael Morrison (better known as John Wayne) during the filming of the movie "They Were Expendable."

time as a teacher's aide. I was able to pick up odd jobs as a carpenter. I enrolled in the Reserve Officers Training Corps and could have been commissioned a second lieutenant. But I waived it (the commission) in order to complete law school.

We had been able to complete the four-year program in three because we went the year around, didn't take any summer vacations. Ruth graduated in the spring of 1942 and got a full time job as a teacher at Tuscaloosa County High School. One of her students was Lurleen Burns, who would later marry George Wallace and one day become Alabama's first woman governor.

But even with the full time job, we were having a rough go of it. Ruth as a teacher was making only eighty dollars a month. The war, by then, was a part of everyone's life in one fashion or another, and we both knew that as soon as I finished law school that I would be high on the draft list.

One morning in April 1943, a few months before I was to get my diploma, she told me that since I was going to be going away, and we had no children to encumber her, she had decided she wanted to join the Navy WAVES.

She graduated from the Women's Officers Candidate School at Smith College and was sent to Florida, then Washington. Meanwhile, I graduated in June and immediately after told the draft board I was available. In the early summer of 1943, I received my notice and was inducted as a private.

After basic training, I was told I qualified for officers' training if I chose and decided to follow it up, going to the Infantry O.C.S. at Fort Benning, Georgia. After several years of studying, the rugged training was a welcome change. I enjoyed the running and climbing and was the top student in a class of three hundred.

I was shipped overseas and given the command of an infantry platoon with the Fifth Division, stationed in England. It was less than a month after arriving that we again packed up, this time told we were headed for combat. We embarked and unloaded at the Normandy beaches five days after the D-Day assault of June 6, 1944.

What I saw there will always be a part of my memory: The bodies of those boys who went in on the original assault were still lying on the beach where they had fallen; they were swollen and stinking. It was a terrible, sickening thing. We were moved up to the front and began crawling our way through the hedgerows. For the first time in my life I really understood what fear was. If a combat soldier isn't afraid, then he's insane.

I was wounded twice. The first time a German soldier fired at me with a submachine gun from about twenty yards away; the bullet struck me in the left leg. I was crawling across a hedgerow in Normandy at the time. He fired, then disappeared. I was dragged back, bandaged and sent to an aid station. The wound kept me in a hospital for a few weeks. When I returned to duty we had pushed on and were driving the German army back at a faster clip. When the winter set in they were getting desperate. They began firing at us with anti-aircraft guns . . . fired them flat trajectory, right down our throats. One cold, rainy afternoon outside of a small German town — I don't remember the name — the Germans began firing those anti-aircraft guns at us as we tried to advance across a farm field. One shell exploded shrapnel right in front of me; the impact staggered me and knocked me to the ground. At the same time, chunks of metal tore into my chest and mid-section. For a few moments there, I thought my time had come. A long hospital stay took me out of the war, which was beginning to wind down. But I wouldn't be going home as fast as I had hoped.

Noting I was an attorney, the Army assigned me as part of the defense team for a group of enlisted men charged with beating stockade prisoners at the Lichfield prison in England.

The prisoners were American soldiers who had deserted; their complaints, which received attention from the news media, said they had been subjected to terrible beatings, made to crawl on the floor for food, and some had been force-fed cigarette butts.

After talking with the defendants, it became clear to me that they had been encouraged by their officers to be harsh on the prisoners, so as to dissuade other soldiers from deserting. Like the German officers who would be tried at Nuremberg, these soldiers were "merely following orders." I made motions to call the commanding generals into the court martial proceedings, but was denied. The commanders, I told the judges, were the ones responsible. We managed to get rather light sentences for the men, and created some uneasiness among the Army Command. I think everyone was happy when, in June 1946, the Army discharged me with the rank of captain, with two Purple Hearts, a Bronze Star and Combat Infantryman's Badge.

I was told to catch a boat back to the states, but I didn't want to waste thirty days on the water in a Liberty ship and instead caught an Army plane going to Orly in Paris, France. Once I got there I hitched another ride going to Iceland and from there to Goose Bay, Labrador, then another one to Presque Isle, Maine, and then on to New York. Total travel time was about three days. I wired Ruth, who was still in Washington with the Navy, told her I was on my way. I rode a train down to Washington and went to where she was assigned with the Joint Chiefs of Staff office. Ruth was an aide to a Navy Captain Herman. So I walked in, saw Captain Herman, popped him a salute and said, "Sir, I've come for my wife." Ruth heard me and came running from an adjoining office. I think the first thing he said was something about her being a lieutenant commander and outranking me, an infantry captain.

The Navy began processing Ruth for discharge which would require a few days, so I caught a train back to Alabama, visited my parents for a couple of days, borrowed their car, then drove back to Washington. Ruth and I took a ten-day vacation, which was the first we'd had.

We then came back to Walker County. I was ready to begin my private law practice in Jasper.

8

I T WAS AT THAT TIME that Johnson's career reached a pivotal point. He had been hired by the law firm of Curtis and Maddox in Jasper, Alabama. The senior member was James Jackson Curtis, then eighty years old, a former state circuit judge. He was a man Johnson had admired since he was a boy. Often in those years he had gone to the courthouse to watch Curtis preside over trials. Johnson felt hanging around the courthouse was better than loitering around pool halls.

The Johnsons rented an apartment in Jasper and things looked bright. He was young and full of energy, eager to earn his wings in law. He also showed a strong interest in golf. Sometimes after work he would stop by the course and hit a few. One day a local group sponsored a tournament and Johnson entered.

JOHNSON

Well, to my surprise, I managed to get into the finals. In such things, I suppose, golfers lose track of time. I didn't bother checking with the office, I was so caught up in the games; played three straight days.

When it was over, I went back to the office, sunburned and worn out. First thing, Judge Curtis calls me into his office.

"Frank," he says, "I think the time has come for you to make a decision."

"A decision? What's that, Judge?"

He looks me square in the eye and says, "You must decide whether you're going to spend your time hitting golf balls or being a lawyer."

It wasn't a suggestion; it was an ultimatum.

I nodded and says, "Judge, I think I'll practice law."

After that conversation, I didn't touch a golf club for over ten years; in fact, I didn't play again until I was a federal judge.

In 1948 Curtis died, but he had made such an impact that when Frank and Ruth Johnson adopted an infant son they named him James Curtis Johnson (though he would be called Johnny more often than James).

On Saturday nights the Johnsons would go grocery shopping, bringing in a week's supply of food.

JOHNSON

At the time, we were living in an apartment not far from the downtown section of Jasper. Christmas had just passed, and we were getting back into the routine of post-holiday living. Well, we got the groceries and I suggested that we eat out. Ruth readily agreed. We went to the Collins Hotel which had a reputation for serving some of the best steaks in Northwest Alabama. They charbroiled them . . . big, thick juicy steaks. They gave you a big platter for just two dollars. So we started eating and I had just commented about how good the steak tasted when, all of a sudden, we heard a siren.

Ruth chuckled, "I'll bet that's our apartment burning."

She was joking, of course.

But I shrugged and said, "I don't care if it is, I'm not leaving until I've finished this steak."

And that's what we did. We finished our meal, paid the tab, then went to the car. Driving to the apartment we saw police cars and fire trucks, their red lights flashing.

They had the entrance to our street blocked and I drove up to a police officer, rolled down the window and asked, "What's burning?"

Well, he told me, all right. It was our apartment building.

They wouldn't let me get by the roadblocks, so Ruth and I stood there watching. The fire got everything, including a brand new Stromberg-Carlson radio and record player. We didn't have a cent of insurance. Ruth and I had spent almost all of our military mustering-out pay on clothes and furniture and they were gone.

The fire had started when a boy had ran by the apartment building throwing firecrackers and one of them had gone through an open window. The firecracker landed in a Christmas tree that someone still had standing. Naturally, it was dried out and when the explosive went of, it caught the tree afire. The apartment with the burning tree was directly below ours.

The apartment was destroyed. For the next few days we stayed with an aunt, then got us a room at a boarding house. It was then that we decided we should have a house built. It was completed before the apartment was rebuilt.

One of the few civil rights cases I handled as a private attorney took place in the late 1940s when I filed suit against the sheriff of Franklin County, Alabama, a man named Byars. My client said that he had been driving through Franklin County and was, no doubt, speeding. He said the sheriff started chasing him and fired shots, four of the bullets striking the car. The driver stopped, but later we filed suit, charging the sheriff used deadly force in a situation that didn't call for it. You don't shoot at speeders. But the sheriff's lawyer met me and agreed to settle the case out of court and that ended the case.

But a few months later, along about February of 1950, Lecil Gray and I were up in the northwest corner of Alabama, fishing for jack salmon on the Tennessee River, coldest place in the world when the winter wind gets up. Lecil was a short, stout man with a quick wit and a big talker. He was also the probate judge of Walker County, and a big Democrat.

Anyway, late in the afternoon we got cold and went in. Lecil was gathering up some equipment and I walked toward the boathouse. About that time the owner, a man named Cain, comes out and says to me, "Want a drink?"

Well, I sure did and I took a big swig of Jack Daniels whiskey. Fortified, I walked back down to help Gray unload gear from the boat. But he was already on his way up. And he stops and stares at me, then he says, "Where'd you find some whiskey?"

Even in that cold wind he could smell it. I laughed and pointed toward Cain. Lecil got a drink and then threw the equipment into his car, a new Nash.

It was nearly dark when we left. Lecil drove and I sat in the passenger seat, one of those which could be let down into a reclining position. I was cold and tired and felt like sleeping.

To get back to Jasper meant driving through Franklin County and as we moved down the highway it turned dark. I was nearly asleep.

Suddenly there was a loud banging sound and I was knocked forward, then back again. We had hit something. I shouted at Lecil as he slammed on the brakes and for just a second I saw a big mule straddling the hood of the car, then it slid off onto the highway.

"Lecil, you hit a mule," I hollered. "Why didn't you watch where you were going?"

So we got out of the car and stood looking at the mule that lay dead in the highway.

In the headlights we could see it had been split nearly open and the contents of its bowels were splattered across the hood of the Nash.

Lecil's car had considerable damage, including a smashed-in grill, and one fender that was crumbled back so far it was shoved against the left tire. I got the jack handle out of the trunk and managed to wedge the fender away from the tire enough to allow Lecil to pull the car off the road.

Even in the cold air the smell of the fresh manure

was overpowering; it was all over the hood and even up
on top of the car.

"We gotta get the mule out of the road before someone else comes along and hits him," I said. So we dragged
him out of the road.

I noticed a metal tag on the mule and took a closer
look. The words "Walston Heston" were stamped on it. I
knew there was a mule barn around that area and apparently that mule belonged to Mr. Heston.

Well, Lecil keeps saying that we have to call the
sheriff. So a car came along and we flagged it down and
asked the driver to call the state patrol or the sheriff. As
we waited I took a closer look at Lecil's car.

"Looks like we can drive it all right," I said. Then I
say, "I'll pay half the cost of the repairs."

"That sounds fair," he said.

About thirty minutes later the sheriff's car pulls up.
Well, since I had once sued the man, I told Gray, "I think
I'll wait in the car. If he knows who I am, he's liable to put
you in jail for awhile."

Gray laughed. He thought I was joking. But I got in
the car and sat there with my hat pulled down over my
face so the sheriff couldn't see me. But a little while later
I hear a knock on the window and look up and there is the
sheriff. He says, "Good evening, Mr. Johnson. How are
you?"

So I told him I was fine and got out of the car. And
Lecil is standing there grinning at me. I figured he had
told the sheriff who I was. When the sheriff completed his
investigation, he left. Me and Lecil drove back to Jasper.

We went along a way and finally Lecil says, "Frank, I
managed to miss the first mule, but I couldn't dodge the
second one."

"The *first* mule," I said in disbelief. "Lecil, there
wasn't a first mule. There was just one mule and you hit
him."

"I swear, Frank, there was another mule," he said.
"But I managed to dodge him."

"Well, then you dodged the wrong mule," I said.

Later, I changed the subject and said that even though I agreed to pay half the damages to the car, there might be a way to get the mule's owner to pay the entire cost. Lecil agreed it was worth a try.

"I'll write a letter first thing in the morning," I told him.

Next day I was at my office and Lecil calls and says, "You wrote that letter yet?"

I told him I hadn't yet, but I was fixing to.

"Don't write it," he said.

I asked him why and he says, "Because I found out that the guy that owned the mule is the Franklin County campaign manager for Carl Elliott."

Elliott was a Democratic congressman from Alabama who was seeking reelection; Gray, of course, was a staunch Democrat.

So I said, "Is Carl Elliott going to pay for the car?"

"No, but I don't want to hurt his chances," Lecil says.

Well, I reminded him that I was a Republican. I didn't care who the mule's owner supported for Congress, I thought he should pay for the damages.

But Gray tells me, "I don't want to sue him."

So I told him I wouldn't write the letter. Then I said, "If you don't want to make a Democrat pay for the damages, then I don't think that I, as a Republican, should have to pay either."

"That's fine," Lecil said. "I'll take care of it."

And that ended the mule affair. Except for one thing. For week after week, Gray would drive that Nash to the Walker County Courthouse and park it right in front. And he never did wash the mule manure off it. It stayed there in caked form until a heavy spring thunderstorm finally washed it away.

Years went by and often when I saw Lecil, he would mention the incident. And he insisted until the day he died that there had been two mules that night and he had managed to dodge the first one.

Johnson was rated a solid lawyer by his peers in Northwest

Alabama. He wasn't afraid to take on the establishment. He once defended two brothers who were charged in the murder of the sheriff of Marion County, which adjoins Winston. They were accused of gunning him down with a pistol. Johnson argued self-defense. The jury didn't buy it and found both guilty. Johnson filed an appeal.

JOHNSON

I got looking at things and found that the two special prosecutors, Ernest Fite and his son, Rankin, practically ran Marion County. They were involved politically and they owned the bank. I came across the fact that they kept not only money in the bank but also the county jury rolls. I went to the State Supreme Court with this information, saying it might tend to sway a jury since some of them undoubtedly banked with the Fites. So the Court reversed the convictions and ordered a new trial. In the second case, the jury came out eleven-to-one in favor of acquittal. The State elected not to prosecute again and the two went free.

In 1949, a Jasper police officer, John Brom, was charged with murder in the death of a prisoner at the city jail, Thomas Hardcastle. The prisoner's arms were covered with bruises; the indictment said the officer beat the man to death. It had the community stirred up; they wanted to punish the officer. The evidence did appear damaging. It was going to be tough. Lecil Gray didn't help my morale in the matter. He says, "You ain't got a chance in hell of getting him off."

So I did some homework on the case, had experts examine the body, then produced testimony to the fact that the prisoner had been alleged to have used narcotics. There was testimony to the fact that when he was taken to a medical facility for treatment he had fallen down several times. A jury found Brom not guilty.He later became a state trooper and often stopped by my office to visit. He was a friend even though some of my orders were tough on the troopers, notably in the Selma march case.

In early 1953, Johnson was nominated by President Eisenhower to be the United States Attorney for the Northern District of Alabama.

When the offer came to be the United States Attorney, Johnson had to spend some time thinking it over. Giving up a private practice for such a position was a tremendous financial sacrifice in most cases. Besides, it would mean a commitment of at least four years, maybe eight, if Eisenhower was re-elected. At first, he wasn't sure he wanted to do that. In those days, United States Attorneys were getting a salary of $12,500 per year, which wasn't bad in 1953. But as a partner in a private law firm, he was pulling down between $15,000 and $18,000 a year.

But after a couple of days of thinking about it and talking it over with Ruth, he made up his mind. He walked into the office one day and asked Maddox his opinion.

JOHNSON

So Maddox says, "What do you think of it? It's your decision, Frank."

"Well, I kinda think I might enjoy taking the job, working for the federal government," I said. "I think I'm going to take it."

Maddox says, "Well, it might add some prestige to our firm if you do. You can never tell."

So we sat there for a moment or two and Maddox says, "Frank, why don't you just go ahead and walk out that door and go take the job. Then, in four years, or eight years, you can come on back and just walk right back in that door and take up where you left off."

I nodded. "Sounds fair to me."

And that was that. It might seem strange to say, but there wasn't a whole lot of legal work needed to temporarily undo the partnership. We were never very formal. Even though we were attorneys, we had no written agreement between us. I always figured that if people had to have something in writing, they had no business being partners.

I had enjoyed the way we operated. At the end of each month we would get together, figure up how much money we had taken in, pay the hired help and the bills, and then divide up what was left. It was a pretty good way to do business. So, I just walked out the door that day in 1953. I didn't pack up any books or files. I just left everything where it was.

And he went to Birmingham to be United States Attorney. But he would never return to private practice in Jasper. Nor would his life ever be quite the same.

As the U.S. Attorney, Johnson's toughest case involved the prosecution of a prominent West Alabama family charged with a form of slavery. Oscar, Fred, Grady and Robert Dial owned extensive farming land in Sumter County, the western end of the Alabama Black Belt, along the Mississippi line.

The brothers had routinely paid the small fines of blacks arrested and jailed by a sheriff in Mississippi. The deal was that those prisoners would work out their fine payment on the Dial farms, and stories of beatings and other mistreatment had been quite common.

Then, in May 1953, the body of a Negro identified as Herbert "Monk" Thompson was brought to a funeral home in York, Alabama; it bore evidence of a severe beating and the black couple who operated the funeral home contacted Johnson's office. He sent FBI agents to check it out. Their reports indicated that the Thirteenth Amendment notwithstanding, slavery was still being practiced.

In September, a grand jury in Birmingham indicted the four Dial brothers, plus two cousins from Mississippi. The trial before an all-white jury began May 10, 1954. The evidence showed that Thompson had worked on the Dial farm from March until early May, 1953, then attempted to escape, probably figuring the fifty-five dollar fine paid for his release from the Mississippi jail had been more than paid back by his labor.

The Dials found him, testimony revealed, and he was tied to a bale of hay and beaten ruthlessly by Fred and six black workers who were forced at gunpoint to perform the terrible deed. Thompson died two days later.

In prosecution of the case, Johnson faced one of Alabama's best defense attorneys, Roderick Beddow, Sr., who put on a grand defense, claiming among other things, that the unfortu-

nate Mr. Thompson may have died as a result of pneumonia. He
paraded a host of character witnesses to the stand and they all
said the Dials were fine people. But one old man, named Boyd,
was trapped when Johnson cross-examined him.

"You ever hear of the reputation the Dials have for beating
Negro workers?" It was just an offhand question.

To Johnson's surprise — and Beddow's shock — old Mr.
Boyd casually replied, "Yes, I've heard about that."

Beddow hurriedly called for a recess and followed the old
man into the hallway, storming, "You old son-of-a-bitch, I told
you this morning if you knew anything bad about the Dial boys
to tell me."

Replied Boyd, "But Mr. Beddow, whupping a nigger ain't
bad in Sumter County."

On May 14, 1954 — just three days before the historic
Supreme Court decision on *Brown* — the jury returned guilty
verdicts against Fred and Oscar Dial. Both were to be sentenced
for involuntary servitude. Fred was also found guilty of forcing
Thompson into peonage. Fred faced fifteen years in the pen,
Oscar ten. Months later, Judge Seybourn Lynne sentenced
them to eighteen months in prison.

JOHNSON

There had been a total of five defendants named in
the indictment, but during the trial I asked the judge to
dismiss three of the men, because there was not sufficient evidence to convict them. Anyway, I stood up and
announced to Judge Lynne, "Your honor, at this time the
government moves to dismiss the indictments against
the following defendants." And I named the three men.

Across the room I saw defense attorney Beddow
watching me. Shortly after, during a recess, he saw me in
the hallway and started grinning at me.

"You sneaky rascal," he said. "You knew you could
never prove anything against those three when you indicted them. Then you come in here and dismiss the
indictment. You did that just to show the court and the
jury how fair you are. That's real strategy." He laughed
then and shook his head.

I just grinned at him and walked on, not saying a word. It was an honor to get a compliment from a lawyer like Beddow. He was probably the best-known defense lawyer in the South.

One of my first legal involvements with blacks was in 1948 when I was practicing in Jasper. According to the police report, a black man who apparently was just passing through along the railroad tracks was spotted by a white woman who lived nearby. She told the police that the man was standing alongside the tracks and holding a pole in his hands. At the end of the pole was a pair of woman's panties and the man stood on the tracks waving it back and forth. The police came and took him to jail and he must have been there a couple of days before he got word out to me. Another man who was released from jail came by my office and said the man wanted to see me. So I went down to the jail and I didn't even ask him what he had done or why he had been waving the pole with the woman's panties affixed to the end. It was clear there was no law against standing alongside the railway tracks. It was also clear that the only reason he was being held was because he was black. So I went to the courthouse and filed a motion for habeas corpus, which would force the City of Jasper to show cause why the man should be held and what charges he was being held on. The city attorney sent me a note: "Your issue is moot," he wrote. "We released the man this morning."

It had rankled me to see a man being held in jail for no reason. I didn't care about the fee and I didn't even want one. I just hated the way he had been thrown into jail for no reason.

9

F RANK JOHNSON NEVER had to look very far to see the division the Civil War had brought to the nation. His own great-grandfathers lived not thirty miles apart in Fayette County, which lies just to the southwest of Winston, in the northwestern part of Alabama. Like Winston, Fayette was rugged country, full of hills and ravines.

JOHNSON

Great-grandfather James Johnson had taken up arms with the Union. He was a Lincoln man. Slavery was not the issue with him, I don't suppose, although I'm sure he had feelings about it. There were virtually no slaves in northwest Alabama. I think Great-grandfather Johnson just had a basic belief in preserving the Union. More basically, perhaps, he just couldn't let himself fire on the American flag.

On the other hand, great-grandfather Francis Marion Treadaway chose to fight for the Confederacy.

In my early years, when I was ten, and eleven and twelve, I would spend some summers with my grandparents, William Rufus and Bessie Johnson, who lived near Carbon Hill in Walker County. That was in the late 1920s. Grandfather was a carpenter and one summer he and I built a barn. It was the sort of thing every boy should do.

During those summers Grandmother Bessie would get up early and fix breakfast for us. As she would knead the dough for biscuits, she'd hum or sing. And sometimes she'd sing the words from "Battle Hymn of the Republic."

Mine eyes have seen the glory,
Of the coming of the Lord,
He is trampling out the vintage
Where the grapes of wrath are stored.

I never even heard the song "Dixie" until I was twenty-one years old, enrolled at the University of Alabama.

It was during those summers that she would tell me about her father — my great-grandfather — Francis Marion Treadaway, and what she remembered of the days and nights of Reconstruction, when Treadaway was sheriff of Fayette County. In the Civil War he had been a captain of infantry, and was twice wounded in battle. After the war, however, he accepted the change that had come. He became a Republican and was elected sheriff of Fayette County.

This was Reconstruction and the Ku Klux Klan was terrorizing the South. But Treadaway set out to do some terrorizing of his own against the KKK. One night he was checking a report of a Klan attack. While he was gone, some fifteen or twenty Klansmen, attired in their robes and hoods, came to his house, firing shots into the air and shouting threats. Great-grandmother Sallie was terrified.

She watched through the slip latch as some of the men walked up to the porch and pranced about, telling her that her husband would be killed. She couldn't tell who they were, but she saw that one of them had a clubfoot and she knew that was a man named Luther Ingalls. And she stuck her rifle out the slip latch and said, "Luther Ingalls, I'll blow you off that porch if you don't leave."

Well, he left and took the others with him. When my great-grandfather got home, she told him about it and said she saw one man had a clubfoot. So Treadaway went and got some of his deputies and they rode over to Luther

Ingalls's house and called him out.

When he came out Treadaway tied him up, hanged him upside down over a well and told him to either reveal the names of his cohorts or be cut down into the well to drown. Well, the man poured out the information.

In those days lawmen didn't have to read suspects their Miranda rights.

At daybreak Sheriff Treadaway was on the move, rounding up KKK members and cramming the jail full of them. For a time, the bold action broke the hold of the Klan in Fayette County, but within a few months they came back, threatening, shooting, burning, killing. The sheriff's posse began to waver under KKK pressure and finally disbanded. With only a few deputies to help, Sheriff Treadaway watched law and order begin to erode. The power of the KKK at that time was awesome. At Livingston and Eutaw, in the western end of the Black Belt section of Alabama, the governor of the state was afraid to speak at political rallies of blacks and white Republicans because KKK mobs appeared with guns and clubs and hurled threats at him.

Treadaway's own life became a living hell. He would come home at night and find Sallie sobbing in terror, telling him of Klan visits which included gunshots fired into the house and shouted threats. He had to stay home with her then. Some days, strident KKK members, in full regalia, would parade by his house, waving guns, shooting, hooting and jeering.

The embattled sheriff sought help from the state and federal authorities. He couldn't write very well, and had to have a friend compose a letter for him to send to Governor William H. Smith. In October 1870, he sent this urgent appeal to Montgomery:

His Excellency, Wm. H. Smith
Governor of Alabama.
Sir:
The undersigned, Sheriff of the County of Fayette in the State of Alabama, as such Sheriff, respectfully represents to your Excellency that, there are, and have been for many months past, a great number of lawless persons in said County

of Fayette, who perpetrate acts of violence upon the good and law-abiding citizens thereof, under cover of night and in disguise; that these persons obstruct, hinder, and defeat on many occasions the due enforcement of the law and the executions of its process, by threats, intimidations and actual violence. And, that because of the threats of this vengeance, the good people of said County are frightened to such extent that they are unwilling to aid your petitioner as posse; that said lawless persons, in the belief of your relator, can and will execute their threats in detail, upon such citizens as are willing or might be constrained to act as such posse, whenever disbanded, that several persons within the five months last past have been executed, in disguise by lynch law, so called, in said county; and that many other acts of lawlessness from said persons continue to occur in various locations.

And, to further (illegible) that many of the . . . citizens of said county . . . will not be permitted to . . . cast their ballots at the ensuing general election in this state unless your petitioner procure military aide to co-operate with him as a posse commitatus in the preservation of the peace and in the protection of the citizens regardless of party affiliation, for the reasons above set forth. He, therefore, requests your Excellency, to procure and provide such military aide in the interests of law and order...

The governor dispatched a unit of infantry troops to the county and by late in the month Sheriff Treadaway reported that he and the troops began making arrests of the lawless men, three of whom confessed, he said. But it didn't end the problem, he said, adding that after making bond, the KKK members would continue their nighthawk activity. He asked Governor Smith to "send in the U. S. Marshall (sic) and declare the county under marshall (sic) law, so I can have these lawless ones I catch up punished at once . . . ."

More troops were sent to Fayette County and later the U.S. Attorney for North Alabama — a job Frank Minis Johnson, Jr., would later hold — was sent to begin a probe of KKK activity. His name was George Minnis. He brought KKK members to trial and finally the terror came to an end.

Treadaway's daughter, Bessie, married the son of James Johnson, William Rufus Johnson. That marriage brought forth a son who was named Frank M. Johnson, who would later become the father of Frank M. Johnson, Jr.

JOHNSON

In honor of Mr. Minnis, my father and later I, were given the middle name Minis. For some reason the second "n" was left out.

The terror that pervaded in Alabama during the 1870s was similar in many ways to that which gripped the state in the 1950s and 1960s, the Second Reconstruction. I believe I felt the same concerns that my great-grandfather felt. We both saw white people who were inclined to do right, but were afraid to speak out, afraid of the reprisal that might come, either socially, economically or, more frightfully, in the form of a night visit by hooded hoodlums. In both periods of time, the KKK had run rampant.

I've tried to understand the behavior, the silence of so many whites. I suppose there is a self-preservation instinct in people, and they see something taking place that they know is wrong, but won't speak out. They stand silent, pretending not to see, dreading the prospect that they might be called upon to make a moral judgment and commitment; they do everything possible to avoid that.

Whites faced that dilemma in the Second Reconstruction as well as the first, and turned away, blinded and speechless.

Heading the list, in my opinion, would be the organized religion groups and their ministers. According to their charge, as I understand it, they are to carry out God's work here on this earth. With few exceptions, they did not carry out the Lord's work when it came to the rights of black people. I can often recall sitting in my office weighing an emotional, potentially explosive civil rights case and wondering — never hoping, just wondering — if some ministers or church groups would cry out to their followers about what was right and just. I never heard it, except on occasion from a few, most of them from outside the South.

What was different between my situation and that of great-grandfather Treadaway was that I had more power than he did. I had the advantage of living in a modern time. I could pick up the telephone and get the FBI, the U.S. Marshal, the Justice Department, even the President of the United States, whatever was needed to ensure the support of an order.

But there were many times, even with this force in support of me, that I felt alone. I don't care who you are, when something happens and the entire state rises up, through its politicians and its press, and lambasts you and the Klan is making threats, you become apprehensive for your family, sometimes waiting for something to happen.

At such times I would be supported by my own family, especially my wife, Ruth, who always supported me.

The lonely struggle of Treadaway, his wife Sallie, and their children, including Bessie, who would become my grandmother, is one of the true stories of courage that has never really been told.

Great-grandfather James Johnson, though not facing the challenge Treadaway did, nonetheless was a man of courage in his own right. After the Civil War, he became a pillar in the community, becoming one of the poll officials in Fayette County.

One of my favorite stories about him involved his preparations for celebrating the Fourth of July. It was back when ice making was first introduced to that part of Alabama.

The ice maker was located in Carbon Hill in Walker County, about twenty miles or so from where the Johnsons lived. So late one July third afternoon, he and some friends drove their mule and wagon over to Carbon Hill and bought a fifty-pound block of ice, put it in a croker sack, then hurried back home with it. They were going to make ice cream.

Trying to figure out how to keep it intact for the July Fourth picnic, they devised a plan of tying the sack to a tree limb and letting it dangle down into the waters of Boxes Creek. The water was cold and great-grandfather Johnson surmised that it would serve as a natural refrigerator. Next day they go back to the creek and get the sack out. Naturally, the ice had melted away. They thought some neighbors named Kelly had stolen it.

They, like many others in Tennessee and North Alabama, were basic, primitive people, the Johnsons. I heard the story passed along about great-grandmother Suzanne Johnson, who killed a deer one day. Seems she had gone to the creek to do the laundry and had placed one of her babies down on a blanket near the creek. While she was busy with the clothes, she heard a noise and turned to see this big buck nosing around the blanket.

I don't know what intentions the deer had, but Mrs. Johnson just acted by instinct. She was afraid it meant to harm the baby. So she grabbed up a pine knot and charged the deer, hitting him with it. I guess she must have whacked him a number of times, because it killed him. She came home that day with clean laundry and some venison.

10

W HEN JOHNSON WENT to Montgomery in 1955 he found a haphazard operation in the office of the U.S. District Judge. His first impression of the place was not positive: he found a desk and a chair in his office, but there wasn't a piece of paper in or on the desk; not a pencil to write with. Records were in a state of disarray; some case files were as much as seven years behind. Everything about the place appeared outdated, even archaic.

JOHNSON

It wasn't Judge Kennamer's fault. He hadn't even been given a law clerk; instead, a son of his served as both clerk and secretary. The court reporter, a woman in her seventies, had made a good effort at doing her job; it had been poor, at best.

And the probation officer didn't find it necessary to put things in writing. I remember there were a number of cases piled up in which the defendants simply wanted to enter guilty pleas. But before I could sentence them, I wanted to know something about their backgrounds. So I called the probation officer in one day and asked him for a pre-sentence report for the first defendant.

He looks startled, says, "Judge, we don't make pre-sentence reports."

78

I couldn't believe it. "No pre-sentence report?"

So he reached into his pocket and pulled out a personal letter he had received. On the envelope he had scrawled some notes and he hurriedly read over them. Then he says, "Judge, you just ask me anything you want to know about this man and I think I can tell you."

"That's not satisfactory," I told him. "I have to sentence a man and I want to know something about him before I do. I want solid, comprehensive reports from now on and I want them in writing."

Then, there was the referee in bankruptcy for the district, a Mr. J.O. Middleton, who was in his eighties. I had serious questions about his ability. This man had to do comprehensive reading of figures and make decisions.

One day about two months after my arrival, I was getting on the elevator at the courthouse and Middleton walked up and stood beside me ... and looked and looked; practically put his face up into mine. Then he says, "I believe I've seen you around here before, haven't I?"

The man was almost blind. And his wife, also in her eighties, who served as his assistant, couldn't see much better. Johnson did some replacing of the staff, bringing in professionals to do the job. He was going to need them.

JOHNSON

One of the first things I did as a federal judge was to see that women were included on jury rolls. At the time, the law prescribed that federal court jury rolls would follow the state law. In Alabama, that meant men only.

But in 1957, Congress passed a new law regarding federal juries and it said that the jury selection process would be available to all citizens of the United States. I read the law and noted that it did not say anything about women. But at the same time, it didn't say that juries had to be composed of men. It said citizens.

I immediately entered an order directing the federal jury commission for the Middle District of Alabama to

draw up a new list of prospective jurors and to include
women as well as men. A Montgomery woman named
Olive Andrews became the first woman to be selected to
a jury in Alabama. Interestingly enough, the case was
appealed on the grounds that a woman had sat on the
jury. At the time, State of Alabama courts did not allow
women. The appeal didn't hold water.

A short time later I also entered an order to the jury
commission that they would increase the number of
blacks listed to the jury rolls, the number reflecting as
nearly as possible the proportion of blacks living in the
Middle District of Alabama, roughly 25 percent.

In November 1957 something happened that almost forced
Johnson to step down as a federal judge. It was a mild heart
attack, but serious enough to put him in a hospital and give
sober thought to his future.

JOHNSON

I was told that maybe it was time for me to either quit
smoking or cut down. I was smoking two packs of Home
Run cigarettes a day.

When the attack came and I was put in the hospital,
Ruth called Dr. Tinsley Harrison of the University of
Alabama Hospital in Birmingham. He had been one of
President Eisenhower's physicians when he had had his
heart attack in 1955.

So Dr. Harrison came down and looked me over and
somewhere in the conversation he says, "Judge, you
need to cut down on the smoking. Now I smoke cigarettes myself and here's what I do: Each day before I
leave the house I take ten cigarettes with me and budget
myself. I ration them during the day because I'm not
going to smoke more than ten. See, ten cigarettes a day
won't hurt you. So you do that and you'll be doing all
right."

So I told him I'd try it; meanwhile I asked him to
remain as my physician and he said that would be imprac-
tical since he lived in Birmingham. Instead, he recom-

mended a Montgomery doctor whom he said was an excellent heart doctor, Dr. John Wade. And he was right, it turns out. Well, we contacted Dr. Wade and before long I was out of the hospital and the two of us decided to go fishing together. A weekend of fishing is good therapy no matter what your problem might be, the doctor had told me, and I agreed.

I told Ruth, "Now Dr. Wade smokes cigarettes, too. So what I'll do is watch him. If he smokes one, I'll smoke one."

Well, it turned out to be a bad idea. Dr. Wade smoked one cigarette after another the whole day, practically smoked me out of the boat. So I knew such systems wouldn't work. And I continued with Home Run cigarettes, firing one up whenever I wanted to smoke.

I never did stop smoking until 1974. And what stopped me was the death of Dr. Wade . . . he died from lung cancer. That told me something.

A short time after his death, I had to go to Texas for a hearing and a U. S. marshal rode out there with me and we both smoked . . . filled up an ashtray the size of a watermelon. Well, I had been giving a lot of thought to quitting and that trip did it. When we prepared to drive back to Alabama my mouth was sore, my throat was sore and I couldn't taste food very well. So all of a sudden I just took the pack of cigarettes I had and handed them to the marshal, said, "I quit smoking just this minute. You can give them to some of the prisoners when we get back."

I decided to stop and I stopped; no cut-down programs, no rationing. The only way to quit is to quit, just throw them out the window. I've felt better since I've quit. But I haven't lost my desire for tobacco. But instead of smoking it, I chew it. Chewing is a little less dangerous and almost as enjoyable. I've been chewing Levi Garrett since 1975 or so and enjoy a good chew. And when you're fishing, chewing doesn't tie up one of your hands.

After the 1957 heart attack, I began to have some second thoughts about being a federal judge. I think any judge will have that sense of uncertainty gnawing at him.

A federal judgeship is a lifetime appointment; when something's for life, you do some soul-searching, wonder if you've made a mistake. I was raised to believe that you get paid what you're worth. But in this job you're paid without regard to your production. Then, too, your social life has to be altered, perhaps; you should not be socializing with attorneys that practice before you on a regular basis.

And you cannot be an advocate on public issues — for or against something. An attorney can get out there for some cause — civil rights, or anything else — and plow some ground. But a judge can't do that. So I was wondering about things. But the workload had nothing to do with my heart attack; it had been a rather uneventful period, actually.

So, from all the pondering on it, I decided that I would remain a judge. But the only change that came about was that I became a fisherman again . . . something I had been out of touch with for several years. And if I wasn't fishing, I'd try to spend some time golfing or gardening. The main thing was to try to do something different, something relaxing and enjoyable, on weekends.

I've worked hard on this job; I've never felt I had to hang my head down or back up to the paymaster. But I've rarely taken the job home with me. I would work twelve hours a day and if I couldn't do it in that time, I needed to get another job.

Part III

'A carpetbaggin',
scalawaggin' liar

Wallace vs. Johnson
on voting rights
1958-1963

Viola Quinn was twenty-two years old. And on this day, in June, 1960, she had, along with other Negroes, waited more than six hours in the hot, musty corridor of the Macon County Courthouse at Tuskegee, Alabama. A yellow-brick building, it sat facing the town square, a quiet, grassy area centered by a statue of a Confederate soldier. A neat town with tree-lined streets, Tuskegee was nearly 80 percent black and the home of famed Tuskegee Institute.

Finally, Miss Quinn was called in to take the test to see if she could become a registered voter. For nearly an hour she wrote on questions concerning the Constitution, then filled out a personal questionnaire. Registrar Wheeler Dyson took note that she was single. He also observed other things. To his colleague, Charles Scott, he said, "You notice that Quinn girl? Her breasts were running." Scott also had detected the tell-tale sign of motherhood. "Well," said Dyson, "we can't have the city supporting illegitimate children." Miss Quinn was rejected.

—FROM AN AFFIDAVIT FILED IN JOHNSON'S COURT.

11

F ROM THE MID-1870s until 1951, blacks were kept off
the voting rolls in Alabama by the mere fact that the
white governing bodies in many counties simply refused
to allow them to enter the courthouse on registration day. It
could all be summed up by the incident at the Bullock County
Courthouse in Union Springs when a black man walked into the
registrar's office one day, hat in hand, and stood meekly under
the glare of the officials.

"Luke, what business do you have here?" one asked. "Didn't
I tell you once before not to come around here?"

"I come to try to register to vote," came the reply.

The registrar rose, pointed toward the door, and bellowed:
"To hell out of here!"

Period. It was an especially effective tactic in maintaining
white supremacy in the Black Belt counties — Lowndes, Wilcox, Perry, Bullock, Barbour, Macon, Hale, Greene, Sumter,
Marengo and Dallas — where blacks outnumbered whites by as
much as four to one.

(In Mississippi, one registrar merely pulled a pistol and
shot a black who had sought to be registered).

In 1951 Alabama began applying a new four-page voting
questionnaire which required applicants to have some knowledge of the Constitution as well as other things decided upon by
the whim of the individual registrar. As far as blacks were

Johnson's former law school classmate, George C. Wallace, became his constant adversary over a turbulent two-decade period.

concerned, it didn't mean a great deal. In Bullock County, from 1952 through 1959, a total of five blacks were registered. In 1960, a minister attempted to become the sixth. He was rejected twice; his failure so demoralized the others, that not another even tried.

There were no blacks registered to vote either in Lowndes or Wilcox counties, both areas where black families picked cotton by hand, most of which was used to pay the rent of the shanty located on a plantation. Although slavery had been legally ended since 1865, there was some truth to the whispered observations of many Negroes: "If you can't vote, you ain't free; if you ain't free, you a slave."

The battle against voting discrimination in Alabama began rather routinely in 1958 when the United States Commission on Civil Rights began looking at the problem in the eastern Black Belt counties. Things came to a head when a former law school classmate of Johnson's — George C. Wallace, the circuit judge for Barbour and Bullock counties — refused to turn over voting records to the commission.

Known to his constituents as "the little judge," Wallace had been viewed as a comparative liberal. In May 1958, he had lost in his bid to be governor to John Patterson and vowed after that defeat "I'll never be out-segged again." He began implementing that pledge when the request for voting records was made. On October 28 — with more than a little fanfare — he announced he was impounding all Barbour County records. Several weeks later he likewise took possession of voting records in Bullock County. This, just two weeks before the commission was to hold public hearings in Montgomery on voting discrimination.

The pending confrontation shaping up between Wallace and the federal government caught the attention of the press. There was still hope that Wallace would yield to pressure and cooperate, but when the hearings began on December 8, he refused to attend. Nor did he allow the records to be turned loose.

The Commission notified Judge Johnson of the impasse and on December 17 he issued an order to Wallace and the registrars of the two counties to turn over their records. They had until January 12, 1959, to comply, the judge said.

JOHNSON

That Sunday evening Ruth and Johnny and I went out for supper and when we returned we found Glen Curlee parked in front of the house. Glen was an old law school friend of both mine and Wallace's. In fact he and Wallace had roomed together.

When we pulled into the driveway he got out of his car and came over. After exchanging greetings, he asked if he could talk to me.

So I asked, "What do you want to talk about?"

He says, "Little George asked me to ask you if he could talk to you."

"What about?"

So Curlee says, "He's afraid you might send him to the pen."

Well, a judge isn't supposed to be talking about a case to the parties involved. I stood there for a moment thinking it over. But George had been a friend in law school; even though we had lost touch with each other, he had sent a letter of support to President Eisenhower for my nomination as federal judge. So I told Curlee, "OK, I'll talk to him. Does he want to come here?"

"Let me call him," he said, "and I'll get back to you."

So Curlee left and in about fifteen minutes he called me from a telephone booth. He had talked with Wallace. He says, "Little George is over at his home in Clayton and says it'll take him a little while to get here."

"That'll be all right," I said.

"Says it might be eleven-thirty or so," Curlee says. "That OK?"

"I'll wait up for him," I said.

But I couldn't figure why it would take him so long to get to my house. Clayton is only about seventy miles from Montgomery. It was then only about eight o'clock and if he left then he could have been at my place by nine-thirty, at the latest. But I watched some television with Ruth and Johnny for a while. When they went to bed, I sat up reading, then put on some coffee. I figured George would need something to keep him awake, as he would be driving back home and it would be late.

It was close to midnight when the doorbell rang. It awakened Ruth and she came to the bedroom door. I went to the front door. And George is standing there, his coat collar turned up high. There have been stories that he had his coat over his head, but I don't recall that being the case, just had the collar turned up high.

So I said, "George, come on in. It's too cold to be

standing out there."

Well, we shook hands and he says, "Judge, my ass is in a crack. I need some help."

Ruth later told me she heard the remark and decided to go back to bed.

I took his coat. "I fixed us some coffee. Why don't we sit in the kitchen."

We went in and I poured two cups; George sat at the table. When I sat down he says:

"You know I'm running for governor." He looked at me for some reaction and I shrugged. He continued, "I ʼnk this is going to help me get in."

ʼ shook my head. "George, you know I don't care ʼt."

ʼt want to violate your order," he said. "I'm ʼre some way to comply."

ʼe way to do that is turn the records over," I saʼ ʼll you have to do."

ʼd that for a minute or so. Then, he says, "I think ı ıʼ to comply. That'll help me. If you'll just give me ten or fifteen days, I could stand that. But anything more than that would hurt me politically and it would kill my mother."

His words puzzled me. He had, within a few moments, done a complete about-face.

"George," I said, "I just will not talk to you about a sentence. We shouldn't even be talking."

"You can't give me ten days or so?"

"George, if you don't comply," I told him, "I'll pop you hard."

He just sat there staring at me. He knew he could get up to six months. I told him I couldn't bend the law. And I wouldn't bend it. Talking with him was as far as I would go.

Finally, he says, "What if I turn 'em over to the grand jury in each county and let them turn 'em over to the Civil Rights Commission?"

I shrugged. "That'll be OK. I don't care how you do it, just so you do it before the hearing."

That ended our conversation. Next morning he sends the sheriffs of the two counties scurrying across the countryside, rounding up members of each grand jury for emergency sessions. Then he gave them the records and suggested that they could do what they wanted to do with them. Apparently he made it clear he was leaving it up to them to comply with the federal government request.

What George had hoped for was to be able to defy the government — at least outwardly — come before me and be found guilty, then go to jail for a couple of days and come out a hero to the white people of Alabama. But even though he wouldn't get it his way, he would turn the situation to his own advantage, as he would often do in later years.

The first inkling of the kind of politician George Wallace would be was shown to me during that case. And he was a good politician, I'll grant you that — the best I've ever seen. No matter how high up you threw him, he landed on his feet, like a cat. But I would detest the way he would go about misleading the people of Alabama for the purpose of pursuing his political career.

On the day of the hearing, George came into the courtroom and, much to my surprise, his attorney, John Kohn, a tall, stately man, rose, lifted his arms grandly upward and intoned, "We plead guilty. We plead guilty."

I stared at him in disbelief. I had already been told by the U. S. Civil Rights Commission that the voting records of Barbour and Bullock counties had finally been turned over to them by the grand juries.

So I refused to accept the guilty plea and, instead, asked the government attorneys to call their witnesses. They testified that the order for Wallace to surrender the records had been obeyed; that the Civil Rights Commission had possession of the records.

After a short hearing, I called Wallace to the bench and read my findings. He stood before me, his head down, his hands clutched behind him, listening as I read:

"This court finds that on January 12 and 13, George C. Wallace, after receiving actual notice, for some reason judicially unknown to this court, attempted to give the impression he was defying this court's order. As to why the devious methods were used this court will not now judicially determine. In this connection, this court feels it sufficient to observe that if these devious means were in good faith considered by Wallace to be essential to the proper exercise of his state judicial function, then this court will not and should not comment.... However, if these devious means were used for political purposes, then this court refuses to allow its authority and dignity to be bent or swayed by such politically-generated whirlwinds."

In essence, Wallace had raised a cloud of dust but still managed to walk the narrow path within the law. He followed this same sequence many times during his political career. The "stand in the schoolhouse door" and then withdrawing was a typical ruse. As he emerged from the court building that winter morning in Montgomery, he was greeted by a band of supporters who cheered his "state's rights" stand. Quick to recognize the opportunity, he began the oratory that would become familiar across the land — how he had stood up to the government and backed it down.

Wallace flashed the V-for-victory sign, then went to the Jefferson Davis Hotel to prepare for a press conference. There were stories as he drew up his statement, he became so wound up that he thumped his head against the wall. When he met with the news people, he was in rare form. His statement in part read:

I pled guilty to failing to deliver the voter registration records to agents of the Civil Rights Commission. Since there was a grave Constitutional question involved . . . I believe this justifies my militant stand against the Civil Rights Commission to take over the courts of Alabama . . . [W]e have here a case of federal authority against state authority and I was willing to risk my freedom in order to test the question . . . These characters from the evil Civil Rights Commission and Justice Department were backed to the wall — they were defied and backed down. It has been apparent that they were hunting a way out. This 1959 attempt to have a second Sherman's March to the Sea has been stopped in the Cradle of the Confederacy.

And later, he would refer to the hearing and declare that he had stood up to the federal court and the government and backed them down. And anyone who said he didn't, he would declare, was a "carpetbaggin', scalawaggin' liar." He was obviously talking about Johnson.

JOHNSON

I wouldn't be human if I hadn't been disgusted by some of the statements he made. I hadn't seen that side of Wallace before and didn't know he could be so vicious. I had never seen it that starkly displayed in anyone, conduct that was both Machiavellian and mendacious.

And the majority of the white people of Alabama bought every word he said; they believed it when he said he had taken on the federal government and won. George just simply misled the people. He couldn't have believed the things he was saying then and would say later. He hoodwinked and duped the white people of the state and they ate up every word.

Maybe it was just the times. I guess if George Wallace hadn't been there ranting about these things, somebody else would have been doing it.

But whatever, it would be the first step in getting George into the statehouse as governor of Alabama and put him in a position to verbally challenge my orders at every step as the battle to end segregation heated up. Much of that struggle in the South would be centered in Montgomery, Alabama.

My first contact with George Wallace was when I enrolled at the University of Alabama in 1939. George was in pre-law, too, and we became acquainted.

What I recall about George in those days was that he was such a liberal; believed in the New Deal concepts of President Roosevelt. I was a conservative, naturally, and we had debated the issues. But mostly the friendship between all of the law students was based on the social events that college life brings.

George and Glen Curlee occasionally visited our apartment for student social occasions. But there was never any doubt that George intended to be a politician. Ruth recalls that the first time she ever saw him he was actually standing on a "soap box" making a speech about some campus issue. Once, while at our apartment, he placed a long distance call to the president of Mexico. I never knew what he was doing — there was a lot of talking going on and nobody paid much attention — until I saw the phone bill. Ruth and I refused to pay for it; we didn't make or authorize the call. I never did know why he called or how the bill was resolved.

Glen and George remained friends; but the voting case wiped out whatever friendship George and I had in college. We just never talked after that, except briefly on two occasions.

During the 1962 gubernatorial campaign in Alabama, Wallace rallies featured scores of supporters brandishing Confederate flags, the playing of "Dixie" and lots of country music. When the crowd was ready, he would step forth and assail the federal courts and "the carpetbagging, integrating federal judges."

In Haleyville, Johnson's hometown, Wallace proclaimed to a cheering throng: "I will, if elected, refuse to obey any federal judge's integration order. They won't put their filthy hands on the governor of a sovereign state. This Washington crowd and the federal judge backed down, and when they say they didn't they are integrating, carpetbagging, scalawagging liars!"

At Talladega, accompanied by KKK leader Robert Shelton, he exploded: "We got a lousy, irresponsible federal court system that's trying to tell us how to run our schools, our state government and our social life. There's a bunch of sissy-britches in Alabama who say we've got to conform. I say we don't! I am unalterably opposed to mixing the races in the schools and I will go the last mile in stopping the no-count federal court system

from running our lives. If I were a federal judge I would resign
and eat acorns and run rabbits rather than serve."

And Seymore Trammell, who would be Wallace's finance
director after he was elected, said in a speech in Selma: "Federal
judges should be scorned . . . and they and their families should
be ostracized by responsible Southerners."

JOHNSON

No matter how thick your hide, such talk hurts. Any
judge who handles cases that deal with human emotions
can expect some harsh verbal treatment from time to
time. But in those years in Alabama it went on and on. It
was something I tried to ignore. But it had its impact,
mostly, I think, because I realized it might have been
bothering my family. I felt, too, that it was beneath the
dignity of a judge to get into name-calling spats with state
officials, or to use the press to retaliate. A federal judge in
those days didn't have a press corps to carry his side; I
probably wouldn't have said very much anyway.

George and his followers were going around calling
"Nigger! Nigger!" and the people of Alabama didn't knock
themselves out looking for the truth. If you were a federal
judge, it was open season.

There were some ludicrous elements to it, however.
George was going around taking potshots at me, then,
when there was a school desegregation case against the
state of Alabama which named him as a defendant, his
attorney asked me to recuse myself from hearing the
case.

So I asked John Kohn, Wallace's attorney, why I
should step aside. And he told me Wallace had been
making derogatory statements about me — he admitted
it publicly — and said, as a result, I would not be able to
render a fair decision. Well, I told Kohn that if that was a
valid reason, then it might follow that no judge could ever
hear a case because all a defendant would have to do is
make some bad remarks about a judge and then ask him
to remove himself from a case because he might be
biased.

12

THE JUSTICE DEPARTMENT, meantime, began laying the groundwork for suits to attack counties on voting discrimination. Cases were aimed at Barbour, Bullock and Macon counties, east of Montgomery.

The latter county was the location of Tuskegee Institute, one of the Negro "Ivy League" colleges; it was a community where the level of education of blacks was higher than in many other towns in Alabama or the entire country.

Of the 26,700 living in the county, 22,300 were black. Yet, only ten percent of the black people were registered to vote.

Johnson set a hearing to be conducted at the satellite courthouse at Opelika, in Lee County, which adjoins Macon on the east. The date was February 20, 1961.

JOHNSON

This would be the case where I realized the time had come to start wearing glasses. I was then forty-two. There was such an enormous pile of material for me to read that my eyes were starting to feel the strain. The State of Alabama, for instance, submitted a 103-point response to the government's complaint. State attorneys also questioned my jurisdiction in the case. The government had filed thousands of pages of evidence.

The Macon County case would be the one that

began to erode Southern voting discrimination. People talk about voting rights, and they automatically think of Selma. But Macon County was the case that began to give blacks the right to vote. I called the efforts of the Macon County Board of Registrars to prevent blacks from registering "puny," and I used that word in my decree. It was the only way to describe it. They tried everything over there to keep them out. The Middle District of Alabama federal court took the lead in voting rights and the Fifth Circuit and the Supreme Court consistently upheld those rulings. When the Selma demonstrations started in 1965, the black citizens in my section of the state of Alabama had already won their right to vote.

"Puny" excuses? Registrars Dyson and Scott (and others who preceded or followed them) were super meticulous in finding ways and reasons to reject black applicants.

Mrs. Ola Sullins, sixty-five, was turned down because she failed to fill out the exact date indicating how long she had lived at her present address. "I didn't know for sure," she said. "I've lived there since 1915." Later, after a pain-staking search of records, it was determined that the exact date was October 30, 1915. But she was not allowed to correct her form.

Such miniscule errors — and even larger ones — were routinely overlooked for white applicants.

Nellie H. Kelker, thirty-seven, a divorcee and a registered nurse in Tuskegee, wrote that she had resided at her address since April 21, 1945. It should have been 1954. She was rejected.

Mrs. Eddie J. Driver was denied registration because she did not know in which ward or voting precinct she resided. In trying to explain to them she said: "Since I have never voted, I never knew what ward I lived in, although I had lived in the same house for thirty-one years. After that experience (she had been trying to register for more than a year) I became so discouraged that I have not been back to the courthouse. Perhaps if I was younger I would have tried again."

Annie R. Johnson, thirty-eight, a registered nurse at the Veterans Administration Hospital, was breezing through the test until she came to question nineteen which asked if she would give aid and comfort "to the enemies of the United States Government or the State of Alabama?" That "or" confused her, as it did others, and many failed because of it. "I thought I had to make a choice," Mrs. Johnson said. "I thought the answer they wanted was that I would help Alabama, so I put down the 'government of the State of Alabama.' After we completed the forms . . . we were called in individually and the registrar (Dyson) asked me about my answer to question nineteen. I think I explained that I thought I was being given a choice and now I realized that the answer should have been 'no.' I thought my explanation was satisfactory because he gave me the oath. But evidently it was not, because I received a notice of rejection. Of course, I support both Alabama and the United States."

Mrs. Dorothy McCutcheon Ivy, forty-six, a dental hygienist and a graduate of the Temple School of Oral Hygiene was rejected because she too did not know the precinct in which she resided.

She had waited four days to take the test, she said, and was exhausted. Failing meant the wearying process of waiting to begin again.

There was cruel irony in the rejection process. A Mrs. Johnnie Mae Baskin, fifty-five, was turned down on a slight error regarding a date. When the rejection notice was sent it was addressed to "Mrs. Johnnie Mae Bascomb." The board members demanded perfection from the blacks, but were prone themselves to err on trivial matters.

One of those who missed the "aid and comfort" question nineteen was William S. Morgan, thirty-six, who held a masters degree. "After waiting all day," he wrote in an affidavit to the federal court," we were pressured to finish. The heat and the long hours made me careless."

The frustration and degradation of waiting in the registration line is poignantly revealed in Essie M. Rivers' affidavit. "My husband died in 1948. I have three children, ages nineteen, eight and three. All three live with me. I first tried to register in 1957. It was before they gave numbers. The first time I did not get in, although I waited most of the day. The second time I went down in the morning and was taken in that afternoon. But I had to write on two or three pages of the Constitution and filled out the form, but I never heard from the board. I went back on the next registration day and asked whether I had passed. The registrar said 'no,' but he refused to tell what I had done wrong. So before July of this year I went down again and got number 739. On July the fifth and again on July the seventh, I went down to wait for my number to be called, waited two hours each day. I returned on August the seventh and about 9:30 in the morning one group was called. I was among the six called. After we copied a part of the Constitution, we were given instructions about filling out the blanks. We all waited until we were finished. And we went before Mr. Dyson one at a time. He gave me the oath and he began to ask me questions. He asked how long had I been a widow. I told him 13 years. And then he asked if I had any children. I told him three. He asked their ages. I told him. Then he said, 'You've had two children since your husband died?' I told him, 'Yes, sir.' Then he asked if the younger children had the same father. I asked him if I had to answer that question. He asked me if I didn't think this should keep me from registering. I told him it had nothing to do with it. Meanwhile, Mr. Smith (an associate registrar) was thumbing through a book and he pointed out something to read which he said was a part of the Constitution. I just glanced at it and saw that it was something about moral character and adultery. I got a notice from them on the third Monday that I was rejected."

Dyson had an unusually strong desire to keep unmarried mothers from registering; it was almost a fetish. He once saw Mrs. Willie D. Bentley, a black nurse and the night supervisor at the Veterans Administration Hospital. They were watching the line form for registration. He asked her how she felt about the subject.

"When the child gets to be twenty-one," she replied, "nobody asks him about being illegitimate when they send him into the battlefield in time of war."

"That's different," Dyson replied.

"Why? What's different?"

And Smith, who was nearby, answered: "We have to be careful about who we let vote. We don't want the communists to take over."

What made Macon so different from the other Black Belt

counties was the fact that blacks with college educations were failing the tests with such regularity that there was no question racial discrimination was behind it. In other counties where the education level was often below the sixth grade, it was difficult to prove. But in Macon, when a man like William Bailey Hill, the state leader for Negro work in the Alabama Cooperative Extension Service, a man holding a masters degree from Cornell and a doctorate from the University of Wisconsin, failed for some minor detail, then the discrimination which was suspected, could be nailed down as a fact by the Justice Department.

"The evidence was overwhelming," Johnson wrote in his order of March 17, 1961, "that the State of Alabama, acting through its agents, including former members of the boards of registrars in Macon County, had deliberately engaged in acts and practices designed to discriminate against qualified Negroes .... The tactics include a 'double standard' and even a slowdown in 1959. The 1960 board, consisting of Wheeler Dyson and Charles D. Scott, invariably made certain that the first applicants to take the time-consuming qualification tests were whites. The discrimination against these Negroes (many with college educations) has been so effective that many have been unable to qualify, while many whites, who have not even finished grammar school, have been registered."

The order, directing the board to apply the same standard to blacks that it had consistently applied to the "least qualified white" later became a part of the 1965 Voting Rights Bill drawn up by the administration of President Lyndon Johnson.

Johnson's rulings on voting rights in Macon, Bullock, Barbour and Montgomery counties once again put the power of the ballot into the hands of black people, a right they had known only briefly following freedom from slavery, nearly a century before. Interestingly, the cases were largely overlooked by the public because the voting rights were secured without a prelude of marches and demonstrations.

Not until 1965 at Selma, when Martin Luther King led hundreds almost daily through the rains of January and February, did the issue of voting rights surface and touch the conscience of the nation. Selma, located in the west-central Black Belt county of Dallas, was in the federal court's Southern District. In Johnson's Middle District, blacks by 1964 had largely won the right to vote.

What happened in Macon County, therefore, set the stage for the Selma marches, where blacks wanted to obtain a right without waiting years to get it. Because those Selma marches would ultimately be aimed at Montgomery and the State Capitol, Johnson would be thrust into that saga of American history, where he would render a remarkable decision. That case will be detailed later.

Part IV

'The tamers of the South'

The Freedom Riders
1961

13

B Y EARLY SPRING, 1961, places with such hauntingly familiar names as Gettysburg, Shiloh and Bull Run were being resurrected in schools, town squares and park sites across the land. America's observance of the century-anniversary of the Civil War was in full blush; little boys and grown men alike donned the Yankee Blue or Rebel Gray to take part in countless mock skirmishes; the clatter of musketry again filled the air.

In Alabama, Mississippi and Georgia, Confederate flags were flapping in abundance from car antennae, or adorning doors and bumpers. The Stars and Bars was hoisted not only in memory of that momentous struggle, but, for many, served as an emblem of a new Southern resistance to black petitions for full freedom.

The Civil Rights Movement was simmering over Dixie; police had been called to remove small groups of blacks who sought service at department store lunch counters.

To this overall stir of uneasiness came an announcement in late April by the Congress of Racial Equality (CORE) that a group of college students were going to attempt a "freedom ride" through the South, beginning in Washington and ending in New Orleans.

The freedom riders, as they came to be known, began their pilgrimage May 4; their appearance in the Carolinas drew some

103

attention, some harassment, a few arrests. But there was no violence until May 8, when John Lewis (later a member of the Congress of the United States), then twenty-one, a black from Troy, Alabama, was beaten by several whites as he attempted to enter a restroom marked "white only." The incident at the Greyhound station in Rock Hill, South Carolina, was observed by police who reportedly made no effort to assist him until he had been roughed up.

(Lewis would later find an even worse reception waiting for him in Montgomery; four years later, he would be clubbed as he stood in the front ranks of the attempted march from Selma to Montgomery).

But for the most part, reaction to the freedom ride was sporadic, and the chartered buses rolled into Georgia without further disturbance.

Then, on May 14 — a sunny Mother's Day with temperatures to soar into the low nineties — the riders left Atlanta and headed west for Alabama.

Arriving before noon in Anniston, an industrial city of 38,000, one bus, carrying nine riders, was met by a throng of ruffians at the Trailways terminal. Rocks were hurled through some of the windows, and the riders found themselves trapped inside for more than twenty minutes. Police finally appeared and cleared an escape lane. It headed for Birmingham.

A second group of ten found the same reception as they pulled into the Greyhound terminal. White men held clubs and chains and waved them menacingly as the vehicle lumbered into the parking stall. Suddenly, a rock was thrown, then a barrage. There were shouts, screams. Aboard with the riders was Alabama State Investigator Eli Cowling, who, upon appraising the gathering, ordered the driver to move out. A Greyhound official, Roy Robinson of Atlanta, had debarked and found the door to the station locked. He jumped aboard as the bus began to move; the mob surrounded it. But police again cleared a lane, and the long vehicle eased away. Out on U.S. Highway 78, a winding two-lane to Birmingham, the driver noted a white car behind and a green pickup truck in front. When he attempted to go around, the truck would pull out and block him. The game of cat and mouse continued several miles; then one of the bus tires

The Freedom Riders' burning bus after it was attacked by a white mob near Anniston, Alabama.

went flat (presumably due to a gunshot) and it limped to the side, pulling into the parking area of a country store. Cars quickly poured in around it and a cluster of angry white men again cried out for the riders to get off.

Mae Franks Moultrie, nineteen, of Sumter, South Carolina, heard the crash as an object was hurled through the window; at first she thought it was another rock. Then it erupted into flame and acrid smoke. She screamed and the riders scrambled for the door. Investigator Cowling blocked them while holding back a frenzied group of men trying to get aboard. The flames crackled through the rear of the bus, eating at the floor and the seats. Fumes filled the interior. The riders were frantic, almost hysterical. Finally, Cowling's lungs could take no more; he collapsed, falling to the ground. The riders bolted out the door and some were struck as they ran.

By now the bus was burning in a fury, spewing thick black smoke into the hot sky, as riders and their tormentors alike watched in fascination. Two state troopers arrived, assisted Cowling to his feet, then, seeing the ugly mood of the crowd which was again moving toward the riders, pulled their revolv-

With the Birmingham police conveniently absent, members of the Ku Klux Klan assaulted Freedom Riders in the Trailways bus depot in Birmingham on Mother's Day, 1961.

ers; one fired a shot into the air. They ordered the crowd to disperse. Meantime, the Trailways bus was nearing Birmingham.

A group of white men — among them, Robert Shelton, imperial wizard of the Ku Klux Klan — waited at the Greyhound station, unaware that the bus was blazing into a pile of melted metal and rubber, fifty miles away. Then the word spread of the arrival of the Trailways bus. The mob hastened to that station, several blocks away.

Again violence erupted; the riders were set upon by men who attacked in clusters of three, two holding a writhing victim while the third fired his fists into their faces or struck with clubs or chains. One of the injured, James Peck, took such a beating that he required fifty stitches.

The *Birmingham News* in a front page editorial the following day noted that "fear and hatred stalked the streets of Birmingham" and echoed the question raised across the nation: "Where were the police?"To which Police Commissioner Eugene (Bull) Connor responded, "Many were taking the day off because it was Mother's Day."

And then he added, "Both sides were outsiders: The ones that got whipped, and the ones doing the whipping."

In Montgomery, Police Commissioner L. B. Sullivan, informed that his city was next on the freedom ride route, declared: "We have no intention of Montgomery being used as a proving ground for agitators and violence." Attorney General Bobby Kennedy called on Alabama Governor John Patterson to provide protection and was turned down.

Patterson said he could assure no more than the normal security afforded any interstate traveler. And Alabama Congressman George Huddleston, Jr., allowed that the freedom riders "got what they asked for in trespassing upon the South and its well-established customs."

Through the week, tempers and anxiety, like the temperature in Alabama, hovered at the sizzling point. President John Kennedy and his brother, Bobby, were keeping in touch both with Alabama officials and civil rights leaders, trying to work out an amicable solution; Patterson refused to make any guarantees for their protection. The riders themselves vowed the journey would continue; another contingent of volunteers was preparing to come to Birmingham to join, replacing some who were too bruised to carry on.

CORE officials said the ride would resume that Saturday, May 20, with Montgomery the destination; from there they would move on to Jackson, Mississippi.

With neither side backing down, President Kennedy, on the 16th, dispatched John Seigenthaler to Montgomery as his personal representative. John Doar of the Justice Department came with him. Arriving in mid-afternoon, they rushed to the Alabama Capitol to once again implore Governor Patterson to provide security for the riders. The alternative was made quite clear that if Alabama didn't protect them, the federal government would. The governor eased his stance and on the 19th, Seigenthaler called the White House to pass along the governor's view that "Alabama has the will, force, the men and the equip-

ment to fully protect everyone in the state." Furthermore, said
the governor, there would be no need to send U.S. marshals. It
appeared a showdown was going to be averted.

JOHNSON

> I wasn't a fortune teller but I suspected there might
> be some trouble along the way; after what had happened
> in Birmingham and in Anniston, it seemed inconceivable
> that there could be an all-out effort to interfere with them,
> especially in the city of Montgomery itself. After all,
> Governor Patterson had given his guarantee of safe pas-
> sage.
>
> And even if I had known that there would be an
> incident in Montgomery . . . Well, it wasn't for me — or
> any judge, for that matter — to position myself there and
> be a part of the observation. That wasn't my job. The
> police were supposed to provide security, and any ob-
> serving was to be handled by the Justice Department. I
> have never been a part of any demonstrations of any type.
> In fact, I have always made an effort to avoid them. My
> connection, if any, with them was to be in a courtroom,
> not out in the streets.
>
> So on that weekend, I had made plans to go fishing.
> I took my wife and son and headed for the lake and had a
> pretty good day fishing. The first I heard of any trouble in
> Montgomery was when I came in with enough fish for
> supper. And some other people at the lake came up and
> told me what they'd heard on the news broadcast.

As was later revealed in a court proceeding, as the bus had
arrived at the Greyhound terminal — next door to the federal
building — a group of about two hundred white people suddenly
appeared. Trouble started when a reputed Klansman from Montgomery, Claude Henley, a hulking man in his forties, became
angered at a newsman taking pictures of the freedom riders as
they debarked. Henley strode forward, followed by about twenty
others, and began cursing and slapping at the photographer.
That ignited a wholesale rampage; the two hundred swelled into
a hate-filled mob of nearly one thousand. Seigenthaler, the

president's representative, was knocked unconscious. Blacks and some of their white companions on the bus were beaten while Montgomery police officers stood by and attended to such mundane functions as directing traffic.

A young black, William Barbee, was knocked to the pavement, then struck repeatedly with a heavy club; the mob was shouting, "Kill him! Kill him!" It might have happened but for the sudden intervention of Colonel Floyd Mann, the Alabama Public Safety Director, who drew his pistol and ordered the attackers back, threatening to shoot if they didn't. At that point, Mann called for his state troopers whom he had stationed on alert several blocks away. Their arrival restored order to the terminal.

Meanwhile, John Doar, who had watched the incredible events unfolding from the steps of the federal building, hurried inside to find a telephone. He called Attorney General Robert Kennedy: "It's a crowd gone mad," he reported. "They're beating the students. It's the worst thing I've ever seen!" That call prompted the decision in Washington to speed four hundred and fifty U.S. marshals to Montgomery.

Then Doar began drawing up a petition for a federal injunction against the KKK and the Montgomery police. It was late afternoon when he finished. Commandeering a marshal, he was taken to Lake Martin, fifty miles northeast of Montgomery, to find Judge Johnson. After a long boat ride they located Johnson's cabin. Doar presented the judge with a request for a temporary restraining order against the KKK, which the judge signed.

During those crucial hours that Doar was looking for Johnson's lakeside cabin, Governor Patterson was meeting with Deputy U.S. Attorney General Byron White, later a Supreme Court Justice; he had been dispatched to Montgomery when the first report of the melee at the bus terminal had been received in Washington. The governor was agonizing over the dilemma; he objected to the presence of marshals, publicly calling them "interlopers who will be arrested if they violate the law." But privately, he confided in a telephone call to Attorney General Robert Kennedy, "It's as though we're being invaded." He still believed local police could maintain order and refused to call in the Alabama National Guard.

That night about eight hundred blacks gathered at the black First Baptist Church in Montgomery, about three blocks from the Alabama Capitol. Outside, white men began to congregate. Colonel Floyd Mann deployed about two hundred of his Alabama Highway Patrolmen, keeping the throng of whites at bay. By now there were threats being shouted and through the night air came rocks and other objects; one crashed through a church window. While the blacks sang freedom songs, the white crowd, which had now become a mob, grew more intimidating. Mann, tired and sweaty, his white shirt rumpled, feared the crowd might try to storm the church. By then, four hundred U.S. marshals had arrived. The crowd, which had grown to about two thousand, kept threatening to rush the church. They set several cars afire.

Mann was called inside the parsonage where he had a telephone call from Robert Kennedy. He was heard to say, "The crowd is getting ugly." Kennedy told him he was placing the marshals under his command.

Finally, after hours of explosive confrontation, Governor Patterson ordered the National Guard into service. Martial law was declared. Guardsmen, with bayonets fixed, marched into the areas. The show of force took some of the starch out of the mob, which retired into the night. At dawn, the beleaguered blacks were escorted from the church.

That Monday morning, Doar and White went to the United States Courthouse in Montgomery and filed a motion seeking a permanent injunction against the KKK, as well as the Montgomery Police Department. Johnson set a hearing for May 29.

Named as defendants were the KKK, the police, the Montgomery Public Safety Director L. B. Sullivan, Police Chief G. J. Ruppenthal, Birmingham Police Commissioner Eugene (Bull) Connor, Birmingham Police Chief Jamie Moore, and a host of Ku Klux Klansmen, including the imperial wizard, Robert Shelton.

14

THE UNITED STATES ATTORNEY for the Middle District, Hartwell Davis, age fifty-four, represented the government. He was ably assisted by John Doar and Carl Eardley of the Justice Department. About a half dozen attorneys sat at the defense table.

A black woman, Patricia Ann Jenkins, nineteen, was the government's first major witness. As she took the stand, there was a ripple of whispering among some of the spectators. She took the oath. Davis approached.

"Where do you go to school, Patricia?" he asked her.

"Tennessee A and I College," she replied.

"What grade are you in?"

"I'm a sophomore."

"She will have to speak up a little louder," Johnson called. "And let's have a minimum of noise in here."

"Miss Jenkins," Davis said, "are you a member of any group involved in the incidents that occurred here in Montgomery?"

She nodded. "Yes . . . the Student Nashville Non-Violent Movement."

"We can't hear you," someone from the defense table announced. She repeated the answer.

"When did you first become aware of the plan to send what we have read in the papers — freedom riders — from Washing-

111

ton to New Orleans?"

"On the seventeenth of May."

"Who came with you?"

"There were three other boys, another girl, and two white girls."

"And were they all students at the university?" Davis asked.

"No, they were not all."

"Did they come to join the freedom riders?"

"Yes."

"Your honor," interrupted defense attorney Calvin Whitesell, in a somewhat annoyed tone, "we are going to have a definition of this term 'freedom riders'?"

"Well, objection is overruled," the judge said. "Go ahead."

"Did you make an effort to get a bus to Montgomery?" Davis continued.

"Yes, we did," she said. "On the nineteenth of May."

"And were you successful?"

She shook her head. "Not until after eighteen hours."

"You stayed in a bus terminal for eighteen hours?" he asked. "Where was this?"

"In Birmingham," she said. "Yes, we did . . . eighteen hours."

"Now, what kind of bus was it?"

"Greyhound."

"Going to Montgomery."

"Yes."

"All right. These students . . . were they —" and Davis's eyes lifted for moment in thought, "— were they . . . were there mixed races on the bus?"

"Yes, sir."

"How many whites . . . white people?"

She pondered for a moment. "There were . . . there were three whites."

"Do you recall what time you arrived in Montgomery on the twentieth of May, 1961?"

"I . . . it was," and she shrugged, "approximately eleven-thirty in the morning."

"Now what happened, in your own words, upon your arrival?"

"Wait a minute, your honor," defense attorney Clarence

Atkeison said, rising. "We object. He is leading this witness. He is suggesting that something did happen."

"Your objection is overruled," said Johnson.

Miss Jenkins glanced up at him and he nodded for her to continue. "We got . . . we arrived in Montgomery," she went on. "The bus driver pulled into the bus terminal. Before he let us off, he said, 'This is Montgomery, and we will be here for ten minutes.' He also said —"

She was cut off by a chorus of protests from the defense table and one of the attorneys, Morris Dees, was on his feet. "Your honor," he said, "we object to anything the driver might have said."

"Overruled. Go ahead."

"He also said, 'These are the freedom riders, the tamers of the South.'"

"I beg your pardon," Whitesell declared, his voice edged with wry humor. "The *what* of the South?"

His reaction stirred some subdued laughter from several in the audience.

"The tamers," she repeated somewhat hesitantly.

"What?" asked Dees. "The tamers of the South?"

Dees, twenty-five, represented Henley, who was a neighbor. In later years the young attorney would found the Southern Poverty Law Center, and become an anti-KKK champion.

"Go over that again," Johnson instructed. "The bus driver said that?"

"Yes, he did," she said. "The tamers of the South."

The judge stared at her. "And what bus line was it?"

"Greyhound."

"All right, go ahead," he told her.

Miss Jenkins gazed out over the spectators. "We got off the bus, and as we got off, there was around eighteen people standing around, and we proceeded to one corner. We got there and we stood there . . . stood around. Well, while we were there a man came up, he had on a white shirt and had a cigar in his mouth, and there was a photographer taking our pictures and this man (Claude Henley) asked what he was doing there, and he was using some vile language talking to him and then he smashed—"

"Objection, your honor, please!" cried James Venable (the

Grand Dragon for the Georgia KKK), from the defense table. He was on his feet. "This testimony not being made in the presence of these defendants, which we represent as the strictest, rankest type of hearsay evidence . . . she hasn't identified this man as one of the —"

"You gentlemen need not state your grounds for any of your objections," Johnson said. "Your objection is overruled." Venable sank back into his chair. "Go ahead," the judge said, nodding at Miss Jenkins.

She nodded. "Well, this man slapped the photographer, and the photographer began to back off. Meanwhile, a lot of people began to gather around, and they just kept egging this man on, and he kept pushing him and slapping on him, and some of the mob went up where he was and they began—"

"Now we are going to object to the use of the word 'mob,'" your honor," Whitesell said. "She has testified—"

"All right," said Johnson. "I sustain it. It will be excluded for the time being."

Miss Jenkins waited until he motioned for her to continue. "Well, these *people*," she said, stressing the word, "began to follow this man, and a lot of people began to jump on him, and—"

"Lot of people began to what!" Dees cried.

There were more snickers and Miss Jenkins, her eyes wide, stared at him. "They jumped on him," she said. "You know, jumped on him."

"Jumped on him?"

Miss Jenkins stared at him. "On the cameraman," she explained.

"Go ahead," Johnson said in an annoyed tone. "Let's get along."

"And we were standing in the corner," she continued. "Well, this . . . they went on up the street and he dropped a . . . they took his camera, and some boys began to smash it. It was around six or seven boys and they smashed it and stomped on it. Then a cab came up and the boys — the ones who were with us — told the girls to get in the cab. Well, there was two white girls with us and we . . . they proceeded to get in the cab also, and the cab driver said he could not drive them. So the five Negro girls got in the car. We started out one exit out of the bus terminal and a man stood in front of the car with his hand up something like this—" and she extended her arm in front of her, held firm to display the signal to halt — "so we backed up to the other way out, and we were blocked there for about eight or ten minutes. While we were blocked there, well, the group of people turned around on the kids who were with us, and they took suitcases and threw them over the railings, and they proceeded to hit some of the boys, and we saw them beating Jim Zwerg. And they . . . then we saw them hit John Lewis and we saw suitcases going over the rail. And then the cab driver pulled out and we got away."

As she had told of the suitcases going over the rail the hushed giggling and nudges moved through the crowd again. Davis finished his questioning and defense attorney Atkeison went forward. He stood for a moment or two, appraising the slim black girl.

"Patricia," he said in a congenial, down-home manner, "what was the plan that y'all had when you left your destination headed for Alabama?"

"Headed for Birmingham?"

"Yes."

"Well, we . . . to catch the bus out of Birmingham to Montgomery, then from Montgomery to Jackson."

"All right. Was it your purpose to integrate the waiting rooms in Alabama?"

"Our purpose," she replied evenly, "was to prove that some persons in the United States could not travel interstate with being...I mean, without —"

"You just answer my question," he said. "Was your purpose to integrate the facilities at the bus stations and cafes?"

"No."

"That wasn't your purpose for coming?"

"No."

"Did you . . . when you left your destination, did you know that the CORE organization was sponsoring this trip?"

She shrugged. "They did not sponsor us."

"They didn't? When they say that they sponsored you and that y'all were members of CORE, do you say that they are incorrect?"

"Yes."

He puzzled for a second or two. Then: "You are a member of NAACP?"

"Yes."

"How long you been in the NAACP?"

"For . . . I have been a member since I was in . . . my first year in high school."

"All right. Now, all of you that were on that bus had discussed the trip many times prior to leaving your destination, had you not?" (It was the third time Atkeison had misused the word "destination.")

"Discussed it how?" she asked.

"With each other," he said. "You had talked about it with each other, hadn't you?"

"Yes, we had."

"And you planned it with each other, hadn't you?"

Miss Jenkins turned her head slightly, as though she had not heard him clearly. "Planned it?" she asked.

"Yes."

A puzzled pause. "What do you mean, 'planned'?"

He tossed his hands up impatiently. "Well, you're a college student. You know what 'planning' means, don't you?"

His question touched off another subdued burst of chuckling.

Miss Jenkins' eyes darted from the attorney to the crowd, then back to him. She shook her head. "Yes — I mean —" and she wrinkled her brow. "What do you mean, planned what we were going to do?"

Her confusion further delighted some of the spectators.

Johnson had heard enough. He signalled the attorney to hold up.

"All right, Mr. Atkeison," he said. "That just brings me to the point that had been arriving ever since we started this case." There was absolute stillness. "You people that came for the purpose of expressing hilarity and frivolity, you are going to stop it or I am going to exclude you from the courtroom. You are welcome to come, if there is room for you, as spectators. You are not welcome to come for the purpose of exhibiting during this trial; that is the last time I'm going to mention it." He pointed to the rear of the room. "You marshals exclude those that violate that instruction from the courtroom immediately." He glanced at Atkeison. "All right, get along."

"Yes, sir." He approached the girl again. "Now, on this occasion, y'all had discussed it and had planned to make this trip, had you not?"

"Well, it was organized by CORE," she replied, "and we just . . . we followed CORE, we took our . . . I guess we took interest in it . . . in the movement, and then we decided that we would enter into this also."

"Un-huh. Did officials of CORE ask y'all to do this?"

"No."

"Well, who asked you to make this pilgrimage to Alabama?"

"Well, we . . . we have offices in Nashville, and we discussed this among ourselves after the incident happened in Anniston, Alabama, on the fourteenth."

Dees was next to cross-examine and he produced some photographs of the melee at the Montgomery bus station. He questioned in a low voice.

"Mr. Counselor," Johnson said, "I believe you better stand over yonder, so all the litigants can hear the testimony."

"Yes, sir. I want her to look at some of these pictures."

"All right. But speak up."

"Now, Patricia," Dees said, lifting his voice, "you say you saw the man with the camera pointing his camera in the face of the man with the cigar?"

She shook her head. "I didn't say that. I said—"

"You just got through saying—"

"Wait a minute," Johnson snapped. "Don't argue with the witness."

Miss Jenkins tried to continue. "I said—"

"Wait a minute," said the judge, looking at Dees. "You question her, and question her properly. Don't argue with her."

"Thank you, sir," Dees replied, nodding his head.

"I said," the witness went on, "that the camera was pointed *towards* the man with the cigar. I did not say he pointed it at him."

"Miss Jenkins," Johnson said, glancing sideways at her, "do these pictures accurately portray what events were occurring at the bus station?"

She nodded. "Yes, sir. They . . . yes, sir."

"All right," he said, gesturing toward Dees. "Get along."

Dees appeared a bit flustered then. "Patricia, I'd like to ask you this question: The man that had the white cigar — I mean, the cigar with the white shirt on—" He was now flushed. "I mean, did you see him hit or kick or in any way harass any of the students or group that you rode down from Birmingham with?"

"No, I didn't," she said. "Just the cameraman."

"But not the students?"

"No, I didn't."

15

THE GOVERNMENT'S NEXT witness was William Barbee, a theology student from Nashville. He had been clubbed senseless that day and may well have been beaten to death by men with baseball bats had not Alabama Public Safety Director Floyd Mann intervened.

He appeared apprehensive, and when John Doar asked him his name he stood up to answer, "William Barbee."

"You may remain seated when you answer," Doar said. "And will you speak up in a loud voice so you can be heard?"

"Yes, sir."

"What do you do, William?"

"I am a student at the American Baptist Theological Seminary in Nashville."

"Were you in Montgomery, Alabama, on May twentieth, 1961?"

"Yes, sir. I came on May eighteenth."

"And were you," continued Doar, "in the vicinity of the bus station on that day?"

"Yes."

"Will you describe to the court what happened after you got there?"

"After I had gotten there, the . . . there were two students that were badly beaten up, and there was a gentleman laying in

the street . . . laying there in the street, and there wasn't any
transportation for the students to go to the hospital or the like.
There were policemen standing around in the vicinity, and I
asked them to see that the students were taken to the hospital
and they refused . . . they made negative gestures and the like.
After that I tried to secure other means of transportation, which
were the taxi cabs, but . . . my first attempt to get a taxi, well, the
driver refused to drive because there were two students of
different racial groups . . . there was a Negro and a white boy."

"What were their names?" Doar asked.

"Their names were Jim Zwerg and John Lewis." Barbee
paused until Doar nodded for him to continue. "After failing to
get transportation, I then tried other means. And a Mrs. Gregory helped me, also. There was this minister who had come to
help take John Lewis, and I was helping him to take the luggage
to the car that was parked on the street around from the bus
station. Before this incident there were some students in the
post office. They were unable to get transportation also. I went
there and secured a taxi. They were afraid to come out at first
because of the mob in the street—"

"Wait a minute, your honor," Atkeison said, "we are going
to object—"

"I sustain it," Johnson said. "It will be excluded."

"Just tell what you saw, Mr. Barbee," Doar said. "Not what
the other students thought or said. Do you understand?"

"Yes," he said, nodding. "We went out to the taxi and I left
the students in the cab and told the driver to take them to a
church. After that the mob grabbed me. I think it was at first
about three gentlemen, and they threw me to the ground."

"Did he say three *gentlemen*, your honor?" Whitesell asked,
his voice polite but incredulous. "I couldn't understand."

"That is what he said," Johnson said. "Go ahead."

Barbee continued. "And they threw me to the ground and
broke several buttons of my clothing, but I wasn't seriously
injured. I regained my balance and walked to . . . to the other
end of the station, and there I was helping John Lewis to take
some of his suitcases — I think it was one suitcase — and on my
way to the car I heard the mob making gestures and different
types of noises towards . . . and statements, towards the Negro

race and the like."

"Your honor," interrupted Atkeison, "I don't understand whether this mob had come in on the bus he heard or some other mob."

"You can cross-examine him when it gets your time," the judge said.

"Then what happened, Mr. Barbee?" Doar asked.

"After this, after I had been walking down the street behind this minister and John Lewis for about seven minutes, well, not exactly seven minutes . . . but about that vicinity, the . . . the mob must have gotten closer to me then . . . I realized I must have passed out when they struck me the first time, because that is all I remember."

Doar nodded. "As I understand it, you walked out of the bus station and down toward the post office on Court Street?"

"Yes."

"And that is the last thing you remembered?"

"That is the last thing I remember."

"Now were you taken to a hospital?"

Barbee nodded. "Yes . . . to St. Jude."

"And how long did you stay there?"

"I remained until —"

Whitesell was on his feet. "That has nothing to do with this, if the court please . . . how long he stayed."

Johnson nodded. "I don't see that it's important. I sustain."

"All right," said Doar. He turned and ruffled through some papers, and returned to the witness chair holding a picture. "Would you look at this and tell me if you recognize it?"

Barbee studied the photo. "Yes. That looks somewhat like the incident that took place. I don't know if this is me or not, but it . . . this is the type of thing that happened to me. I was thrown to the sidewalk by a . . . a gentleman dressed similar to . . . to this in this picture."

"That is all the questions I have, your honor," Doar said.

Atkeison stood to cross-examine. "What was your purpose in coming to Montgomery, Alabama?"

"My purpose in coming," he said, speaking rapidly, "as a free moral agent . . . it had been known in the past that there had been certain racial disorders in the community . . . and my purpose in coming was to try to . . . to see that these disorders were not continued in my own little way . . . as a free moral agent."

Atkeison nodded. "Um-humm. And you came down here to see that these race disorders didn't happen anymore, is that right?"

Barbee studied the question, gazing nervously at the attorney who was pacing.

"William, is that right?" Atkeison pursued. "Is that what you tell this court? Is it or isn't it?"

"I came down to see," the witness said.

"And you were going to enforce the law if it took that," Atkeison said, "is that right?"

"I . . . no, I didn't say that. I came down to do what I could in my own feeble way. Not enforcing the law by force or any . . . any of that type of thing."

"Had you had contact with this group known as CORE?"

A silence. Then: "Indirectly."

"Well, what was the connection between you and this organization known as CORE?"

"The connection that I have with CORE is the fact that they try to see a better means of—"

Johnson interrupted, "He asked you what your contact and relationship was with the CORE organization."

"I have . . . have no contact at all."

"Did you state you had indirect contact with them?" Atkeison asked.

"Yes."

"What was that?"

"That was the Student Non-Violent Movement in Nashville."

"It is not a part of CORE, is it?"

He shook his head. "No, it is not."

"Who paid for your trip to Montgomery?"

"The Student Non-Violent Coordinating Committee," Barbee said. "I received it in the fact that transportation was provided . . . I was driven here in an automobile."

"By who?" Atkeison asked.

Barbee appeared hesitant. "By . . . by a gentleman that goes to school in Nashville."

"Well, will you tell his honor, please, the name of this gentleman that drove you down?"

"I don't remember his name."

Atkeison lifted his hands in a gesture of bewilderment. "You tell the court now that you drove down from Nashville with a gentleman that you don't even remember his name?"

"That is what I said."

"All right. Would you tell whether he is a white gentleman," Atkeison coaxed, "or a colored gentleman?"

"He is a Negro."

"And you don't remember his name?"

"I remember . . . I know his name, but I—"

"What is his name?"

"At the present," Barbee said, struggling with the words, "I don't like to—"

"Wait a minute now Barbee," Johnson said. "Now you answer the questions. If they are not admissible, then one or more of the lawyers will object; do not be evasive. Answer this lawyer and any other lawyer's questions directed to you concerning this case."

"I don't mean to be evasive," Barbee said, addressing the judge.

"Well, he wants to know the name of the man that drove you down here," Johnson said.

Barbee nodded again, and turned his eyes to the attorney. "I . . . it is not that I . . . I do have quite a bit of trouble remembering names . . . this is not . . . this is not evasive at all."

"Uh, huh," Atkeison said. "But you did say you remembered it just a few minutes ago, didn't you?"

"No. I wasn't trying to evade your question. I do not remember the gentleman's name."

"Oh, all right," Atkeison said irritably. "When you said a few minutes ago that you did remember it but didn't want to divulge it, then you were not telling the truth, is that right?"

"We object," said Eardley. "It is argumentative."

"I sustain it," Johnson said.

Atkeison paced about. "I will ask you, which time are you telling the truth: When you say you remember it but don't want to divulge it, or now when you say you don't rem—"

"Same objection," Eardley intoned.

The judge nodded, staring at Atkeison. "It is argumentative."

"Your honor," the attorney cried, "one time he said he didn't remember it, and—"

"I have just sustained objection for your arguing with the witness," Johnson snapped. "Now don't argue with me!"

There was a stir again in the courtroom. Atkeison rubbed the back of his neck and paced. Then he looked up at Johnson somewhat meekly and asked: "Well, may I ask him which time he is right, when he says he don't remember it or now when he—"

Johnson glanced at the witness. "Barbee?"

The witness raised his eyes. "Yes, sir?"

"Do you remember the name of the man that drove you down here?"

"No, I don't."

"Who introduced you to him?"

"I was introduced to him by some members of the Student Non-Violent Coordinating Committee."

"Who were they?" the judge asked.

"I was introduced to him by . . ." Barbee clenched his hands and gazed at the ceiling, pondering. "I will get you the name . . . student was Diane Nash."

"Who was with you?"

"In the automobile?" Barbee asked.

"Yes."

"There was another . . . another student from my school which was —"

"Name?"

"Bernard LaFayette."

"And the purpose in coming?" Johnson asked.

"I believe he had the same purpose that I did."

"And what was your purpose?"

"And my purpose was to . . . to see about the racial disorders."

"Well, did you come in advance of the group that was to ride the bus to make any arrangements for them?" Johnson quizzed.

"That is what the lawyer wants to know."

"No, we . . . we came in an automobile because we could not . . . we thought that it was not probable that we could come on the bus. We thought we might not get out of Nashville if we rode the bus."

The judge nodded. "Go ahead," he told Atkeison.

"All right," said the attorney. "Now did you know that this group that you met at the bus station was coming?"

"Yes."

"What agreement had you had with them to meet at the bus station?"

"Would you rephrase that?" Barbee asked. "I didn't understand it."

"No, I won't rephrase it," Atkeison drawled. "I will ask the reporter to read it back if you don't understand it."

Reporter Glynn Henderson looked up at Johnson, eyebrows raised, questioningly. The judge nodded, and he read it back.

"My job was to find transportation in case of any type of violence," Barbee answered. "I was to telephone them . . . but I didn't get a chance. They had already left Birmingham and there did not appear to be any signs of trouble at the station here in Montgomery."

"Well, when you arrived at the bus station this little incident in which two or three folks had a little fight was already occurring?"

"Yes, sir."

"Did you anticipate there might be trouble?"

Barbee shrugged. "It was already taking place."

"Uh, huh. Did you at any time call on the chief of police or any of his assistants to do anything that they weren't already doing?"

"Yes."

"Who was it? Which policeman?"

"I didn't know their names, so I can't tell you that."

That ended Atkeison's cross-examination. Calvin Whitesell approached to continue. He was representing Sullivan and Ruppenthal.

He sized Barbee up for a moment. "Did you arrange transportation or were you to arrange transportation for these people when they arrived in Montgomery on May twentieth?"

"Yes, sir. That was my line."

"Did you meet with Reverend (Fred) Shuttlesworth in Birmingham and discuss it with him?"

"I had been at his house, yes."

"Had he been in contact with your group to get you to continue this so-called freedom ride into Alabama?"

Barbee blinked. "Pardon me?"

"Just answer the question," Johnson said.

"Yes, sir," he said. "I didn't understand it."

"Wanted to know," Johnson said, "if Shuttlesworth had been in touch with your concerning the students riding in Alabama such as occurred on the twentieth."

The witness gazed at him. "Me directly?"

"Yes."

Barbee nodded. "Yes."

"How about Martin Luther King?" Whitesell asked.

"I don't know."

"How about Ralph David Abernathy? You discussed it with him?"

"I didn't meet with him."

"You didn't?"

"I discussed it with him."

"You have his phone number?"

"But I didn't meet with him."

"I beg your pardon?" Whitesell asked.

"He said he talked with him," Johnson said, "but he didn't meet with him."

Whitesell nodded. "And he knew about it, and he did cooperate with you, in making your plans to transport this group? Did he cooperate with you?" He watched the witness who again seemed confused. "Your honor, would you instruct the witness to answer?"

Again Johnson turned to the witness. "Barbee? Do you understand the question? Whether or not Abernathy cooperated with you?"

"Yes. I was going to answer," he said, "but it was like this: There was Mrs. Hazel Gregory who did the contacting for me, so I didn't act directly with him."

Whitesell nodded. "Is Charles Conley your attorney?"

"Yes."

"Did you discuss it with him?"

Barbee hesitated.

"Do you understand the question?" Johnson asked.

"Not exactly."

"He wants to know if you discussed with Conley the matter of riders coming here on Saturday, the twentieth. Did you or didn't you?"

Barbee shrugged. "Well, because he is an attorney, he . . . he wasn't supposed to —"

Johnson was plainly irked by Barbee's evasive answers and delays. "Barbee, you are taking up a lot of the court's time," he said sharply. "Now you start answering these questions. And I am not going to tell you any more."

"Yes, sir."

"I am going to put you back there in jail if you don't," he said, "and that is the last time I am going to tell you. Now you start answering these questions, and answer them right off."

"OK."

Barbee's testimony ended in the afternoon.

16

TUESDAY, MAY 30, WAS clear and hot in Montgomery. By 8:45 a.m. the courtroom on the second floor of the federal building was packed; the air conditioning did little to erase the heat which, by noon, would be almost stifling.

The first witness was Roy Franklin Robinson, a white man from Atlanta, regional manager for Greyhound Lines in the South. He was aboard the bus when it left Georgia that Sunday morning, May 14, bound for Alabama. He testified that the driver was afraid to leave without a police escort. So, after Sunday school, Robinson said, he told the driver he would accompany him.

"In your own words, Mr. Robinson," said John Doar, "describe what happened when you arrived in Anniston."

"There were ten in the group," he said. "Three white and seven colored. We arrived in Anniston at one forty-five p.m. Eastern time. And we traveled down the street directly in front of the bus station and when we passed in front there was a large group of people assembled in front. And we went around to the rear of the terminal and this group assembled all around the bus and there was some shouting." He shrugged slightly. "I can't remember all the words but the main thing they wanted . . . they wanted the freedom riders to come off the bus. But I got off in an effort to go into the bus station and use the telephone. And I worked my way through (the crowd), but when I got down to the

128

door, the bus station was closed. So I went back to the bus and told the driver to start up, that we were departing immediately." He gestured briefly with one hand. "But when we tried to pull out of the terminal, the people moved back to let the bus out, but there was a young . . . one young fellow that was sitting in the sidewalk directly in front of the bus, and he refused to move."

"And then what happened?" asked Doar.

"When we tried to back up there were people down there that sat down in the drive," continued Robinson. "So we couldn't get out. About that time the City of Anniston police arrived and once they had arrived they just issued orders out there for the people to back out and let the bus out and the people obeyed."

"Was there damage to the bus?"

Robinson reflected a moment. "I believe there was four windows broke."

"Did you see," Doar asked, "or did you observe any clubs, or pipes or chains . . . in the possession of members of the crowd at Anniston?"

"Yes, sir."

"What did you see?"

"Well, I saw . . . it looked like a homemade club or two, and I saw some lengths of chain, and pieces of metal, like a wrecking bar, and I saw some blackjacks."

"Will you tell what happened to the bus after it left the station?"

"Well, going out of there was a green . . . a light green pickup truck that was directly ahead of us, and he would drive slow, and when we would speed up to pass him he would speed up and pull across the center line . . . and each time we would try to pass him he would cut over on us. Then he went on and a white car did the same thing. This went on for four or five miles and when we reached Forsyth and Sons Grocery store the left front tire went flat, and we pulled into the area in front of this store and parked. I left the bus to help the driver, and we had been there a minute or two when the Alabama Patrol car drove up. I asked him if he would radio in to Anniston, but in the meantime somebody had slashed the rear outside tire. I don't know who. And I asked a trooper if he would contact the patrol office and get some additional help there, that the mob seemed to be out of control and I was fearful that somebody would be seriously injured and he said that there was only three men on duty in the area." Robinson shook his head. "Well, when he told me that, I left but just then I noticed some smoke coming out the windows of the bus. The passengers opened the windows and I could see the smoke coming out. But I . . . thought occurred to me maybe it was somebody had set a piece of paper on fire or something, but I went to the store and asked a person if he would permit me to use the telephone. He said it was a pay phone so I put a dime in and placed a call to our office in Birmingham. But somebody apparently cut the wire someplace because the phone went dead."

"Then what happened?" asked Doar.

"Well, I came back out of the store and saw Mr. Cowling who had been on the bus from the time we left Atlanta . . . I understand he is with the Alabama Patrol and he — I hope the judge won't call me down now — (is) one of the bravest men I have contacted in my life . . . he knows no fear . . . he stood in the door of the bus and had not permitted anyone to enter . . . and about that time he just fell out of the door down on the ground, apparently overcome by smoke. And then the rear of the bus was in flames and smoke completely engulfed it inside and when he tumbled out the door, the other passengers on the bus got off, and most of them ran towards the house that adjoined the store and one of the passengers was hit with a length of chain . . . and . . . but I wasn't able to identify the person because he ran toward the group of people."

"You see anyone else hit?"

"I saw no other personal injury inflicted on anyone," Robinson replied. "And an Alabama patrol car arrived and a sergeant quickly sized up the situation and ran about middleway of the bus and withdrew his revolver and fired one shot into the air. And some other patrolmen joined him and they told the people in no uncertain terms what would happen if they attempted to injure anyone. And that broke up the party."

Early on Wednesday, May 31, the government began calling persons known or reputed to be Klansmen to the stand. Some were in Birmingham the afternoon of May 14 when the Trailways bus arrived and freedom riders had been attacked by men with clubs and bottles.

The questioning bore little fruit. Typical was this exchange between Doar and James (Ace) Williams of Gadsden.

"Are you a member of the Alabama Knights, Knights of the Ku Klux Klan?" Doar asked.

"Beg your pardon, sir?"

Doar repeated.

Williams regarded him coolly. "Sir, I refuse to answer that question on the grounds that it might tend to incriminate me."

Doar glanced at his notes. "You know a Robert Thomas?"

"I do."

"Were you with him on the afternoon of May 14 in Birmingham?"

"I was."

"Is he a member of the Ku Klux Klan?"

"I don't know, sir."

"How about Hubert Page? You know him?"

"I do."

"Is he a member of the Ku Klux Klan?"

"I don't know, sir."

Doar picked up a paper from the table and handed it to Williams. "You ever see this before, Mr. Williams?"

"I don't know, sir."

"It's a ballot, Mr. Williams, for what appears to be an election in the KKK. You see your name on it?"

"Yes, sir."

"How'd it get there?"

"I don't know, sir."

"Isn't that the ballot that you voted on in connection with the Ku Klux Klan?"

Williams examined the paper, then stared at Doar. "Sir, I prefer not to answer that."

"On what grounds?" Doar demanded.

"It might tend to incriminate me."

Robert Thomas of Birmingham, whose name would come up later in the civil rights drive in connection with the killing of Mrs. Viola Liuzzo, was questioned by Eardley.

"You a member of the Ku Klux Klan?"

"No, sir."

"Ever been a member, Mr. Thomas?"

"No, sir."

"Ever attended any of their meetings?"

"No, sir."

"Or any of the various Klans' meetings?"

Thomas gazed at him. There was a long pause. Then: "Would you repeat that, please, sir?"

"All right. There are several Ku Klux Klan groups. Are you a member of the Alabama Knights of the Ku Klux Klan?"

Another silence. "I am a past member . . . inactively."

"When did you join?"

"About two years ago."

"Who was the president?" Eardley asked. "Or the leader?"

"I don't know, sir."

"You don't recall?"

"No, sir."

"Didn't I understand you to say you were a member there for a year and a half or two years?" Eardley asked.

"Yes, sir."

"And you don't know anybody there?"

"Not by name, sir."

Eardley raised his eyebrows in surprise. "You were never introduced to any of them?"

"Not by name, sir."

Other alleged Klansmen called included Kenneth Adams, Frank J. Tolbert, Cecil Lewallyn, Jesse Oliver Faggard and LeRoy Ducker. All politely refused to say anything of substance.

When Ducker concluded his stay on the stand Johnson said to Doar: "Call the next witness. I don't think I want to hear anymore of that kind of testimony."

But there was to be more. Robert Shelton, the imperial wizard of the KKK, a lean man with rather narrow-set eyes and a long, slightly hawkish nose, was sworn in. He sat with hands clasped, head tilted slightly to one side, and watched as Doar approached.

"How old are you, Mr. Shelton?"

"I'm thirty-one, sir."

"Do you have any connection with the Alabama Knights of the Ku Klux Klan?"

"I do," he replied matter of factly.

"What is the connection?"

"As president of the organization."

"Your honor," said Doar, "I would like the record to show that I am calling Mr. Shelton as an adverse witness."

Johnson nodded. "I understand."

"How long were you an officer in the U.S. Klans, Knights of the Ku Klux Klans?"

"I don't remember."

"Approximately," Doar prodded.

"About four years."

"And . . . did you know Alvin Horn?

"I have met Mr. Horn on various occasions but not connected with the organization."

"Do you know whether or not he is the head of the U.S. Klans?"

"I do not."

"Other than yourself," Doar continued, pacing a little, "who are the executive officers of the . . . of the organization?

Shelton gestured briefly with a hand. "They are listed on the charter, sir."

"And you have — does the Alabama Knights have any local klaverns?"

"Beg your pardon?"

"Does the Alabama Knights," Doar said, enunciating the words, "issue charters to local . . . local organizations, called klaverns?"

"No, sir, we do not."

"You have any types of local organizations?"

"In some areas."

"In Birmingham?" Doar pursued.

A pause. "In the vicinity."

"Is there an organization known as the Eastview Klavern Thirteen?"

"As specifically to the name," Shelton drawled, "I could not determine that fact."

"Well," Doar went on, "do you have . . . you know or recall the names of any of the organizations in the Birmingham area that are part of the Alabama Knights?"

"I have no records involving any names listing numbers of the organization."

"The question," Johnson interrupted, "is do you know the names of the organizations?"

"I do not." Shelton glanced at the judge, then shifted his gaze back to Doar. "I merely act in a public relations position in carrying out the press releases; therefore, I do not know nothing of the inner workings of a local unit, or den...."

"Mr. Shelton, you know Mr. James H. (Ace) Williams?" Doar asked.

"I have met him."

"Is he a member of the Alabama Knights?"

"To my knowledge, I do not know."

"Do you know Mr. Hubert Page?"

"I have met him."

"Is he a member?"

Again the slight shake of the head: "To my knowledge, I know not."

Doar fired the next question. "Do you know *any* of the Alabama Knights?"

"I do not have any records to verify the fact that any individuals are members of the Alabama Knights."

"That is not responsive to the question," Johnson said. "Ask the question again, Mr. Doar."

Shelton stared dully as he listened. He replied, "To authenticate it, I do not."

"That is not responsive," Johnson repeated. "Read him the question one more time, Mr. Reporter."

Court Reporter Glynn Henderson read it back a second time: Did he know any of the Alabama Knights? Shelton furrowed his brow, tilted his head to one side, then answered: "Presumably, those on the charter are the only ones that I am familiar with since they are the trustees . . . the ones I work with."

Doar questioned him more about issuing charters to local klaverns, and Shelton repeated he did not know of any specific klaverns.

"Does anyone know?" Doar asked.

"To my knowledge, I do not know."

"Let me ask you again: Do you know Mr. James H. (Ace) Williams?"

"I believe my answer was that I did not, that I had met him a couple of years ago in Gadsden."

"You had any contact with him during the month of May, 1961?"

"To my knowledge, I don't know of it."

"I believe I will recess at this time," said the judge.

Shelton's attorney, James Hammonds, jumped to his feet.

"May I speak to you, your honor? May I approach the bench?"

"I'll talk to you during the recess," the judge said. "And let me state this as a matter of record: During this recess I suggest you talk with Mr. Shelton about his evasiveness on the questions."

Hammonds nodded briskly. "That was my idea for asking for a recess, your honor."

"Yes, sir," said the judge. "I suggest you take advantage of this recess to do that, because I don't want to put Mr. Shelton in jail until he has been advised by his lawyer."

When the recess ended, Shelton returned to the witness seat and announced: "Your honor, I would like to reconsider my answers."

Johnson nodded. "All right. The witness requests permission to reconsider his answers. So if you will, Mr. Doar, commence his interrogation now."

Shelton's hostile loftiness melted and he became more direct in his replies, although, he testified, he did not know many of the Klansmen; the main thrust of his testimony was that most KKK members were known by number rather than name.

17

LOUIS FISHER, AN AGENT for the U.S. Treasury Department, had been in his office in the Federal Building in Montgomery that Saturday morning; he testified that he had gone to the window when he heard shouting coming from the direction of the Greyhound Bus Station below.

"And what did you observe?" asked Doar.

"I saw about fifty people with three or four of them in the forefront, and these three or four were attacking a white male. I later learned that it was Jim Zwerg. The . . . Zwerg was beaten to the ground and the mob withdrew slightly. I then observed Zwerg stumble to the railing of the dock of the bus station and lean against the rail. My next view of Zwerg was he was in the air as though flipped over the rail."

"Let me interrupt," said Doar. "Were you able to identify any of the people you saw beating Mr. Zwerg?"

Fisher nodded. He spoke in the quiet voice of a trained observer. "At that moment I don't recall the man that I saw actually hitting Zwerg, but in the front of the crowd was a man whom I later learned to be Thurman Ouzts."

"Is that man in the court room this morning?"

"Yes, sir, he is."

"Would you point him out?"

Fisher aimed his hand at Ouzts. "In the blue sport shirt at the corner of the table." Ouzts stared straight ahead, his hands

136

folded on the table.

"What next did you observe?"

"I saw three colored males running toward Court Street from the area of gate five of the terminal."

Doar leaned slightly on the prosecution table. "And then what happened?"

"My . . . I saw a young white boy about fourteen or so stomping on a suitcase. My next view was directed to an area near the western exit of the terminal near Moulton Street. There I saw a mob of men and women—"

"Now we are going to object," Whitesell said, "to the use of the word 'mob.' Let him tell how many, if the court—"

"I sustain," Johnson said. "Tell the number."

"I observed a group of people," Fisher continued, "some fifteen or twenty, on Moulton Street, pursuing a white girl south . . . north! excuse me, on Moulton Street. Near the western exit of the station I saw a man step from the crowd, take the girl by the arm. He was dressed in a light-colored sport shirt. He took her by the arm and attempted to lead her back in the direction that he had just come, and I saw him attacked by the group."

"Were you able to rec— . . . just what happened to him?" Doar asked.

"Wait a minute, your honor," Atkeison cried. "He's leading the witness. He's suggesting something did happen."

Johnson turned to Fisher. "What, if anything did happen to him?"

"The man (Seigenthaler) that had took the girl by the arm fell from my view into the crowd. I did not observe him anymore."

"Were you able . . . to observe any particular person in the group near that man?" Doar asked.

Fisher nodded. "I observed Mr. Ouzts."

"Then what did you observe?"

"At this time more and more crowd was gathering, getting angry, and I also observed more and more police arriving on the scene. And the next scene I viewed was immediately under my office window on . . . near the eastern entrance to the post office driveway and the Moulton Street sidewalk. My . . . when I first observed this scene, I saw a young colored male dressed in a suit lying on the sidewalk, apparently unconscious. He had a suitcase beside him. I observed him for some few moments and as he stirred on the sidewalk, the crowd around him apparently became enraged at that time. I heard screams of 'kill him! kill him!' The mob . . . the crowd grabbed the colored male and drug him into Court Street, and there was various people kicking and beating him at that time. I also . . . I saw a slim youth take an object resembling a baseball bat and strike the victim several times on . . . on the head and body. About that . . . as the assailant was using the bat, I saw Mr. Floyd Mann, the public safety director, step into the crowd and with his sidearm subdued the attackers. This victim was carried off by Mr. Mann and some of his assistants."

"Did you see any other person being attacked at about that time?" asked Doar.

"In the immediate vicinity of the terminal," said Fisher, nodding. "I saw several fist fights breaking out. They were among the bystanders and some of the attackers of the victim."

"Did you see any more violence that day?"

Fisher cocked his head sideways, thinking. "A little later I observed a crowd pursuing two or three colored males east on Adams Street. They ran from my view. Shortly after that the Highway Patrol and the Sheriff's posse and more and more police arrived . . . and I saw no more violence that day."

"What, if anything," Doar questioned, "did the police . . . the city police do to stop the violence?"

"After I heard the screams, I saw two motorcycle patrolmen park their motorcycles on Court Street and start directing traffic at that time."

This incredible description of the scene hung over the courtroom for several seconds.

"What, if anything, did the police do during the period from ten-twenty to twelve o'clock?" Doar asked. "The City of Montgomery Police?"

"Well, as I saw, there was a group of them there . . . and there were scattered police in the area that I observed off and on."

"Did you see the police take action with respect to these violent . . . this violence that you have described?"

"I . . . at the time I observed the colored male lying on the sidewalk unconscious, I saw a policeman walk by the victim and look at him and then disappear. He was immediately on the scene. And my next police action was observing Mr. Mann saving the victim there."

"Can you . . . are you able to tell the court when . . . the time of the last act of violence?"

"This was approximately twelve-thirty," Fisher replied.

Doar nodded. "That is all."

Atkeison approached. "Mr. Fisher."

"Yes, sir."

"You don't know what transpired down at the bus station before you say you heard some noise?"

"No, sir. I do not."

"But you did see some fights breaking out all around, didn't you?"

"Yes, sir. That is correct."

Atkeison waved some notes. "People fighting backward and forward between each other?"

Fisher nodded. "Yes, sir."

"And you don't know who most of the people were, do you?"

"No, sir."

"And you don't know," the attorney continued, his voice rising, "whether these people were fighting a bunch of communists that had come in here or not, do you?"

Fisher stared at him for a moment, then shrugged. "No, sir," he responded somewhat wryly. "I haven't . . . no knowledge of that."

"At that time, could you identify any of the . . . the integrationists from anybody else?

"No, sir."

The attorney resumed his slow pacing and gazed out over the spectators. "Are you originally from Alabama?"

"Yes, sir."

"Do you know," Atkeison asked, a smile spreading over his face, "what the word 'possuming' means?"

"Yes, sir."

"And that fellow laying there in the street," Atkeison said, thrusting a finger toward the window, "could have been 'possuming' for all you know, couldn't he?"

Fisher shrugged. "Could have been," he muttered.

A reputed member of the KKK, Jesse Oliver Faggard, who had been present in Birmingham during the beating, was slow in some of his answers, so Doar provided him with a copy of a police report to refresh his memory.

While he pored over the document, a restless quiet stirred the courtroom. Johnson watched Faggard. Ten minutes, then fifteen passed.

Finally, the judge inquired, "How much of that have you read, Faggard?"

"I'm on the seventh page, Judge."

"Found any errors yet?"

"No, sir."

"That's all the time we're putting on that," the judge declared. "Let's move along."

Among the witnesses the defense called was Colonel Floyd Mann, who had personally saved the life of William Barbee on the twentieth, and who had brought the state troopers in to restore order to Montgomery. Privately, Mann told friends that the Montgomery police had virtually abdicated their responsibility that day. But on the witness stand, in response to specific questions, his testimony would be used to speak favorably of the local law enforcement officers. He had been called as a witness for Montgomery Public Safety Director Sullivan and Police Chief Ruppenthal. Whitesell arose to question him.

"You're the director of the Alabama Department of Public Safety ?"

"That's correct."

"Were you present at the Greyhound Bus Station somewhere between ten-thirty and eleven on the morning of May twentieth, 1961?"

"Yes, sir, I was."

"Did you see the Montgomery police?"

"Yes, sir."

"Do you recall a photographer, I believe, being beaten?"

"Yes."

"Do you recall anyone being there with you?"

"I know at the time we got those people off Mr. Atkins (the

photographer) I turned and Chief Stanley was standing there."

"Chief Stanley was standing there?" Whitesell asked.

"Right. Those men were turned over to Chief Stanley and Mr. Atkins said 'I want those men arrested.'"

"Now, let's talk for a minute about an occasion that happened down here in front of the Toddle House," said Whitesell, "where a Negro boy named Barbee was beaten by some people and another Negro jumped in to help him. You recall that?"

"I do," answered Mann in a tone that suggested he would always recall it.

"And you went to his aid?"

"I did."

"And drew your revolver?" Whitesell asked.

"I did."

"At that time, do you recall if the Montgomery police assisted you in getting this man from the area?"

Mann's eyes narrowed for a moment while he mentally reenacted the incident. "I recall at the time," he said slowly, "the crowd backed up where you could see. I looked behind me and Mr. W.R. Jones (Mann's assistant) was standing there, and I asked he and this other boy that was on his knees — not Barbee, the other one —"

"The other Negro?"

Mann nodded. "Yes. I asked them to pick that boy up, and when the crowd opened up I saw (Montgomery police) Lieutenant R.D. Moody there, and he assisted us in getting the boy out of the crowd."

Whitesell paced slowly gazing at the floor. Then: "Was the Montgomery police standing there, opening the crowd so that they could move this boy through?"

"Well, when ... " Mann stopped, wrinkled his brow and asked, "Would you repeat that, please?"

Whitesell asked the question again, whether Montgomery police officers overtly opened a hole in the crowd to help facilitate the removal of William Barbee after Mann had rescued him.

The red-haired public safety director seemed to choose his words carefully. He spoke slowly. "When the crowd opened up, I saw Lieutenant Moody standing there. Then he helped get him (Barbee) out."

With the exception of the one Montgomery officer, Lieutenant Moody, Mann's testimony had done little to make the department look good. The police had not opened an escape avenue that day . . . it had just simply opened.

Whitesell resumed his questioning. "Now, did you talk to any policemen at any time during the morning on that scene and ask him why Mr. Sullivan didn't send more officers there?"

"I did not. I had talked with Sullivan earlier, and I had told him at the time he asked for help he would get it. After we brought that boy out of the crowd, Mr. Sullivan met me and says, 'It is time we had some assistance,' and our state police was called for immediately."

"At the request of Mr. Sullivan?" Whitesell inquired.

"Yes, sir."

"Mr. Sullivan was on the scene when you arrived?"

"Yes, sir."

John Doar questioned Mann briefly about any conversation he may have had the morning of the 20th of May with Montgomery Police Commissioner Sullivan.

"I got word that the bus would leave Birmingham at approximately eight a.m. I got that word, in my best judgment, around five-thirty in the morning. I dressed, went to our office, and called Mr. Sullivan's home around seven."

"Did you advise him the bus was leaving at that time?"

"I did."

"Did you talk with him again that morning?"

Before Mann could answer, Johnson intervened. "Just a minute. Mr. Mann? Did you advise Mr. Sullivan what time the bus was expected in Montgomery?"

"To . . . well, there was a change in plans on that bus. It was first set to leave at eight and then they changed to eight-thirty. I discussed that with Mr. Sullivan. Yes, sir."

"What time did you discuss that eight-thirty leaving time with him?" the judge asked.

"Mr. Sullivan was to make a welcome address to some organization at the Whitley Hotel," Mann replied. He thought for a moment. "I believe it was about nine . . . a little after when Mr. Sullivan came and talked with Chief Stanley and Chief Joe Smelley and myself."

"All right. Thank you."

Whitesell came back for some further questions. "Mr. Mann, did you notice anything unusual at the station?"

Mann shook his head. "I drove by there ten minutes before the bus arrived and I saw nothing unusual."

"Let me ask you this: You have been through all of that situation on that Saturday morning. And as a police officer, do you have any reason to believe that the Montgomery Police Department deliberately failed to send people out to that station?"

The question hung a moment. "I do not," Mann responded in a firm voice.

"Did they deliberately fail to provide protection, do you have any reason to believe?"

"I do not."

18

THE HEARING ENDED ON the afternoon of June 1, a Thursday, but Johnson told the parties to be back at nine a.m. Friday for his findings. He wasn't going to spend a lot of time on a case that had been so volatile; there was more than a question of law at stake; there was also the urgency of cutting off any further acts of violence. He worked late that night — one of few times he didn't make it home for supper — and his staff stayed with him, typing the order which he wrote in longhand.

JOHNSON

I can't say enough about the people who worked with me those years in Montgomery; they were, simply stated, just the most loyal and dedicated court employees and other government workers you could have. There are those who say I was one man against the wrath of the old order of the Southern aristocracy. But I was never alone. My staff assisted me through some of the harshest times, when the attitudes of many white Southerners were hot with anger; they never flinched, the U. S. marshals who were with me never batted an eye; the FBI agents were always nearby. So I wasn't alone.

The next morning all parties reported back to the federal

building. The attorneys for both sides were there at the tables, and Johnson glanced at them and said:

"All right, gentlemen. All right, now. To you gentlemen representing the plaintiffs, and you gentlemen representing the defendants, and you defendants: I had you to return this morning with the idea that it would be impossible for my office staff to transcribe the findings and conclusions and order that I have entered in these cases. They worked way into the night and got it done. So it will not be appropriate or necessary for me to read to you my findings and conclusions, and the injunction that I am issuing against each defendant in this case, and the injunctions that I am issuing against the Congress of Racial Equality, the Southern Christian Leadership Conference, the Montgomery County Jail Council, the Nashville Non-Violent Movement, the Reverend Fred Shuttlesworth, the Reverend Martin Luther King, the Reverend Ralph D. Abernathy, Solomon Seay, and Wyatt T. Walker.

"Now gentlemen, if there is any misunderstanding after you read my findings and conclusions, and injunction and restraining order, on the part of any defendant against whom this temporary restraining order has been issued, it simply means this: That if there are no other occurrences like the ones involved in this case, then this temporary injunction and this temporary restraining order will amount to nothing. But if there are such other occurrences — and let me impress upon each of you that this injunction is going to be enforced by the U.S. Government — if there are such other occurrences, I am going to put some Klansmen, some city officials, and some policemen, and some Negro preachers, in the U.S. penitentiary in Atlanta, Georgia. And that is all I want to say about it. Court is in recess."

ORDER

This court finds that on May 20, 1961, it was a matter of public knowledge that was known to the Montgomery Police Department that a Greyhound Bus carrying ... student passengers ... was coming. The evidence is abundantly clear ... that L. B. Sullivan, as police commissioner, was advised by Floyd Mann, director of the Alabama Department of Public

Safety . . . that the bus in which this group was riding was en route from Birmingham to Montgomery . . . the likelihood of violence was known to the Department of Public Safety and that through its head, Floyd Mann, had taken the necessary precautions. (Mann) had 16 patrol cars and one airplane to accompany this bus. Sullivan had not even alerted the Montgomery Police Department on this morning of May 20 and no special plans had been made . . . to ensure the safety of the group of students.

The court specifically finds that the Montgomery Police Department under the direction of Sullivan and Chief Ruppenthal willfully and deliberately failed to take measures to ensure the safety of the students and to prevent unlawful acts of violence upon their persons. From the testimony of witnesses and the radio log of the police department, no police car was dispatched to the area of violence until Car 19 was sent at 10:33 a.m. to investigate. At 10:37 Car 25 was sent also to investigate. It is significant that none of the officers in these two cars testified in this case. At 10:30, Car No. 29 was sent to the general area to "direct traffic."

This court specifically finds that the U.S. Klans, Knights of the Ku Klux Klan, and the Alabama Knights of the Ku Klux Klan, conspired to and did commit acts of violence upon these interstate student-passengers in Anniston and Birmingham on May 14, and in Montgomery, Alabama on May 20. The failure of the defendant law enforcement officers to enforce the law in this case clearly amounts to unlawful state action in violation of the equal protection clause of the 14th Amendment . . . the willful and deliberate failure on the part of the law enforcement officers was also unlawful in that it deprived the passengers of their rights without due process of law . . . .

The order enjoined the KKK from "conspiring to interfere with the travel of passengers, committing acts of violence upon, or threatening or otherwise obstructing, impeding, or interfering with the free movement of interstate commerce."

A preliminary injunction was also aimed at the police officials of Montgomery for "refusing to provide protection for all persons traveling in interstate commerce." As for the freedom riders and their supporters, the order read:

> Those who sponsor, finance and encourage groups to come into this area with the knowledge that such publicized trips will foment violence in and around the bus terminals are just as effective in causing an obstruction to the movement of bona fide interstate bus passengers . . . this court now specifically finds that the so-called "freedom riders" and other groups sponsored by CORE, SCLC, Martin Luther King and Ralph D. Abernathy and other officers of such groups . . . even though it is agitation within the law of the United States, is agitation that constitutes an undue burden upon the free flow of interstate commerce at this particular time and under the circumstances that exist. The fact that this agitation on the part of the members is within the law . . . the right of the public to be protected from the evils of their conduct is a greater and more important right. All are due to be enjoined and/or restrained from such further activities that produce this evil result.
>
> While it is true that this violence is caused directly by the Klan groups and has been allowed by the willful failure of the police authorities . . . it is equally true that the CORE and SCLC and others, by their actions in financing such non-bona fide trips are directly causing an undue burden and restraint upon interstate carriers . . . .

JOHNSON

> Some northern newspapers were dismayed that I included the freedom riders in my restraining order. And the reason I did is that I felt they went about pursuing their rights in the wrong way. When they ran into trouble in Anniston — their first stop in Alabama — they should have quit and come to the courts. That's why we have courts. But they did not do that. Instead, they kept on and it not only created strife, it also interfered with the other passengers who were riding buses. It impeded the normal flow of interstate commerce.
>
> They should have come to the courts and presented their grievances.
>
> Now what made the freedom riders different from

the blacks who took part in the bus boycott in Montgomery is that the boycott was a negative protest, so to speak. People just quit riding buses. But they did not bother anybody else; did not interfere with others riding them.

But in the freedom rider case, people who were not part of the protest activity were afraid to get on the buses when they knew the freedom riders were there. They were afraid of trouble. And that's what there was, trouble.

Even the Greyhound people were afraid. They had a bus burned and after that they didn't want to charter any more buses for the riders. So Bobby Kennedy hears about it and he calls up Greyhound's headquarters and asks them why they can't provide a bus.

And they tell him that their drivers are all scared. So Bobby gets mad and says, "Why, hell, can't Mr. Greyhound get out and drive one of 'em?" And one of the drivers had said something like, "I've only got one life to give for my country, and I'm not giving it for the NAACP or CORE."

But this court entered a ruling in November, 1961, that stopped discrimination at all levels in interstate transportation. And it would have happened without all that trouble. They didn't have to push as hard as they did.

They could have achieved their goals just as effectively if they had come to the courts in the first place. As it happened, there was a terrible wave of violence here and we were lucky we didn't have some people killed, because the Klan went into action without any interference from the police. When the riders entered Alabama they had one state investigator with them. After the trouble in Anniston on May 14, Floyd Mann began taking measures to prevent anything further from happening.

But Bull Connor, who was in charge of the Birmingham police, didn't do a thing. On that same day, an hour or so after the bus burning at Anniston, he did nothing to alert his men to trouble. So the riders came in and were beaten. Then six days went by and the Montgomery police knew the riders were coming. They had six days to get ready. Six days. And didn't do a thing. When the riders got here the Montgomery police had virtually abdicated their responsibility. And the Klan moved in and rode roughshod at the bus station.

If it hadn't been for Floyd Mann, there would have been some folks killed that day. He had to take over with his men and do the job the Montgomery police should have done. Instead of protecting people, the police were directing traffic.

This freedom riders thing should have been stopped in its tracks right after the trouble in Anniston. Anyone with any sense could have seen the threat of violence was at the exploding point.

But nobody did anything until Bobby Kennedy sent the U.S. marshals in and John Doar of the Justice Department came to me with his petition for an injunction. The freedom riders — or their supporters and sponsors — should have done it at the first hint of trouble.

I was told that as part of the Justice Department's preparations for potential violence on May 20, 1961, a van was parked in the vicinity of the Greyhound Terminal in Montgomery and FBI agents were stationed inside with a movie camera. Not one frame of the film was presented as evidence. It seemed, so some agents said at the time, that all the footage had been exposed and ruined. Whether it was an incredible coincidence or photographer's bad luck or sabotage, no one to this day will say.

I had heard such a report in some conversations. But I don't know what could have happened to the film; seems strange that three cameras would all go haywire at the same time. I know the only pictures available of the violence outside the bus station were taken by an agent of the Alcohol, Tobacco and Firearms Department who was standing in the window right in this building, looking down on the bus station. He saw it all.

19

A S AN INTERESTING sequel to the freedom riders episode, Claude Henley, the burly Klansman who wore the
white shirt and had a cigar clamped in his mouth that
day at the station, and who slapped the news photographer
about, later used his friendship with George Wallace to land the
concessions franchise at Montgomery's Garrett Coliseum.

Some years later Johnson would run into Claude Henley
again.

JOHNSON

I had gone to West Bay, Florida, to do some fishing.
I got up early that morning and headed out at about five
o'clock. I was by myself and had gone about three miles
out and was catching several large trout. Suddenly I
noticed a fairly big boat moving off to my left and it stops
about fifty yards or so away from me. At the time the sun
was just getting ready to rise. I glanced at the boat and
noted four men in it. I didn't pay them any particular
attention.

But a short time later one of them — a big man —
calls out, "Hey, Judge! You havin' any luck?" Well, it
surprised me that he knew who I was. It surprised me and
bothered me, too, because I hadn't told that many people
I was coming down there. So I answered, "Nope." I didn't

extend the conversation. Just minded my own business. I
had lied, of course, because I had been catching some
fish. But a fisherman doesn't tell other fishermen that
he's getting fish ... they'll invade his territory if they
know. But these men kept sitting there and pretty soon
the big guy calls out, "Hey, Judge, you want a beer to
drink? We got plenty over here."

Well, I told them no thanks, that I had a jug of water
with me. It disturbed me some that they knew who I was,
because I was several miles out in the bay and was alone.
Then he hollers, "You're gettin' some good distance on
those casts, Judge. What reel are you usin' there?" And I
called back, "A Johnson spinning reel." And he says,
"That must be a pretty good make of reel." And I said,
"The best."

Well, they continued to sit there for a while, watching me. Finally, they cranked the boat up and went on
their way. So I finished a couple of hours later and headed
back. The guy that owned the fishing camp was standing
there on the dock and I asked him, "Did you tell some
people I was out there?" And he says, "Well, yes. Was
there any harm in it? They had asked if there was anybody out there from Montgomery, because that's where
they're from. And I told 'em you was out there."

Well, it turned out the big guy was Claude Henley.
And his fishing buddies were two Montgomery police
officers and Gerald Wallace. "Don't ever tell anybody
when I'm out there," I told the owner. He didn't understand that Henley had once been in my courtroom and I
had slapped him with an injunction. Nor did he understand the philosophical differences.

Somewhat ironically, a week or so after that little encounter, Henley returned to West Bay, Florida, with his sons for
some more fishing. Outside the camp office, his sons became
engaged in an argument with two men.

Henley hurried to the verbal fray and became involved.
When it ended, he returned to the camp office and was going to
buy some fishing supplies. Suddenly, he collapsed and hit the

floor, dead of an apparent heart attack.

JOHNSON

He didn't mean me any harm out there. I think he was trying to be friendly . . . but mostly, I guess he just wanted me to know that he knew who I was.

The freedom riders were zealots, young and full of vinegar and they weren't afraid of getting whipped. Now, a lot of the white people in Alabama as well as other places were saying that they came here to cause trouble.

After what happened in Anniston and Birmingham, the fact that they continued on to Montgomery led me to believe that was true. I wouldn't argue with them that there was segregation and they had a right to ride those buses. The threat of violence by whites would not have been reason to halt them. But when the violence occurred that changed things. It was no longer just a threat of trouble — there were people beaten, rocks thrown, a bus burned, homes and cars set on fire, and bomb threats. So the trouble was here. I had to think of the other people who wanted to ride buses and use the terminals.

Under the particular set of circumstances, I had to issue an order against everyone to allow a cooling off period until a court decided the legal issues.

It was an irony of the Civil Rights Movement, that when it came to the white Southerners' view of Northern civil rights workers, it was much the same as mine. I felt they should have stayed home and let the issues be settled in court.

These young people — most of them were college students — who came South were well-intentioned, but sorely misguided; any good they may have done was badly offset by the turmoil and strife they helped create. Now I would be the first to recognize their right to be here, but there is a world of difference between what is "legally right" and what is good judgment.

I saw some of these young people in my court from time to time. My impression of them was that they had an attitude that said, "If you rule for us, you're not doing us a favor, as we're entitled to it."

Further, there must be some question raised as to whether black Southerners such as Andrew Young and John Lewis really needed that much help from the North . . . I suspect they didn't.

I came to respect these young men; both were courageous and courteous. They were non-violent and used good sense most of the time.

Years after the troubled times in Alabama, Young was elected mayor of Atlanta and Lewis was elected a member of the city council there and later to the Congress of the United States.

Part V

'When I heard 'em say "Wallace," I knew we weren't getting in.'

School desegregation
1963-1967

The Johnsons with their son, Johnny, about 1972.

20

AMONG JOHNSON'S FOND memories of the turbulent civil rights years in Montgomery were the Christmases the family would spend together. Brothers and sisters and nieces and nephews would come to Montgomery and would all go to the home of Frank, Sr.

JOHNSON

It was tradition that the oldest man was Santa Claus and that was Daddy's job. My chief function, according to Ruth and my sister, Jean Johnson McCoy, was to carry the turkey in that Ruth had cooked and then eat up everything in sight without ever offering to help clean the dishes.

We didn't draw names, but everyone would just buy presents for everyone else and we'd all arrive in time for breakfast. After the meal, we would gather around the tree and Daddy would pass out the gifts.

We'd make a day of it, eating the main dinner shortly after the noon hour.

After Daddy died in 1965, the job of Santa Claus fell to my hands. I didn't wear a red suit or anything like that, but they still called me Santa. I liked to play with the kids. I'd get a present and call one of their names and they'd have to say "Here!"

And I'd pretend not to hear and call out the name again. Next time they'd yell louder, "Here I am! Here!"

And I'd say, "OK, but you've got to speak up or I'll give your present to somebody else."

The first year I had the job it took some determination on my part to try to keep the children laughing. I couldn't help but think of Daddy and also my brother Dock who died the same year of a heart attack. He was forty-five at the time of his death.

My brothers and sisters would join me and Mother and Daddy during those Christmases and recall the early days of our family in Winston County.

The Johnsons' Christmas tradition ended when their son, Johnny, took his own life at the family home on Haardt Drive October 13, 1975. He was then twenty-six, and seemed to be headed for a legal career. In the years after, the judge and his wife often left Montgomery during the Christmas season. They told friends it was too sad to remain in town without their son. In 1977, the judge's mother, Alabama Long Johnson, became ill and had to be placed in a nursing home in York, Alabama.

JOHNSON

My sister, Jean, ran a drug store in York, in Sumter County. She kept me supplied with fresh Home Run cigarettes during the years I smoked. She'd mail me a carton every four or five days and I'd send her a check. But once in a while she'd slip up and I'd run out of cigarettes and have to buy them at a store in Montgomery, which I didn't like to do because I'd never know if they were fresh or not. Sometimes a pack of Home Runs might sit on the store shelf for a year. So I'd call Jean up at the store — usually when she was busy — and all I'd say was, "What's the matter? R. J. Reynolds gone out of business?" She'd get the message. I'd say that even though Liggett & Myers made them. But sometime I think Jean would hold back on mailing them just to make me call her.

Those Christmas gatherings were some of the rare

The Judge and the famous half-a-fish.

times we'd play Christmas carols instead of Bluegrass, which is my favorite. All hillbillies like Bluegrass. It was part of my growing up and it's never left me. I have a tape player in my Lincoln and when I'm driving somewhere the only time I turn on the radio is for news. For music, I play tapes of Chet Atkins or something like Flatt and Scruggs.

I used to like to watch them on television on Saturday nights. To me, that's what music is all about. It's got a rhythm to it that gets the blood moving. But Atkins is the king of them all. To me there are only two kind of guitar players in the world: Those that imitate Chet Atkins and those that ought to.

Fishing sometimes gave me time to think about some of the cases I'd have before me; it's just a good time to think about things. At other times it gives me time to pause to appreciate the majesty of life and how tentative things can be, how vulnerable we all are at one time or another.

I was in the Gulf of Mexico once with a former law clerk, Pat Sims of Mobile; we were off the Chandelier Islands, about forty miles offshore below the Mississippi Coast. I had just caught a beautiful redfish weighing about five pounds. We put it on the stringer and let it stay in the water, trailing behind our boat.

We were concentrating on catching some more when, whoosh! All of a sudden there was a tremendous splashing sound. I glanced around and saw the water boiling up behind us. In the same split second, I saw a huge grayish thing right in the center of the spray and foam. Shark! It must have been fifteen to twenty feet long; its mouth looked as big as a barn door. In that fleeting moment it appeared it was coming into the boat. I saw it had something in its mouth; then it disappeared in the water.

For a moment Sims and I didn't move. We were stunned. A shark coming up like that will get your attention — and keep it — for a moment or two. Then we ran back and pulled the stringer in. My beautiful redfish was no longer a five-pounder. About half of the fish was gone.

Some of the most fun I've had fishing has been in the Gulf of Mexico off the Northwest Florida coast. I'm not talking about getting one of those charter boats where people wait on you hand and foot. I mean going out in my own seventeen-foot boat that I'd use at Lake Martin. My brother Jimmy and I would haul it down to Panama City, get us a motel room, then get up at first light and head out. We'd put the boat in right on the beach, getting out through the rough breakers which would sometimes be five or six feet high.

It was a challenge just getting out sometimes. But once we did, we'd get into the calmer waters out beyond the surf line and we'd have the gulf to ourselves. Then we'd usually strip down to our shorts and spend the entire day fishing. Several times I caught over seventy pounds of the best king mackerel I've ever tasted.

Now it's tricky getting out through the waves in a

small boat, but it's even more so trying to get back in. There's a knack to it; everything has to be synchronized. You have to have the motor going full blast as you head in. At the precise moment, as you get to the breakers, you have to cut it, then jump into the water and keep the boat from turning around. If you don't, the waves will catch the wide stern and might flip it over or sink it.

So one day we were coming in — we'd put our clothes back on— and we'd reached the point where it was time for me to leap into the water to hold the boat. As I jumped out, my little toe on the left foot got caught in an oar lock. There was this sudden, jolting pain that ran through my body; at the same time I heard a loud crack . . . heard it above the roar of the surf. I flopped into the water, got a mouthful, but managed to regain my balance.

I shouted at Jimmy to take over.

"What's wrong?" he says.

"Broke my toe," I said. The pain was so excruciating that I didn't care what happened to the boat. All I could think about was getting in.

I knew for sure it was broken when I tried to walk into the beach through that surf. The undertow rushing back to sea would turn the toe completely around, causing unbearable pain. So the only way to get in, I figured, was to walk backwards. Which is what I did. People on the beach were staring at me . . . it must have been a sight.

Finally I got in and was able to turn around and walk forward like a regular person, limped right on across the road to the motel. I had a couple of drinks of Jack Daniels bourbon, then got to studying the toe. I took it and forced it into the position I thought it should be, painful as it was. Then I just left it alone.

For several days after I came to court in soft shoes. Well, it so happened that in one case the defense called a doctor as an expert witness. It turned out that Dr. Glenn Palmer was an orthopedic surgeon. After he testified I called a recess and sent a marshal to bring him back to my office. When he came in I took off the shoe and showed him the toe, and told him what had happened.

He looked at it closely, then started laughing.

"Judge," he says, "next time I have a broken toe to fix I'm going to call you in. This is a perfect job."

The toe got better and never bothered me. But a few years later when Jimmy and I were back down in the Gulf, we had another accident as we were coming ashore. Jimmy broke two ribs. I didn't attempt to set those.

Mrs. Johnson's favorite photo of her and the Judge, taken along the Gulf Coast.

21

GEORGE WALLACE WON the governor's race in 1962 after a bitter campaign against former Governor Jim Folsom and Tuscaloosa attorney Ryan deGraffenried. Like so much else in those days, the campaign was full of great oratory, rebel yells, Confederate flags, and calls by some of the candidates to "secede again if necessary" to preserve the traditions of the South.

Wallace was inaugurated in January 1963, and on that chilly, gray day made his heralded "segregation forever" speech.

Early in the spring of that year, Johnson went to Washington on business and took Johnny with him. Somehow the word got out to Attorney General Robert Kennedy that the judge was there and he sent a marshal to ask Johnson to come by for a visit.

JOHNSON

Johnny and I walked over to his office and we had a casual, friendly conversation. He spoke of some of the voting cases in Alabama and made note of Wallace's speech. Then he looks at Johnny and says, "How'd you like to meet the President?"

Well, Johnny beamed and says, "I'd like that fine."

Bobby got on the phone then and talked for a while, then he says, "We'll have a car pick you up at your hotel at two o'clock."

That afternoon a black limousine pulled up and a chauffeur gets out and holds the door for us. It was pretty stylish travel for a Winston County boy. Arriving at the White House we were met by Bobby who escorted us in, introduced us to the President's secretary, Evelyn Lincoln, then took us in to the Oval Office. The President stood up and extended his hand to Johnny first, then me.

At that time, Birmingham was already having some of its racial demonstrations, but he said little about it. We didn't discuss business.

We talked about general things for perhaps a half-hour. I knew he was busy so I stood then to leave. But President Kennedy says, "Hold on a minute." Then he reached into his desk and got a fountain pen. He handed it to Johnny. "Here's something you can take home with you."

It had his signature embossed on it; Johnny would treasure that gift.

In June of 1963, Governor Wallace prepared to make his "stand in the schoolhouse door" at the University of Alabama which was prepared to admit two blacks. One morning I received a call at the office. It was Attorney General Robert Kennedy who had come to Montgomery to meet with Wallace.

"I'm out here at Maxwell Field," he said. "Could you come and have breakfast with me?"

I said I would and drove out there. Between bites of bacon and eggs, Kennedy says, "I'm meeting with Governor Wallace today and wanted your expertise. How do you think I should approach him? What advice do you have?"

I shrugged. "Governor Wallace is making as much political hay out of this as he can. I know you know that."

Kennedy nodded, grinning ruefully.

"You should proceed on the basis that anything you say which might be construed by Wallace as helping him, will be used by him for that purpose."

"I'll be careful," he said.

Then I told him, "You should not hope to accomplish

anything at the meeting."

I probably didn't give him any advice that he didn't already know. Kennedy was a shrewd man. Later that day he went to the Alabama Capitol and walked around a black wreath that somebody had placed by the marker where Jefferson Davis had been inaugurated as President of the Confederacy. Whatever transpired at the meeting, it didn't deter George from making his grandstand show at the University. Hundreds of National Guardsmen were activated to prevent violence. When Vivian Malone and James Hood were driven to the campus by FBI agents, they saw the guardsmen going through close-order drill and riot-control training.

President Kennedy, meanwhile, federalized the guardsmen and Wallace, after making his defiant speech, stepped aside when requested to do so by the commanding general of the guard. Even so, Wallace declared himself the winner.

A few weeks after the University of Alabama event, Johnson received a note from Robert Kennedy. It said simply, "You were right. There wasn't much accomplished at the meeting."

Even though Wallace had to step aside at Alabama ("I can't stand up alone against bayonets," one newspaper quoted him to say), his cavalier act was clear warning of the resistance he intended to raise when black children would attempt to desegregate the public school at the elementary and secondary levels. And that day was not far away.

22

*"The first thing that impresses the student of school desegrega-
tion in the Deep South is the slowness with which it has proceeded.
No Negroes attended white primary or secondary schools in Alabama until 1963. The record elsewhere was little better. When
resistance finally began to crumble, the meager result of massive
litigation was token. In the 1963-64 school year, the eleven states
of the Confederacy had 1.17 percent of their Negro students in
schools with white students. By the following year, 56 percent of the
South's school districts had desegregated schools. In 1966, 97
percent . . . were in official compliance with the HEW guidelines
or under court orders, but the actual attendance of Negroes in
formerly all-white schools was less than 16 percent.... There are
reasons for the long delay between the declaration of the right to
attend desegregated schools and its implementation. The profound
disagreement of most regions of the Deep South is probably the
most important single factor. Resistance took many forms; some
were spectacular, like sending state troopers and governors to
stand in school house doors . . ."*

—Excerpt of a speech made by Judge Johnson
at the University of Minnesota Law Forum,
April 17, 1970

The effort to integrate public schools began in Little Rock,
Arkansas, on September 11, 1957, when nine black children

tried to enter Central High School. They had a federal court order to back them, and when whites turned them away, the government stepped in, sending paratroopers to the school. Bayonets were used to force the state of Arkansas to desegregate.

That case shows the strength we Americans place in the law. The court order was not to be trifled with. And without it, chances are those students would have met the same fate as did four black children in Birmingham, Alabama, who tried to enter all-white schools on that same date — but without a federal court order.

On September 11, 1957, Ruby Shuttlesworth, twelve, her sister, Patricia, fourteen, and two other black children went to all-white Phillips High School in Birmingham. They were driven by the girls' father, the Reverend Fred Shuttlesworth and his wife, Ruby, plus another minister, J. S. Phifer. As they pulled up in front they were met by a group of about thirty white men, some of them wearing brass knuckles, others carrying chains and clubs. They advanced, shouting threats and cursing. Then they broke out the car windshield.

Shuttlesworth got out of the car, knowing what awaited him. He was set upon and knocked repeatedly to the ground. His wife and the girls attempted to get out and run to the school, but were forced back inside. Birmingham police, meanwhile — and there were only a few of them on hand — attempted to radio for reinforcements. The call was held up, they said, because the radio was airing a routine stolen car report. Later, the report was found to be false; the car reported "stolen" actually was the property of Police Commissioner Eugene (Bull) Connor.

Bleeding and bruised, Shuttlesworth managed to get back into his car and was driven by Phifer to University Hospital. While most of the news media centered its attention on Central High in Little Rock, the attempt by the audacious Shuttlesworth to implement the *Brown* order in Birmingham and Alabama ended in one day.

Ruby and Patricia Shuttlesworth returned to the all-black schools they had been attending.

Sizing up the racial situation of the day, President Eisenhower uttered a statement that was less than profound when he said, "Patience is the key word in integration."

To the average black person living in the South then —
ninety-four years after Abraham Lincoln put his signature on the
Emancipation Proclamation — it was hardly an encouraging
word.

The angry resistance Shuttlesworth encountered ended
the integration drive in the education arena for six years.

Then, in the spring of 1963, Mr. and Mrs. Detroit Lee of
Tuskegee entered a suit asking that their son, Anthony, and
other blacks be admitted to all-white Tuskegee High School.

On July 22, 1963, Johnson entered an order directing the
Macon County School Board to open its doors to black students.
It would be the beginning of a long and bitter struggle in
Alabama.

On a sultry, thunder-filled night a few weeks later, several
hundred blacks gathered at Greenwood Baptist Church in
Tuskegee. It was not a freedom rally, but a business meeting.
Marsha Sullins, then thirteen, vividly remembered the night —
and the days and nights to follow:

"We had to come to the church to see which of us wanted to
try and go to the all-white school. At that time, we were attending Tuskegee Institute High, which was for blacks. So that
night, Fred Gray, our attorney, and other leaders were up on the
altar and they asked which of us wanted to try. So about a
hundred of us raised our hands. I did because my mother had
just told me that I was going to try to go. And the more I thought
about it, the more I knew she was right. So I got one of the forms
and filled it out."

The board of education ordered examinations to be admin-
istered to the applicants; Miss Sullins and twelve others, including Anthony Lee, the chief plaintiff, passed.

Superintendent C. A. Pruitt then interviewed each of the
thirteen individually. "I admit," he would say later in a hearing,
"that I recommended to the board that the Negro students be
accepted at Tuskegee Public High School. It . . . I did these
things that I felt I had to do under the court order . . . not what I
wanted to do."

At the same time, there were several black students in
Birmingham and Mobile assigned to attend previously all-white

schools; this, all on the heels of the dramatic developments the previous June at the University of Alabama when Governor George Wallace stood in the door to keep two blacks out.

The majority of the high school students in Alabama were to enter at Tuskegee, in Judge Johnson's Middle District. The action, *Lee vs. Macon*, was to be the central battle of school desegregation in Alabama, and ultimately would spread as the case of precedent for the entire state.

School would begin September 2, 1963, in Tuskegee; Mobile and Birmingham would start the day after.

JOHNSON

I awoke early as usual, feeling pretty good about things in Tuskegee. I had issued the orders and the people there were working it out among themselves to comply. Lawyers like Fred Gray and other Negro leaders were meeting with people like Allan Parker, the white president of a bank, and Broward Segrest, a white attorney. They seemed to have the thing worked out and everyone was prepared for the school bell to ring. But during the night of September the first, Governor Wallace sent his supporters over there and they began stirring things up. Early that morning, around dawn, state troopers appeared at the home of the superintendent and gave him an executive order from the governor that the school would not open.

In a lightning display of force, trooper car after trooper car sped through the morning mist into Tuskegee; by 7:00 a.m., there were more than two hundred lawmen fringing the sprawling, oak-studded school yard, prepared to carry out Wallace's order of defiance ("Goddamnit, we just ain't," *Time* magazine quoted him to say).

About twenty minutes before eight, the school yard was full of white students, most dumbfounded by the presence of the troopers. A moment later, at the Board of Education building located about a half-block away, the thirteen Negroes arrived. The girls were dressed in skirts and blouses and most wore brown-and-white penny loafers and white anklets.

"Nobody was saying much," Miss Sullins would recall. "We just stood there. And then a bus pulled up, with Mr. Whitlock, a Negro, the driver. We were told to get aboard. I didn't know what was going on. But I got on with the others, and the bus started up and just swung around across the street and stopped in front of the school. It seemed silly for them to put us on a bus to ride just that far. But before we could get off, a trooper came on and he had this long piece of paper. And he started reading . . . saying something that Governor George Wallace was issuing some kind of order. Well, when he said 'Wallace', I knew we weren't getting in."

She and the others listened with sober faces as the trooper read: "Whereas, there now exists in the State of Alabama conditions calculated to result in a disruption of the peace and tranquility of this state and to occasion peril to the lives and property of the citizens thereof, this situation resulting from the threat of forced and unwarranted integration of the public schools, now, therefore, I, George Wallace, do hereby order the Macon County Board of Education . . . to delay the opening of Tuskegee High School for a period of one week . . . ."

The reaction of the governor sent ripples of uneasiness over the state, then turned to bristling anxiety as a pending showdown loomed.

On September 9, the black children — Marsha Sullins, Shirley Chambliss, Anthony Lee, Patricia Jones and her sister, Wilma, Robert Judkins and his sister, Carmen, Willie Wyatt, Heloise Billes, Harvey Jackson, Janice Carter, Eddie Mathews and Edith Henderson — again boarded the bus and made the ridiculous half-block ride to the school. Another order was read. Wallace was forbidding the school to be integrated. The driver was ordered to move the bus.

As it eased away, white students cheered and hooted.

"I looked at them," Miss Sullins said, "and some of them were hanging out the windows and carrying on. I didn't feel anything in particular at that moment. I could only think to myself that it was silly the way they were acting."

Through the week, tensions began to build; there were angry demonstrations by flag-waving whites at Birmingham's West End High School.

The Justice Department asked Johnson to declare a state-wide injunction against Wallace and the local school boards who were refusing to admit blacks. He didn't have the authority, he told them, but the Department of Justice called other district judges and a five-judge panel convened in Montgomery — the first time such a judicial body had been called into session. They issued a restraining order, enjoining Wallace and his troopers from interfering with the desegregation of the schools in Tuskegee, Mobile and Birmingham.

Wallace responded by removing the troopers but replaced them with Alabama National Guardsmen, activated the same afternoon.President John Kennedy, watching the development, promptly countered by federalizing the Guard troops, reversing their role of prohibiting blacks from attending class, to protecting their right to do so.

But the pressure applied to local citizens by the tactics had an impact. When classes began, only thirty-five whites showed up at the high school. Before Wallace made his grandstand play, most of the people were prepared to give the thing a real try. After all, whites and Negroes had been living there for a long time, they said. But the tensions and fears aroused by the governor's inflammatory remarks and actions undid the efforts.

(In Birmingham, on Sunday morning, September 15, a bomb ripped through the basement of the Sixteenth Street Baptist Church, killing four black girls and injuring another twenty persons, most of them children. The girls had just finished Sunday school and were preparing for the regular worship service when the blast erupted. It was believed an outgrowth of the heat generated by the school desegregation demonstrations.)

At Tuskegee High, the efforts to achieve harmony began to crumble; the captain of the football team quit school and soon the other whites began leaving classes. They registered at nearby Shorter or Macon County High in Notasulga; some enrolled at a hastily created private academy.

To further dramatize his resistance to Johnson's orders, Wallace directed state troopers to carry white students to their new classrooms. The thirteen black students, meanwhile, had the entire Tuskegee Public High School to themselves.

"The teachers never said anything about the small classes or the general situation," said Miss Sullins. "They just went about their business, loading us down with work. I worked hard, determined not to give in. I wasn't going to have them say I wasn't a good student."

During the latter days of October and through November, the situation at Tuskegee remained unchanged, a tense truce.

JOHNSON

I was conducting a jury trial on Friday, November 22, when a marshal approached the bench and handed me a note sent by my secretary, Helen Cosper. It was hurriedly written: "President Kennedy has been shot in Dallas."

I seldom let anything interfere with a trial, but the news left me with such a profound sense of disbelief, shock and a terrible feeling of loss that I quickly raised a hand and interrupted one of the attorneys who was questioning a witness.

"I have just been advised that President Kennedy has been shot," I said. "We're going to adjourn court for now and will resume next week." I then hurried to my office to try to find out more of the shooting.

A number of things were running through my mind; I could recall the meeting we'd had that spring . . . for a moment I thought about Abraham Lincoln.

President Kennedy's death also had an impact on Ruth and Johnny. My son, I remember, got the pen the President had given him and held it that night of November 22 when we watched the television reports.

At my office, two of the treasured articles are pictures of both John Kennedy and Robert Kennedy. I also have a photograph of President Eisenhower, and on my desk, a paper weight bearing a quote by Lincoln.

Shortly after the funeral for the President, I sat down and wrote Robert Kennedy a letter, expressing my sadness over his deep loss. A short time later I got a thankyou card from Robert and Ethel Kennedy and Robert had affixed a few handwritten lines. My secretary filed it with the other letters I had received. One day my son was looking through the letters and he saw the note from Robert. When another assassin shot down Robert Kennedy, Johnny remembered the note and asked me about it. I went to the office and got it out of the file and had it framed, then put it on my office wall. To me and my family it was an historic thing. Robert had written simply, "Dear Judge: I just wanted to thank you personally for writing me in November. It meant a great deal. Robert."

In Tuskegee, after the holidays passed, the black children returned to find a note on the front door. It said, in effect, that the Macon County Board of Education could no longer maintain a school for only a dozen students (the thirteenth, Eddie Mathews, had been expelled earlier for "insubordination").

The Alabama State Board of Education ordered the children to return to Tuskegee Institute, where they had attended previously. At the same time the board voted to provide grants-in-aid for whites who chose to attend private schools.

In a resolution, the board declared: "The State Board ... deplores the order of Judge Johnson and pledges every resource at our command to defend the people of our state against every order of the federal court in attempting to integrate the public schools of this state and will use every legal means at our command to defeat said integration order."

JOHNSON

I set a hearing for the satellite courthouse in Opelika, fifteen miles east of Tuskegee, and subsequently enjoined the state from providing aid to students in private schools; I then ordered the local school board to transport the Negroes to the nearest public school of their choice. George Wallace was talking about freedom of choice all the time, so these twelve Negro children made a choice. Six of them chose to go to the Macon County High School at Notasulga, the other six to Shorter. Both schools are about five miles or so from Tuskegee. If the state didn't want desegregation at Tuskegee, then they could have it at the other two schools.

23

I T WAS A CHILL rain that swirled from the leaden skies that morning of February 5, 1964. Before 7:15 a.m., Marsha Sullins, Patricia Camille Jones, Anthony Lee, Shirley Chambliss, Robert Judkins and Willie Wyatt huddled near the school board building, waiting on bus No. 27. They were going to Notasulga to once again attempt to attend classes with white students. Six other blacks had left earlier for Shorter.

With the Notasulga group was a photographer for *Life* magazine, Vernon Merritt. He was going to record on film this episode of the desegregation struggle in the South. They boarded the bus, and it moved off through the drizzle for Notasulga.

As they entered the town, they saw a group of lawmen wearing yellow rain coats; some carried sticks and cattle prods. Sheriff Jim Clark of Dallas County (Selma) had led a group of volunteer possemen to "assist" local police. The officers flagged the yellow bus to a halt about a block from the school. Clark and several others boarded. They dragged Merritt off the bus, threw him to the ground and broke some of his camera equipment. Then somebody shouted at Whitlock to drive on, and the bus moved up to the school.

But the mayor of Notasulga, James Rea, was standing in front and as the students got off he stopped them and began reading from a piece of paper, saying that to admit them would mean too many students in the building and would be a fire hazard. They were told to get back on the bus and returned to Tuskegee.

JOHNSON

When I heard what happened, I set a hearing for the following day in Opelika and drove over there. It was easy to see what had happened. You had somebody pulling another schoolhouse door stand. The mayor had come up with this ordinance about fire safety . . . but it was just a ruse to thwart a lawful order of this court. So I got Mr. Rea in there that day and I slapped him with an injunction. Well, that cooled him off in a hurry. And I directed the school board to open that school up to those Negro children.

The order directed the mayor and the lawmen to stand clear as the bus entered.

The children returned on bus No. 27 on February 13, passing through a gauntlet of armed men lining the main street. The Alabama and Confederate flags were at half-staff above the school. But nobody blocked the six students as they debarked and walked quickly to the front door.

But they were far from accepted; within a few days the whites began to leave and before long, the blacks were alone.

In later years, Mrs. Marsha Sullins Slocum would recall those days at Notasulga: "We would ride by these people every day and they'd be standing out there with their guns. Mr. D.W. Clements, the principal, tried to help us. I think he was threatened also; in fact, I know he was. Some days people would throw rocks through the windows, and they'd have firecrackers tied to them and they'd explode. We began to get jumpy. We could not go outside because there was fear for our lives. I was afraid they might shoot me. Almost every day when we arrived there would be fresh signs painted on the school — ugly things, calling us names. At night, I would receive phone calls; it would always be a man or woman, warning me not to appear at school the next day or I might not ever return home. People would drive by the house and throw firecrackers in the yard. Some of us really began to get nervous. But we stayed with it. The more they did,

the more determined we became. John Doar of the U.S. Department of Justice sent marshals to watch over us; I know I'd look
out the window sometime at home and see them standing out on
the street. I was concentrating on being the best student I could
be; the more work the teachers gave me, the harder I worked.
The others did the same, because we had something to prove."

Patricia Jones, her parents said later, would develop a
stuttering problem from the emotional strain.

Then, on the night of April 17, 1964, a portion of the school
(where the six blacks attended classes) was burned, the obvious
work of arsonists. Once again, they were ordered by the local
board to stay home.

At Shorter, things hadn't been much better for the six
blacks there; all seventy-eight whites had departed within a few
days. But before they left, the Negroes had been ordered to use
only certain toilets in the restrooms; they were mostly segregated during class sessions. For several days the school was
closed by a bomb threat. At the school in Notasulga, signs had
been crudely painted by the arsonists: "Judge Johnson and
Bobby Kennedy's school. Godfathers of all niggers." There was
a rough wreath-like circle around the word "niggers." And
below it: "Step by step, one more day, nigger. Damn nigger,
damn nigger, damn nigger. You done been told once and that's
all."

Once again, the school board attempted to assign the Negro students back to the all-black Tuskegee Institute High
School. Johnson, Judge Rives and Hobart Grooms, sitting as a
three-judge panel, issued another order, which took note of the
fact that the fire had not rendered the building at Notasulga
unuseable. The students were ordered to return to the school.

"We went back a few days after the fire," Mrs. Slocum
recalled. "We kept on and soon it was May. So one day,
Mr. Clements, who had been the principal there for twenty-three
years, called the six of us together in the auditorium. Three of
the boys — Anthony Lee, Willie Wyatt and Robert Judkins —
were seniors. So Mr. Clements says that he had received a
threat — and you could see it in his eyes — and that if he
attempted to hold a graduation ceremony the place would be
blown up. And he said, 'I am sorry that there isn't time to invite

your parents and friends, but I'm afraid for your lives.' So he shook hands with the boys and told them congratulations, that they had graduated."

It was one of the most unusual graduation ceremonies in Alabama history. There was no one in the audience save the three girls who were underclassmen, the principal, and several teachers. One young white man from Notasulga, Robert Anderson, a student at Auburn University, came out of curiousity; he sat in the back.

Anderson would later recall: "I just wanted to come by and see what would happen. I knew there had been all the anger over these students, but in my heart I believed in the public education system. So I sat there and these six Negroes came in, three girls sat in the audience section, the three senior boys sat up on the stage. There was a brief ceremony, very brief. There hadn't even been time, I'm told, to invite the parents to the ceremony. And almost as quickly as it began, it was over. But then one of the girls (Patricia Jones) got up and walked to the stage, followed by the other two (Marsha Sullins and Shirley Chambliss) and they all three began singing the song, 'No Man Is An Island.' I don't think anything has ever moved me as did that song. The entire issue of desegregation of schools seemed to hang in that moment. Here were these kids singing a song like that, one with hope in it, after all that they'd been through. I knew then that I wanted to help in some way and restore some order to our town, because I had been born and raised in Notasulga. I made up my mind that I was going to be an educator and work in my hometown."

Anderson would later return to Notasulga and become the principal of the school, which would be renamed Notasulga High School. In the first few years after the desegregation order, the school became almost entirely black. But by the mid-70s, whites began returning and in 1979 it was roughly forty-five percent white; townspeople boasted they had the best integrated school in the state.

But in 1964, Wallace appeared totally committed to battling integration to the last. In a speech in March 1964, he declared: "We stand a chance to lose millions of dollars in federal aid because there is no Judas Iscariot among us who will sell our racial integrity for the proverbial thirty pieces of silver."

But during the summer of 1964, some whites and blacks again held meetings in Tuskegee to attempt to reach a solution to the school problems; most agreed it was absurd to send students to Shorter and Notasulga when Tuskegee had its own public high school.

"There were meetings in the homes of Negroes and there were meetings in the homes of white people," recalled Douglas Jones, the father of Patricia and Wilma Jones. "Everyone seemed dedicated to carrying out Judge Johnson's orders."

When classes began in September, the black children returned to the reopened Tuskegee Public High School, as did a number of whites.

"Some of the white kids," Marsha Sullins Slocum said, reflecting on those times, "came up to me and — quite to my surprise — told me they were sorry for leaving the year before, but said they had been pressured to do so. They began to accept us. Things were a great deal better then. I graduated in 1967 from Tuskegee High. There were four other blacks in the class and, I think, seventeen whites. A lot of the whites didn't return, but preferred the private schools. I was asked by some of those in my class if I hadn't been used by Judge Johnson, that my life had been threatened because of his orders. But the threat didn't come from Judge Johnson. It came from some of the white people who refused to acknowledge the law of the land."

Johnson summed up the problems of desegregation in a speech at the University of Georgia.

"If we, as judges, have learned anything at all from Brown vs. the Board of Education, *it is that prohibitory relief affords but a hollow protection of citizens to equal protection of the law. Once a constitutional deprivation has been shown, it becomes the duty of the court to render a decree which will, as far as possible, eliminate the effects of the past deprivations as well as bar like deprivations in the future. Utilizing their powers, the federal courts in the South pursued the only reasonable and constitutionally acceptable alternatives — fashioning relief to fit the necessities of the particular case. I submit that history has shown, with few exceptions, that decisions of the federal judiciary over a period of time have become accepted and revered as*

monuments memorializing the strength and stability of this nation."

JOHNSON

I avoided the word "integration" in my court orders, preferring to use "desegregation" instead. To desegregate means to open a public facility to all people, or rather, to prohibit one race from denying another race entry into a public facility because of the racial factor. Integrate, on the other hand, means the social interaction between members of different races. I think of it in more social terms. My purpose in the school cases was not to integrate the school system — putting blacks in just to be putting them in — but rather to disestablish an illegal system, which is what the segregated system was.

I was sensitive to the interchangeable uses of the words, and there was some conflict within the federal judiciary itself. For instance, the U.S. Fourth Circuit Court of Appeals in Richmond was of the opinion that *Brown* simply said a system could not deny black children from entering because of their color. But the U.S. Fifth Circuit in New Orleans shot that down by saying the fulfillment of *Brown* went beyond that. The Fifth said the states were REQUIRED to disestablish a segregated system. The Fifth's interpretation called for an affirmative effort to bring blacks into previously all-white schools.

24

DESPITE THE DETERMINATION and courage of those black children at Tuskegee, Mobile and Birmingham, the schools of Alabama remained basically segregated for several more years. But in March of 1967, Johnson was joined by Judge Rives and U. S. District Judge Hobart Grooms in issuing a statewide desegregation order that applied to all school systems, except some in Huntsville that were doing it on their own.

The reaction was hysteric; whites lamented that all the treasured traditions of high school — the senior prom, the sockhops and such — were a thing of the past; that whites would not be safe with blacks in the same schools.

There was open defiance from the state's leadership; in some school systems, particularly in the state's Black Belt counties, private schools sprung up like mushrooms, almost overnight. White parents feared their daughters would be raped.

JOHNSON

I could not personally buy those arguments. In my mind, if security could be maintained in a school hall for white children alone, it could be maintained on the same basis if black students were there as well.

Ed Livingston, the chief justice of the Alabama Supreme

Court, declared: "I'm for segregation and I don't care who knows it. I'd close every school from the highest to the lowest before I would go to school with colored people."

Governor Lurleen Wallace, in April 1967, addressed the Legislature; so wrapped up emotionally was she that she stamped her feet and said state leaders and parents would "go to jail before permitting their children to attend desegregated schools." While the legislators whooped, stomped their feet and issued rebel yells, she added that Johnson's court orders "were the final step toward a complete takeover of our children's hearts and minds." She equated the court order to a decree by Hitler. "They've made their decree . . . now let them enforce it."

The state's superintendent of education, Austin Meadows, went on to explain that "segregation was a perfectly good word" and added that the Lord "segregated fruit in the Garden of Eden." To explain further to the unenlightened, he said, "Red birds mate with red birds."

It was against this background that, on the night of April 25, 1967, a bomb exploded at the home of Johnson's mother.

JOHNSON

I lived about six blocks from her home and at about ten p.m. was in bed nearly asleep when the telephone rang. It was my sister, Ellen Harvill.

"F. M., get on over to Mother's," she said. "There's been an explosion."

Johnny had picked up the extension in his bedroom and heard her. He and I quickly dressed and sped over there. At first I thought it might have been a gas explosion or the hot water heater. I wasn't sure.

The first thing we saw was the red lights flashing on the fire trucks and the police cars. Johnny shouted that he saw his grandmother standing in the yard. "You OK?" I asked. She nodded.

Mother was unhurt, but angry. A fireman told me he thought the explosion was caused by dynamite. I was enraged.

"Give me your flashlight," I told him and started poking around the wreckage to look for clues, although

I'm not sure I could spot anything.

I was sure the bomb was meant for me. My telephone was unlisted, but Mother's was still listed in the directory under my father's name, "Frank M. Johnson." Some deranged person or persons thought it was my address. The device had been placed on the ground near the house. Mother had just left the kitchen and gone upstairs to her bedroom when it exploded.

The force of it swept all the way through the downstairs, tore the carpet up, broke windows, knocked the chandelier down from the ceiling of the dining room. Mother was living alone then. Daddy had died two years before. But she was rational; it didn't scare her. The news reporters and FBI agents were milling around and poking into things and that added to her discontent.

Some of the agents began boarding up the windows, sweeping up the glass and other debris. One of them came up to Mother and said, "Miz Johnson, don't you want to go somewhere and spend the night?"

"Absolutely not," she said. "They're not going to run me away from my home. I'm staying right here."

She even turned me down when I suggested she come stay with Ruth and me for a few days.

She was mad, too, because some of her plants and flowers outside had been ravaged by the explosion.

The agents and the U.S. marshals told me they'd post a couple of people out there and keep watch to make sure the bombers didn't return.

Mother tolerated that for a few nights, but it soon began to wear on her nerves. She didn't like looking out the windows at night and seeing them prowling around, shining their flashlights about. Mother was a very courageous and cool woman.

A couple of days after the explosion I went by to see her and she said to me, "When are you going to take them away?"

I told her they wanted to stay for a few more nights to assure that nothing else happened.

"Well, they're bothering me," she said. "All night long

they go around looking, opening and closing doors . . ."

The cowardly act directed at my mother burned me, made me want to get my hands on the person or persons responsible. I knew the bomb had been intended for me. I had been aware for several years that I might be a target for some lunatic. The murder of President Kennedy in November, 1963, had heightened that possibility. But I didn't run from shadows; you can't live in fear of a sniper or a bomber.

The FBI from the early 1960s kept me supplied with a list of known KKK members. That list gave their name, address, employer. The list was given to me after under-cover agents had overheard KKK members discussing the prospects of bombing my home. While it never happened, the explosion at my mother's house made it clear that it could happen. I can't say the Klan bombed mother's house, because no one was ever arrested and brought to trial.

A few days after the bombing, Governor Lurleen Wallace issued a statement calling the act a "cowardly deed" and offered a reward leading to the arrest and conviction of the person or persons responsible.

It was of little consolation to me. It would have been far too little had my mother been killed or injured. The only thing that saved her was the fact that she had gone to bed. Had she been sitting in the living room she might have been seriously or fatally injured.

When Robert Kennedy and Martin Luther King, Jr., were shot and killed, and later when George Wallace was severely wounded, I felt the same sense of outrage that most Americans felt.

I first heard about Bobby being shot when I awoke the morning of June 6, 1968, and heard the news reports. I felt disbelief, shock and a deep agony about what was happening in a country which has laws to protect human liberties and human life. He and I had been friends and he had been a courageous leader, especially in the field of civil rights. His brother John, the president, had been a strong leader in that area, too.

My feelings about King's assassination were a little more mixed, I suppose. I hadn't known him on a personal basis. I had admired his courage, but at the same time took a dim view of some of his methods. This had nothing to do with the sorrow I felt when he was shot. He was a leader.

Wallace's wounding was also a terrible thing and reflected some of the sickness in the country. In all three cases — King, Kennedy, Wallace — I could not accept the rationalization that a "demented" person had committed the deed.

Part VI

'O freedom's over me'

The Selma to
Montgomery March
1965

JOHNSON

The Civil Rights Movement was a social and legal revolution that shook the nation to its core. It was a drive by blacks to obtain equal rights and civil rights. It was a massive effort for equal rights and an equally massive effort against equal rights, for the white reaction to it was a deep-seated racial fear. White people perceived it as an attack on the social order, on the political order, and the economic order . . . which were the same things that caused the Civil War.

Then, it was the abolition of slavery; in the 20th century it was the abolition of segregation and the hue and cry was just as emotional. We can all utter a prayer of thanks that the battle to end segregation did not result in as much bloodshed as the effort to abolish slavery had done.

Common sense told me that there could be violence, especially if the philosophy of the political leaders didn't change. But a federal judge can't let violence or the threat of violence undermine his decisions in these high-profile, controversial cases. And while I was aware of the threat, I didn't study about it unduly. I never thought that I better start deciding these civil rights cases in a different manner.

25

WHILE BLACK PEOPLE in the eastern Black Belt counties of Alabama were winning voting rights in the early part of the 1960s, those in the central and western counties of that belt were still facing incredible white resistance. Most notable of the sites for avowed white supremacy was Selma, a city of 28,000 and the seat of Dallas County.

Sheriff James Clark, a robust man with a square jaw and reddish hair, used police powers and turned back black efforts to mount a drive for voting rights. The blacks had attempted to get demonstrations going in 1963 and 1964, but Clark swamped them. To back him up, a local judge issued a court order which not only made it unlawful for blacks to have rallies and marches, but further said it was illegal for more than three blacks to congregate at any one place — if they did, they would be arrested.

The leader of the black drive, F.D. Reese, a minister, was jailed and served with that court order while still behind bars. It effectively threw cold water on any other marches and for the last six months of 1964 black churches were silent on the matter of voting rights.

Clark didn't mince his words. He was quoted by one newspaper to say, "Negroes will never overcome us."

For a time it seemed the white power structure had effectively put down black petitions for voting rights. Heeding the court order there, blacks quit holding public rallies; church services stuck to the Scriptures, and let the matter of voting ride.

But in late December, 1964, Reese and other black leaders met in Selma and decided to invite Martin Luther King, Jr., there to lead a renewed effort. King came on January 2, 1965, for Emancipation Day services held at Brown Chapel AME Church.

The church was packed; hundreds pressed around the exterior, listening to a public address system. The meeting broke the injunction against such gatherings. Sheriff Clark was in Miami, Florida, watching Alabama play Texas in the Orange Bowl.

Sixteen days later, King led the first march through the downtown; another followed the next day, and they kept on daily, through the raw, wintry rain that fell almost without letup for the entire month of February.

Sheriff Clark would wait at the Dallas County Courthouse, arresting them by the hundreds. Johnson saw some of the TV and newspaper accounts of what was happening; but Selma was not in his Middle District. Any suits that might arise were to go to the Southern District, in Mobile, Judge Daniel Thomas's district. When they were filed, he issued orders to allow registration of blacks. But there was some balking in Selma; instead of getting registered, the white officials passed out numbers to blacks, telling them to come back on registration day. There were two such days a month. Thomas's orders specified a hundred blacks to be registered each day, which meant two hundred a month. At that rate it would take years to get the black people registered. Dallas County's population was 55,000, evenly divided between blacks and whites.

When the jails were crammed full, Clark opened a dilapidated prison road camp and filled it with singing, hand-clapping youngsters. The situation worsened daily. On February 10, deputies force-marched two hundred black teenagers several miles; they pushed them, used cattle prods on them, and ran them until, panting, most of them dropped by the roadside; some vomited.

On the night of February 18, at nearby Marion, a group of blacks emerged from their church and were set upon by state troopers under the command of Alabama Public Safety Director

Dallas County Sheriff Jim Clark orders protesters to disperse from the courthouse in Selma.

Colonel Al Lingo. Clubs struck heads with a loud popping sound; there were screams; newsmen had their cameras broken or sprayed with black paint by a mob of white men. During the melee, a young black woodcutter, Jimmie Jackson, was shot in the stomach by a trooper. He died a week later.

In the desolate rain of Selma, King announced a march from that city to Montgomery to petition Governor George Wallace on police brutality and the denial of voting rights. It was scheduled for March 7, a Sunday.

While Selma pulsated with the sound of freedom songs sung by a thousand inspired blacks, Wallace met with his staff; at first, he was going to allow the march, but after pressure was exerted by some members of the Alabama Legislature who feared snipers, the governor issued an order barring any march between the two cities.

To back it up that Sunday, he dispatched two hundred state troopers, under the direct command of Major John Cloud; the blue-clad lawmen formed a picket line across U.S. Highway 80 on the south side of the Edmund Pettus Bridge which spans the Alabama River. Colonel Lingo arrived on the scene shortly

The assault by Alabama State Troopers on marchers at Selma's Edmund Pettus Bridge was televised nationwide by newscasters and helped galvanize public support for what became the Voting Rights Act of 1965.

before the march began. There were more than six hundred marchers and when they crossed the bridge, Cloud halted them. They were given two minutes to disperse; when they refused, the troopers slammed into them. The first thrust sent marchers sprawling and running, retreating thirty yards or so where they knelt in a tight circle, praying.

Another assault followed, with troopers lobbing tear gas cannisters; behind them galloped Sheriff Clark's possemen, flailing the screaming marchers with whips and clubs. More than eighty men, women and children were injured in the onslaught.

The next day, attorneys of the Justice Department and the NAACP came to the federal building at Montgomery, seeking an injunction against Wallace, Clark and Lingo.

Johnson issued two temporary orders: one, directed at the troopers, Lingo, Clark and Wallace, enjoined them from interfering with peaceful demonstrations; the second prohibited King's followers from attempting any further marches to Montgomery until a hearing could be held; because of the gravity of

the situation and the explosive atmosphere over Selma, he set it
for that Thursday, March 11.

Meanwhile, President Lyndon Johnson dispatched former
Florida Governor LeRoy Collins to Selma to act as arbitrator
between the opposing sides. Collins was head of the Justice
Department's Community Relations Service. King, who had
been in Atlanta during the Bloody Sunday encounter, returned
to find the people anxious to march again.

On March 9, early in the afternoon about two thousand
walked with King over the same route as the Sunday march;
before reaching the bridge, however, a U.S. Marshal halted
them, read Johnson's order barring marches, then stepped
aside as King strode on. Sheriff Clark immediately took note
that the civil rights leader was violating Judge Johnson's order.

Colonel Lingo had his troopers lined up again. King stopped
short of them; there was an exchange between the two and King
asked permission to pray.

"Pray if you so desire," Lingo said. Then, to the surprise of
many, he ordered the troopers away, leaving U.S. Highway 80
open. Why he did this remains a mystery, unless he was baiting
the blacks to deepen what was apparently a violation of a court
order. But after several minutes of prayer, the singing of freedom songs, and a brief address by King, the marchers turned
around and retraced their steps to Brown Chapel.

JOHNSON

It was all a staged performance; King knew he had to
do something to save face, because his followers wanted
to march again. Actually, King and Wallace were a lot
alike and even worked in concert for that episode on
March 9. I don't know that they talked directly, but they
talked through aides and through Collins.

Both King and Wallace engaged in activity and
speeches for the purpose of stirring emotions. Maybe
King felt it was necessary. But then, maybe Wallace did,
too.

But both helped create an undue atmosphere in this
part of the nation during those times. Both hoodwinked
their followers and didn't always tell the complete truth.

Wallace knew what the law was, yet led whites to believe they'd never have to desegregate.

King's prime example of distorting the truth was on the March 9 event at Selma. His agreement with Wallace and Wallace's aides was that he would pretend to lead a march in apparent violation of my order and pretend to try to go to Montgomery, but would stop when the troopers faced him.

But George double-crossed him and instead of forming a human wall, the state troopers were pulled back. I don't know if Wallace was baiting King into trying to march on along Highway 80 or what, but King turned around and went back to Brown Chapel.

Yet, either way, George Wallace came out the winner. When King turned around, George won. If King had marched on, he would have violated my order and George would have won then, too. It was one of those situations that George created and controlled. It was "heads I win, tails you lose," because that's how George liked to orchestrate things.

My personal feeling about demonstrations is that as long as there are courts in this land, there is no need for sit-ins and marches and such things. I feel there is no justification for any kind of a demonstration so long as there is a court open to define the rights of the people. It wasn't up to Martin Luther King, Jr., or any of his lieutenants to define the rights. That was a duty that judges have.

But even though I personally dislike demonstrations, the law says they can be held peacefully, so I have upheld those rights. I have also upheld the rights of police to arrest demonstrators blocking street traffic.

Nonetheless, Selma was a special situation and I would weigh it in light of those special circumstances.

After King led the march to the bridge and turned around, it seemed that the fury that had hung over the city had, at last, eased. But not so. That evening, one of the scores of clergymen who had come to Selma — the Reverend James Reeb of Boston, a Unitarian — was attacked by several white toughs as he and two other clerics walked along a downtown street. Reeb was knocked senseless by a club; vomiting and muttering incoherently, he was given emergency aid, then rushed to Birmingham's University Hospital where he underwent surgery during the night; several times, his heart stopped. His prognosis was poor.

The incident served to dramatize the urgency of getting the hearing underway.

It began that rainy Thursday, March 11, at 9 a.m.; again, as in other civil rights cases, the courtroom was packed.

Representing the blacks and the United States were Fred Gray, John Doar, Peter Hall, Jack Greenberg, Demetrius Newton and Norman Amaker. Heading the defense for Governor Wallace, Sheriff Clark and Colonel Lingo were Selma attorney McLean Pitts and Montgomery attorneys Maury Smith, John Kohn, and T.G. Gayle.

Johnson dispensed with the formalities that always hamper such proceedings, then looked over the assembly.

"Now there is also presented to me a petition to show cause why Dr. Martin Luther King shouldn't be found guilty of contempt of this court, presented on behalf of the defendant Clark."

Pitts nodded, "Yes, sir. There are now . . . there are other persons now named."

Johnson glanced at him coolly. "Yes, well, let me say this in that regard, that any contempt proceedings or any order to show cause so as to why an individual shouldn't be found guilty of contempt of this court is a matter between this court and the alleged contemptors. It is not a matter that James Clark has any interest in, so the court will, of its own motion . . . will dismiss the petition by Clark."

There were nods from the attorneys, then the judge announced, "All right, gentlemen, we are ready to proceed. Call your first witness."

Gray rose.

"We call Dr. Martin Luther King."

He was ushered into the courtroom, given the oath and seated.

26

"D R. KING, WHAT is your title with the Southern Christian Leadership Conference?" Gray asked.

"I am the president."

"Could you explain the philosophy of your organization?"

"Yes. It says that one must have the inner determination to resist what conscience tells him is evil with all the strength and courage and zeal he can muster. At the same time he must not resort to violence or hatred. It works for the complete integration of the Negro in American life."

"What is your most recent movement the SCLC has been involved in in Alabama?"

"It is the project taking place in the Black Belt counties of Alabama and the voter registration drive in Selma and Marion."

"What was the purpose of this drive?"

"Well, the Dallas County Voters League invited us to aid and assist in getting more Negroes registered to vote."

Pitts raised a hand. "Your honor—"

"Wait a minute," said the judge, gesturing to Gray. Then he turned to Pitts and nodded for him to proceed.

"Your honor," said Pitts, "I think all this is incompetent and irrelevant —"

"Well, I make this comment for whatever guidance it may be to you gentlemen," Johnson injected. "I consider the matter of grievances or alleged grievances that are . . . are being pro-

tested to be a material issue, and I will permit inquiry into it up
to a point."

King's testimony continued in which he stated peaceful
demonstrations were a chief means of dramatizing the plight of
Negroes who were unable to register to vote.

While he answered questions, the crowd that jammed every available seat, sat attentive, almost strained, listening. Then
Maury Smith, one of the defense attorneys, approached to
cross-examine.

"When you came to Selma in January, I believe you said,
you realized that there were ... was a suit pending in the
Southern District of federal court on the matter of registration,
did you not?"

"Yes."

"But instead of presenting the grievances which you observed to the court through either the United States Justice
Department or counsel for the NAACP or your organization,
you felt that in the best interest of those whom you represented
in the movement which you advocated, to take to the streets?"

Greenberg intoned softly, "Object."

Johnson nodded. "That is argument. Go ahead. Don't argue
with him. Question him, but don't argue with him."

"All right, sir," Smith said. Then, back to King, he asked,
"Were you on March ninth, Tuesday of this week, in the morning, served with a copy of this court's order?"

"We object," Greenberg said. "This is a matter which the
court specifically said it will not take up today."

Johnson gazed over his glasses at Greenberg, then in a
crisp tone said, "I didn't say that it was a matter that would not be
taken up. I said it was a matter that the defendant, Clark, had no
right to petition on."

"We — I'm sorry," stammered Greenberg.

"I will permit the question," the judge said. "Go ahead."

Smith turned to the court reporter, Glynn Henderson.
"Would you read the question back?"

As Henderson scanned his notes, Johnson drawled,
"Whether or not he was served with the order (banning
marches)."

Smith looked up with surprise. "Sir?"

"Whether or not he was served with the order," Johnson repeated. "We don't need the question read back."

"Yes, I was served," King said, nodding.

"But you marched anyway, even after a marshal read you the order?" Smith asked.

"Yes, sir. I felt my duty was to lead the march. We intended—"

"Did you make a statement to the press that the unjust order (of Frank Johnson) ... well, did you make that statement?" Smith asked.

King shifted in his seat. "Yes, I did. I made it very clear that I felt that as a result of the order we had been put in a very difficult position. I felt that it was like condemning the robbed man for getting robbed and allowed the robber to be uncondemned, and I made it very clear that this order upset me ... and I always try to act on the basis of conscience ... and it was one of the most painful decisions I ever made."

Smith folded his arms and paced in front of King. "Did you confer with Governor Collins of Florida, one representative of President Johnson, in Selma this week?"

"Yes, I did, on several occasions."

"Did he beseech you in Selma this week not to — did he ask you on behalf of the President of the United States of America not to conduct this march on Tuesday?

"I don't know if he was speaking for the President ... but he urged me not to march."

"He urged you not to?"

"That's right."

"Did he admonish you that it was an explosive situation in Selma?"

"He mentioned that fact."

Smith retired to his table to puzzle over notes. Johnson waited a moment, then inquired: "Does that conclude your examination, Mr. Smith?"

"Yes, sir."

Johnson removed his glasses and turned in his chair, facing the witness. "All right, Dr. King, before we continue with counsel examining you, along this last part of Mr. Smith's examination, let me ask you a few questions, please."

Andrew Young and Martin Luther King, Jr., confer in Judge Johnson's courtroom during the Selma-to-Montgomery March hearings in March of 1965.

King nodded, waiting, leaning slightly to hear.

"On Tuesday when . . . when you did march, prior to the time you marched, did you have any . . . any conversation with Governor Collins concerning the extent of your march, how far you intended to march, and where you intended to march?"

"Yes. I said to him that we felt compelled, as I said earlier, on the basis of conscience, to march, and I said to him at that point that we were aware of the fact at the time that the state troopers were standing at a certain point across the bridge. And when I said . . . said that, I went on to say that I felt that at least we had to pick a point where the brutality occurred Sunday and not only walk to the point, but to be able to make some kind of witness, some kind of testimony, to have some prayers, because of the numerous religious leaders who had come in from all over the country."

"Is it correct to say," the judge inquired, "that when you started to march and you went across the bridge, you knew that the state troopers were approximately five-hundred feet beyond it?"

"That's right, we did."

"And you did not intend at that time to march past the state troopers, is that right?"

"That is correct, we—"

"Had you made any advance preparations for a march from Selma to Montgomery?"

King shrugged. "I think — in the way of food for that day, the way of foods and trucks and things like that?"

"No, we didn't," King replied, shaking his head. "That . . . the predominant opinion was that we would not be able to get to Montgomery, so we didn't even prepare for it."

Johnson then asked: "Now it has been reported to me — and let me ask you if this is correct — that after you reached the state troopers, and while you were there and confronted by the troopers, that they were pulled away and that their automobiles were removed while y'all were still there. Is that correct?"

"That is correct," he replied.

"And then did you go forward, or did you turn and go back to Montgomery — I mean, Selma?"

"We turned around and went back to Selma," said King. In the audience several blacks nodded slowly, as if to reaffirm the answer.

"After the troopers had pulled back?" the judge asked.

King nodded. "That's right."

"And at that point there were no state troopers in front of you?"

"That is correct," he repeated.

"Or on the highway between y'all and Montgomery?

Is that report to me that I have received from the Justice Department correct?"

"Yes, sir. That is correct."

"All right, thank you," Johnson said. "Counsel may continue."

Under questioning by NAACP attorney Jack Greenberg, King testified about the voting rights drive in Selma; the mass rallies, the marches, the singing of freedom songs.

"Did you participate in the planning for another march scheduled for March seventh, 1965, which was this past Sunday?" the attorney asked.

"Yes, I did."

"Would you describe the planning of that march, Dr. King?"

"Well, the plan was to engage in a peaceful, non-violent walk from Selma to Montgomery, where we would present a petition to Governor Wallace protesting the denial of the right to vote and the tragic and terrible police brutality that we had experienced in Selma."

Attorney Pitts snapped, "We object to that. That is a conclusion."

"Your objection is overruled," Johnson said. "He is testifying to what he was going to petition the governor for."

Greenberg continued, "Why had you planned to walk rather than to engage in any other form of demonstration?"

"Well, I think for two basic reasons: First—"

"Wait a minute, your honor," Pitts said, "we object to why the witness did anything."

"I will permit that," Johnson said. Then to King, he said,"Go ahead."

The witness glanced at Greenberg, then looked up at the judge. Johnson nodded at him and said, "That has to do with the planning. Go ahead."

King then continued, saying, "First we were dealing with the whole question of poverty in the Negro community . . . the vast majority cannot afford an automobile. And on the other hand we had to dramatize the condition of poverty, and to engage in the kind of self-inflicted suffering that would be involved in walking fifty miles to call attention to the evils and the injustices that we were facing in Alabama."

King also testified that the process of trying to get blacks registered — even with court orders from Judge Thomas in Mobile — had been appallingly slow.

Then defense attorney McLean Pitts moved forward to cross examine the civil rights leader.

"You knew when you came to Selma," he said, "that there was an injunction against unlawful assemblies, didn't you?"

King nodded. "That's right."

"And you—"

"Well, we went on—"

"Wait a minute," Pitts said. "And you knew that and you marched and carried signs—"

"That's right. I—"

"I am going to ask you . . . and you walked in the middle of the streets, didn't you?"

"At first we walked on the sidewalks," King said. "And I think we followed the sidewalk route until we got to the . . . or rather—"

"Now, listen," Pitts said, his voice testy, "you walked all the way from the depot to Broad Street in the middle of the street, didn't you?"

"Well, I don't know what happened behind, but I am saying that in front of the line—"

"I am going to ask you one more time: You, yourself, marched in the middle of Water Street—"

"I object, your honor," Greenberg said, "because this is repetitious—"

"Wait a minute," Johnson snapped. "I sustain objection to the manner in which counsel conducts part of his interrogation." The silence in the courtroom deepened. He peered at Pitts. "All witnesses in this court, regardless of who they are, are to be questioned with common courtesy."

"I am trying, your honor," Pitts stammered, "but it is a point—"

"Make a little better effort," said the judge, the tone clearly one of annoyance.

It brought a ripple of reaction from the crowd and Pitts, somewhat flustered, said, "Yes, sir. It is a point I want to get over."

Johnson's stern gaze was now on the crowd. Then, his

voice sharp, he said, "All right, all right, let's get going." Then, to
the audience, he said, "We will keep order in this court or you
will be excluded." The room went silent.

Pitts continued in a more respectful manner. "As I understand it, there is an active boycott going on in Selma — is that
right?"

"That's right, uh, huh."

"Uh, huh," the attorney mimicked. "How long has this been
going on? About a month?"

"About a month," King agreed.

"Now all of that has strained the relationship between the
white people and the colored people of Selma, hasn't it?"

King shrugged. "I don't think so. I think instead of bringing
about divided relations, it has caused the community to look at
itself . . . and aroused a sense of shame in the community."

Pitts paced about for a moment. "Now, so . . . now . . . let me
ask you this: Do you know Felton Henderson?"

"Is he working with the movement in Selma?" King asked,
puzzling over the name.

"I mean the Department of Justice attorney," Pitts said.

"Oh, yes, yes."

"Has he conducted any of those meetings?"

"No, he hasn't."

"You . . . that was his car, wasn't it, that you rode in from
Montgomery to Selma, wasn't it? Wasn't that the same Felton
Henderson?"

"Objection, your honor," Greenberg said.

Johnson stared at Pitts a moment. "I can understand your
desire to get into that, but is it pertinent to this inquiry, Mr.
Pitts?"

"Well, the only proposition I am getting at—"

"I ask you that question as an officer of this court: Is it
pertinent?"

Pitts shrugged. "The only point I see it is pertinent as to
whether he admits it or denies it; that is all I am asking."

"Let's get along, let's get along," prodded the judge. "You
know it isn't pertinent."

"Well, what I am getting at, your honor, is . . . is . . . here is
what I am getting at. He has previously denied it. I just wanted—"

Johnson interrupted with a wave of his hand. "I have given both sides some leeway in this thing to develop your background, but it . . . it is not even remotely pertinent to any issue in this case."

When Pitts persisted, saying he was challenging King's credibility as a witness, Johnson shook his head and urged. "Get along . . . let's not lose sight of the fact that this inquiry concerns the petition to have the court adjudicate their constitutional rights with respect to a proposed march from Selma to Montgomery."

Pitts nodded. "That's right, sir."

27

KING'S TESTIMONY ENDED before noon and he asked permission to leave so he could drive to Birmingham and visit Reverend Reeb, who was reportedly near death. Johnson granted the request. Mrs. Amelia Boynton took the stand next, testifying of the day Sheriff Clark grabbed her by the neck and ran her twenty yards to a waiting sheriff's department car, placing her under arrest for refusing to obey his order.

"What had you done?" asked Peter Hall.

"I had walked outside the courthouse after he told me to stay inside," she said. "It was the lunch hour and I went out, and when he saw me ... well, he just got mad, grabbed me, and pushed me along the sidewalk."

She also testified of the Bloody Sunday episode in which she and others had been beaten by mounted possemen and troopers. She had been knocked unconscious and a tear gas cannister placed near her face.

"Before I was knocked unconscious," she said, "they hit me here" — and she pointed to her shoulder — "and on the head and face and they broke my glasses."

John Lewis, who in 1961 had been one of the Freedom Riders beaten at Montgomery, was next; he had been in the front rank with Hosea Williams in the march at the bridge.

"Tell us what happened," attorney Hall said.

"I was in front and when the troopers stopped us, they said

203

they would give us two minutes to disperse. Well, Hosea Williams asked them if we could talk and the trooper — I believe it was Major Cloud — said we couldn't talk. And then they started advancing toward . . . and I heard them saying some things to us, calling us names, like sons-of-bitches and things like that. They started to push us. They hit me twice — when I was falling and once when I was down."

"You said they said things to you when they started?"

"Yes, called us niggers, and sons-of-bitches, things like that."

Hosea Williams testified to much the same thing.

"Were you knocked down?" Hall asked.

"Yes."

"Did you see children knocked down?"

"Correct."

"And did you see the possemen?"

"Yes, sir," Williams replied, shaking his head slowly. "They were on horseback."

"What were they doing?"

"They were whipping people with bullwhips and billy clubs and running . . . and stampeding Negroes, the marchers, with horses."

"Stampeding?" Hall asked, "Stampeding?"

"Correct."

And so the first day ended. The rain persisted as Johnson drove home that evening. As he sat with Ruth in the living room later that night, he heard the report from Birmingham: Reeb had died.

In Selma, more than eight hundred blacks gathered at Brown Chapel for a memorial; most of them, including many children, had maintained a vigil in the street in front of the church, praying in the rain.

The next morning, the courtroom buzzed with the news of Reeb's death; attorney Pitts's face was glum; across the room, Doar and Gray conferred in low tones.

"Call your first witness," said the judge.

Hall rose. "We call Mrs. Margaret Moore."

She was a school teacher at Hudson High in Selma; yes, she said, she had taken part in the Bloody Sunday march.

"I was walking around when I heard the order to go back, and I turned to look around and then I heard the — Mr. Cloud say,'Go back to the church or to your homes. This march will not continue.' Then in almost the same breath he said we had two minutes. And when I looked again, I saw everybody roll . . . just a rolling surf, and something, horses and men and policemen — not policemen, state troopers and possemen, coming. And I turned around and told them, 'Don't run. Stand . . . stand still. You will not get hurt.' And then I turned and three troopers were standing over me, and one hit me in the neck, the neck, . . . the nape of my neck and knocked me down to my knees and another one whacked me on the arm."

"Now when they hit you," Hall asked, "were you hit with the hands or with something else?"

"They used clubs."

"Clubs? You were hit on the back of the neck with clubs . . . a club?"

She nodded. "And on my arm. And in the middle of the back and on the leg."

"Did you observe what was happening around you?"

"I saw Mrs. Boynton and Mrs. (Marie) Foster at the upper end of the highway, and a girl and not far on this side of me a policeman. And I looked back toward the bridge — I had been knocked down on my knees — but I saw the people, and some of them were on their knees and some were running . . . and when they got a . . . and they started throwing tear gas . . . and there were children . . . and these horses and troopers and the children were all excited, and they started beating them. I heard screams, and then I looked to the back, and these people were trying to help Mrs. Boynton to her feet, and tear gas had been thrown at her feet."

Hall waited a moment, pacing, then asked, "Did you then come back across the bridge, into Selma?"

"I came back, but I came back in an ambulance later."

"You weren't able to walk back?"

"Uh-uh," she muttered, shaking her head. "I was afraid of the ambulance at first; I mean there were white people all around and they were jeering. And as we crossed they kept shouting ugly things at us and the driver of the ambulance."

28

I N ADDITION TO THE EVENT at the bridge the previous Sunday, there had been other incidents of brutality in Selma. On the third day, the government, with John Doar doing the questioning, got into it. The first witness was a black teenage girl.

"Would you please tell the court your name?"

"Letha Mae Stover."

"What's that?" quipped Pitts. "I can't hear."

"Stover! Stover! Stover!" Johnson called.

"Did you go to the Dallas County Courthouse on February tenth?" asked Doar.

"Yes. I carried a sign."

"What did it say?"

"It said, 'One man, one vote.'"

"All right, after you got there at the courthouse, what happened?"

"Somebody, one of the sheriff's men, comes out and says for us to turn left. So we turned left. And then they told us to march and we started marching."

"What happened when you started to march?"

"I was cattle-prodded. I was made to run until I dropped out."

"And after you dropped out, what happened?"

She shrugged slightly. "I fell beside the road; I got weak,

206

and I fell beside the road and—"

"Then what happened?"

"One of the officers," said Miss Stover, "one with a helmet on, was trying to make me go on. He told me that I said I wanted to march, so he was going to show me how; he was going to teach me how to march. He kept punching me in the back with his billy club and told me to get up and go on. But I told him he would just have to kill me, because I couldn't go."

There was a ripple in the courtroom.

"And then what happened?" Doar asked.

"Well, he told me to lie there until I rest and then get up and go back toward Selma but he had better not catch me in a car."

The cross examination for the defense was by T.G. Gayle. "I believe you said you belonged to no organization."

Miss Stover nodded.

"Is that correct?" he asked.

"Yes."

He pointed at her. "What is that button you have on there?"

She glanced down at the badge pinned on her shirt. "That is the Student Non-Violent Coordinating Committee button."

"That's an organization, isn't it?"

"But I — I don't belong to it."

"But you are wearing their button?"

"Sure," she said softly.

"And they didn't tell you to march?"

"My conscience told me to march."

"Your conscience told you to," he repeated quietly. "That's all."

Another participant in the forced march was Sallie Bett Rodgers, nineteen. She was a student at Selma University.

"Did you take part in a demonstration at the courthouse on February tenth?" asked Doar.

"Yes. There were about two hundred of us. Mostly teen-agers."

"What was their race?" Doar asked.

"Negro."

"What happened that day at the demonstration, Sallie?"

She bit her lip a moment, thinking. "Well, we stood there for about forty-five minutes and then we were told to — we — we heard a voice say, 'Left face,' and we all turned left face, and then they said, 'March!' And we all started to marching, and we went out in the street. We thought we were going to jail. But we wasn't." Her voice sharpened. "And we was run out of town!"

"Now how — how were you ordered to march?"

"We . . . we was . . . we . . . they just said, 'March,' and as we were marching there were — when the space got between the line, they kept saying, 'Close that gap up,' and that is how we started to run."

"And about how far did you go," Doar asked. "Do you know?"

She narrowed her eyes, pondering the question. "It seemed to be about five or six miles, I guess. I am not sure. We ran all the way."

"And were there other law enforcement officials there along with you?" Doar inquired.

She nodded. "They were in front, beside us, and behind us."

"And did the law officers do anything . . . anything to any of the children in the march?"

"They beat some, cattle-prod some of them, and they cursed some of them, hit some of them."

"Did you — did you observe whether any of the children in the march had to fall out because of—"

"Yes, sir," she responded quickly.

"—exhaustion?"

"Yes, sir."

"Object to that," Gayle said, "that is a conclusion, may it please your honor."

"Sustained," said Johnson.

"Did you observe," Doar went on, "whether or not any of the children were not able to finish the march?"

"Yes, sir."

"What did they do?"

"They — when they fell, they lay beside the—"

Gayle interrupted again. "We object to that, that is her opinion.

"Well, he asked this time what did they do," Johnson said, overruling.

"They fell by the road," repeated Miss Rodgers, "and some of them were sick. Some vomited."

John Kohn, a tall, Montgomery attorney, cross-examined. "How did it happen," he probed softly, "that you took part in this march of February tenth?"

She shrugged. "I just did."

"Who asked you to take place — take part in it?"

"Who asked me to?"

"Yes. Who directed you to take part?"

She shook her head. "I don't remember. I know I was guided by my conscience, but I am not sure—"

"You are not sure," he said, rather sharply, "whether anybody asked you to come down and march and take part in that demonstration?"

"No, sir."

He paced for a moment, lifted his hands slightly. "Was that on a school day?"

She nodded. "Yes, sir."

"Did you have to play hookey in order to take part?"

"That was on Wednesday," she said firmly, "and I don't have classes on Wednesday afternoon." There were a few snickers in the crowd.

Kohn nodded. "I believe you said it was about five or six miles."

"Yes, sir. To my judgment, it seemed to be."

"Isn't it a fact that it is not over two-and-one-half miles from there past where y'all marched?"

Miss Rodgers stared at him. "I don't know if that is a fact or not."

"You just don't know?"

"I don't know."

"You're just guessing at it?"

"I am estimating," she said, her tone almost defensive. "Yes, sir."

"All right," he said, somewhat irritably. "You stated that your conscience told you to march, is that correct?" When she nodded, he plunged on. "If your conscience told you to march or to commit any crime, would you go ahead and do it because your conscience told you to?"

"Your honor!" Hall cried. "We object to that."

"Sustained."

Kohn kept on. "Would you disregard any law if your conscience told you to?"

"Objection," snapped Hall.

Johnson gazed at Kohn. "Sustained."

Kohn turned away. "That's all."

Johnson continued the hearing through Saturday, listening as more witnesses told of the March seventh confrontation at the Edmund Pettus Bridge. On Monday, March 15, while throngs of blacks sang and prayed in front of a line of lawmen on Selma's Sylvan Street, the Reverend F.D. Reese — the man who had organized the voting rights drive and invited King there — took the stand. He told of the early planning, the early marches.

Kohn, who had been asked to join Pitts on the defense team on the first day of the hearing and had received permission from Johnson to do so, cross-examined.

"Besides being president of the Dallas County Voters League,what else do you do?" asked Kohn.

"I'm a teacher."

"Do you draw a salary for your work with the voter league?"

"No, sir."

"Are you on anybody's payroll paying you to agitate?"

"Object," said one of the government attorneys.

"I'm cross-examining him," Kohn announced.

The judge issued his own reminder to Kohn. "You came into this case late, too, with the court's permission," Johnson said.

Kohn nodded. "Yes, sir."

"It should not have been necessary," the judge went on, "but it has been necessary once during this trial for me to advise counsel that when they examine they are to . . . they are to demonstrate common courtesy to all of these witnesses, regardless of who they are or what color they are. And that applies."

Kohn shrugged slightly. "I am not conscious of doing that, your honor."

"And I am — I am — cognizant of the fact that counsel used the word 'agitate.' But it has many definitions. I will permit the question."

Kohn faced Reese again. "Will you answer the question?"

The witness stared with some puzzlement. Johnson saw it and said: "Asked if you were a member of any of the groups that have participated in any of the demonstrations."

Reese nodded. "Yes. I am president of the Dallas County Voter League."

"I can't hear you," Kohn declared.

Reese raised his voice. "I am president of the Dallas County Voter League."

"Any other group?"

"No."

"What is that voter league?"

The government table again erupted with several objections, citing repetition.

The judge nodded. "I will permit a limited amount of this, Mr. Kohn, because you came into this case late. But I will not permit that fact to unduly prolong this trial."

Later, Pitts began his cross-examination. "You say you are a teacher?"

Reese nodded. "That's right."

"Uh-huh. And ... how many days you missed teaching because of these demonstrations?"

"Oh, four or five, I guess. I'm not sure."

"You're not sure?" Pitts scanned his notes. "You advocated juveniles taking part?"

"I have never advocated juvenile delinquency."

Pitts stared at him in surprise. "Haven't you, as a result of the demonstration, been charged with contributing to the delinquency of a juvenile?"

"I have been charged ... yes." Reese nodded. "Yes."

"You were arrested, weren't you?"

"Certainly."

"And that involved you hauling juveniles to the courthouse, didn't it?"

Hall rose:

"Your honor, we are going to object to that ... we—"

Johnson shrugged and spoke to Hall. "Well, one of your theories is that there has been harassment by arrest. I don't see that it hurts your case. It may inure your theory. Your objection is overruled. If Mr. Pitts wants to continue this, let him go ahead."

"Well, your honor," Pitts stammered, "that is . . . that is all I want to say about it."

When State Trooper Major John Cloud was summoned, there was a stir in the crowded courtroom. A man of medium build and reddish hair, he had been the field commander of the troopers that Sunday at the bridge; he was a witness for the government, but in legal terms, a hostile one. Doar watched him take his oath, then advanced.

"Major Cloud, how long have you been with the troopers?"

"Let's see . . . eighteen years; eighteen years in May."

"And you were in charge of the troopers on Sunday, March seventh?"

"Yes, sir."

"And what were . . . tell us what your instructions were on that day?"

"Well, at first we were told that the march would be permitted." Cloud straightened somewhat in the chair. "And then we were told . . . then it was changed."

"Changed? By whom? Who changed it?"

The major shrugged slightly. "By Governor Wallace."

Doar folded his arms and paced. "Now, when you saw the marchers come out on the highway . . . well, did you see them coming?"

"Yes, sir."

"And did you observe their conduct on the bridge . . . as they came across the bridge?"

"Yes, sir."

"Were they peaceful?"

Cloud's face was expressionless, his voice flat. "They appeared to be. Apparently."

"Were they orderly?" Doar asked.

"They were walking on the walkway of the bridge."

"Were they orderly?" Doar repeated.

"As far as I could see, they were."

Doar nodded. "Now . . . and you then lined up your troopers across the bridge . . . the highway just below the overhead signs on the . . . the east side of the highway, is that right?"

"Yes, sir."

"And after the order was given to the marchers to disperse, what happened?"

"Well, they — I — I — let's see." The major pondered a moment."When they ... after the instructions were given to them to disperse and they refused to do so, I gave the order to the troopers to disperse them."

"Then what happened?" Doar prodded.

"Well, the troopers, to the best of my knowledge of it, began to slowly walk into the crowd." Cloud's eyes dropped while he recalled the event. "After they got into the crowd, the front lines of this march began to be a turmoil," and he rotated his right hand to illustrate. "And I called for the troopers to regroup."

"Did you ... had you given the troopers any instructions with respect to striking any of the ... of the marchers at that time?"

"Our troopers are always told not to strike," Cloud said,"but to use their stick as a ... as a means of shoving, pushing or prodding."

"Did you see any of your troopers strike any of the Negroes there in that first advance?"

"No, sir." The major shook his head firmly. Then: "I saw people falling, including the troopers ... troopers fell as well as the people in the march."

"And did you at that time—" Doar hesitated, watching the major. "Did you observe whether there were any of the marchers lying prone on the highway?"

"Yes, sir."

"And what, if anything, did you do about them?"

"Well, some of them were getting up, so we didn't do anything...I didn't at that particular time."The major shrugged. "Of those—"

"Now what instructions did you give the troopers with respect to using gas?"

"Well ... we had told them if they lay down that we would use gas ... if they didn't get up. The thought was that the gas would break this dispersal up, and ... it was to herd them or gather them — head them, rather — back toward town."

"And did you see what happened after the gas was used?"

"Well, some of the people that were in this group that was lying down began to get up and try to run, and . . . some of them did, a lot of them did, in fact . . . I saw one boy come from the front, run around the front end of it, and when he hit the pavement he had a suitcase in his hand and his feet went out from under him and he slid ten feet or so, and he jumped up, ran back, and picked the suitcase up and . . . and went back toward town, along the highway."

"Now did you . . . did you give the troopers any orders to move into these people that didn't move after the gas was used?"Doar asked.

Cloud shook his head. "No, sir."

"You didn't give them any instructions to move in at all?"

"No, sir."

"Had they had any training that indicated that this was standard operating procedure for the troopers to move in and among the persons that were . . . against whom the gas was used?"

"Yes, sir," Cloud said, nodding. "The riot training school that we have had has taught them to try to break groups up, to scatter them out, and get them headed in one direction if possible."

"And did you call for the posse . . . the mounted posse, to go into action that day?"

"No, sir."

"Did you feel it was necessary to control that situation that the posse go into action that day? With your state troopers there?"

"Well, as . . . from the way the things were . . . the people were running, I . . . I kind of feel like it was justified." Cloud's answer seemed to lack authority, and he raised his voice slightly. "I feel like it was justified in using them, trying to contain them."

"But you didn't call for them?" Doar pursued quietly.

"No, sir."

"And your understanding was they would not go into action unless they were needed?"

"Yes, sir."

"And you were in command?"

"Yes, sir."

"Did you give them any instructions out there what they

should do when they went into action—"

"None what—"

"—with respect to the use of force?"

"None whatever," he answered.

Doar nodded. "Do you . . . you know what effect noxious gas has on a person against whom it is used?"

"It makes them ill," Cloud said. "My — I think sick at the stomach."

There were murmurs and nodding of heads in the courtroom crowd.

"In your opinion, is it reasonable to have troopers move into areas where gas was used to use their clubs to disperse a crowd?"

"If they didn't break up," the major answered. "When that thing first . . . when they first lay down —"

"In your judgment," Doar snapped, "was it necessary to use a club on a person?"

Kohn objected. Johnson nodded. "I sustain that."

"I withdraw it," Doar said. "Now, Major Cloud, can you tell me . . . on that afternoon, did you . . . did any of the marchers commit any acts of violence on the east . . . on the Montgomery side of the bridge?"

"I was told they did," Cloud replied.

"But did you see any?"

"I never saw any violence," Cloud said.

"And did you see any state troopers strike any of them . . . any of the marchers?"

"No, sir, I didn't."

Attorney Peter Hall pursued the questioning.

"Did you observe any weapons held by the marchers?"

"Some had walking sticks," the major said, nodding.

Hall's voice was slightly amused. "Any knives, major?"

"Umbrellas."

"Umbrellas? No knives or pistols?"

"I didn't see any," Cloud said in a low voice.

"Did you see any marchers take these . . . these walking sticks and use them in a threatening manner?"

"No."

"That's all. Thank you, Major Cloud."

29

THE GOVERNMENT WOUND up its presentation early Monday afternoon, March 15. In Selma, the rain had set in again. And still the crowds waited, singing in the streets.

That afternoon, Colonel Al Lingo, the Alabama Public Safety Director, who had gone to Selma the afternoon of March 7 to take direct charge of the troops, usurping to a degree Cloud's authority, took the stand.

Johnson watched him with curiousity as he took his oath. Lingo, holding a hand to his throat, turned and announced in a hoarse voice:

"Your honor, I have a bad cold, and I get all choked up and it affects my hearing a little."

Johnson nodded. "Well, now, Colonel Lingo, you just do the best you can and we'll keep you well supplied with water."

"Thank you, your honor."

Attorney Kohn came forward to question him. "You are the director of the Alabama Department of Public Safety?"

"Yes, sir."

"You were in Selma on the seventh day of March?"

"Yes, sir."

"What instructions did you give?"

"I gave Major Cloud orders to disperse the crowd if possible."

216

"This is on the seventh?" Johnson asked.

"Yes, your honor," Kohn said.

"Sunday, March seventh, 1965. All right."

"Colonel Lingo," Kohn said, "did you observe any member of your department . . . any state trooper, actually beating any human being on this occasion?"

"I did not," he said, his voice barely audible. "I wasn't in a position . . . I was fifty yards away. The reason I wasn't up front was that I almost had pneumonia . . . I almost had it," he said nodding.

"Did you hit anybody?" Kohn asked.

"No, sir," replied Lingo, still holding a hand to his throat.

"Did you shove anybody?"

"No," Lingo muttered.

"Did you curse anybody?"

Again, the shake of the head and the weak, "No."

Fred Gray advanced to cross-examine:

"Now, regarding your orders to halt the march on Sunday, March 7: Who gave you the order?"

"I got them from the governor," Lingo said.

"Written orders?"

"No, they were verbal."

"Did you get them directly from him?" Gray asked.

"I talked to him about it," came the reply. "And he said there would be no march."

"And what did he instruct you to do?"

"He did not instruct me. He just said there would be no march."

"And what," Gray continued, with a slight shrug, "did you interpret the governor's statement to mean for you to do?"

There was a brief pause. Then Lingo said, "To restrain them from marching from Selma to Montgomery."

Gray nodded. "Now I believe in that—"

"Regardless?" Johnson interrupted. To Gray he said, "Just a minute," then turned again to Lingo who was sitting there still rubbing his throat. "Regardless what it took to do it?"

The public safety director seemed surprised by the question."Well, I don't mean to kill any of them but to use the means of least force as possible to restrain them—"

"But whatever it took to do it?" Johnson pressed.

"Yes, sir."

"Regardless of what that was?"

"No, sir," he said, shaking his head. "Not regardless of what that was."

Johnson stared at him a moment. "Where were you going to stop, Colonel?"

"Well, I — the reason I did not want to use tear gas . . ." He shrugged. He appeared to be confused. "I . . . I wanted to use a little resistance there to try to break up the crowd, because . . . because I was in Oxford, Mississippi, and I observed Mr. McShane (U.S. Marshal James McShane) use tear gas . . . what it caused, and that is the reason I did not want to use tear gas unless I absolutely had to."

Another defense witness was Circuit Court Judge James Hare of Selma who testified that he had found blacks — adults and children — guilty of contempt of court.

Pitts examined Judge Hare. "Did you ever observe any member of the sheriff's department abuse or intimidate any Negro citizen?"

The words "abuse" and "intimidate" are conclusions, and Doar quickly objected.

"Sustained," Johnson said, gazing at Pitts. "I'll sustain it until next year until you phrase it right."

"Yes, sir."

"It would save a lot of time if you would get away from that," the judge told him. "And phrase your questions right."

Peter Hall cross-examined. "Judge, I believe you testified that you found some of the demonstrators guilty . . . well, were most of them juveniles?"

Hare nodded. "Most of them were."

"And what were they guilty of?"

"Contempt of court."

"How were they in contempt . . . your honor . . . judge?"

"Singing and clapping their hands and creating a disturbance down there in front of the courthouse in the presence and hearing of my court structure. Yes."

"Singing and clapping their hands," Hall repeated softly.

Deputy Asbury Middlebrooks, under questioning by Pitts,

said he had taken part in the March 7 encounter at the bridge. He was a sheriff's deputy.

"Now what happened," Pitts said, "after the troopers moved forward?"

"Some of the marchers started pushing in behind the troopers," Middlebrooks said, matter of factly, "so we rode up and told them to move out."

"Did you follow them?"

"We did."

"On down to Brown Chapel?"

"Yes, sir."

"Did you see any member of the Dallas County Sheriff's Department strike or hit any Negro citizen?"

"I did not," the deputy replied, shaking his head. "I did not."

"Did you chase small children with bullwhips?"

"We didn't even have a bullwhip," Middlebrooks replied, a hint of exasperation in his voice.

"No bullwhips?"

"No."

Pitts nodded. "Now, on that day, were there any deputies injured?"

"There was."

"How many?"

"One."

"One?" Pitts was surprised. Earlier he had been told two deputies had been injured when some young blacks had thrown some objects at Clark and his men. "Well, do you know the extent of his injuries?"

The government attorney objected.

"Well," Johnson said, "he asked him if he knew the extent of the injuries. I'll permit it."

"He was cut up alongside the head," Middlebrooks said.

For the government, Peter Hall cross-examined and produced some photographs which he handed to Middlebrooks. "Would you look at this first picture and tell us what you see?"

"People marching off the bridge and horses going . . . going beside them, behind them."

"Do you see yourself?"

"No, I do not."

"This next picture, please. What do you see?"

The deputy stared at it. "It is part of the same march. Horses up and down the street." He looked closer while Hall waited, arms folded. "And one there . . . it looks like a billy club up behind somebody's neck."

Hall moved closer. "You mean one of the possemen has a billy stick up behind somebody's neck?"

"It is up behind somebody's neck," the deputy said, "according to this picture."

"All right, let's move to another picture." Hall flipped through them. "Look at this one. What do you see, sir?"

"People and horses again."

"What do the people there appear to be doing? Do they appear to be running?"

"Two of them do."

"Do they appear to be chased — being chased by men on horses?"

The deputy shrugged. "There are two horses."

Hall leaned over and looked at the photo. "As a matter of fact, sir, there are five or six horses in the picture."

The deputy looked again, nodding.

"Did you chase anyone on your horse?"

"Well, I rode behind them; I asked several of them to leave. And I rode behind them. Now some people might call that chasing them, but I call it riding behind them seeing that they move out."

"Let me ask you this sir," Hall said. "Were you riding at a gallop behind them?"

"Once or twice," he replied.

"And were there persons in front of you running?"

"They were."

"And you don't say you were chasing them?"

The deputy studied Hall for a moment. "I was riding behind them," he insisted.

It was still raining when the hearing concluded late the afternoon of Tuesday, March 16.

Johnson hurried home through the bleakness. It occurred to him that in Selma there were black children kneeling on the wet pavement of Sylvan Street, waiting on him to make a decision. They wouldn't leave, he knew.

Not only were those children waiting, but, indeed, so was the entire nation. No hearing had ever been held under such a wave of nationwide emotion. A minister had been killed; women and children had been beaten and gassed; President Lyndon Johnson, the night before, had appeared on national television:

"The efforts of American Negroes to secure for themselves the full blessings of American life must be our cause, too," the President had said. *"Because it is not just Negroes, but really, it is all of us who must overcome the crippling legacy of bigotry and injustice.*

"And we shall overcome.

"The real hero of the struggle is the American Negro. The cries of pain and the hymns and protests of oppressed people have summoned into convocation all the majesty of this great government."

At that moment, that majesty rested in Judge Johnson's hands.

30

THERE WERE CONFLICTING rights at stake, certainly: Peaceful assembly matched by the right of other citizens to use the highways without being hampered, and the responsibility of local and state government to keep those highways open.

Johnson made his decision that night. Early the next morning, March 17, Attorney General Nicholas Katzenbach called to inquire when the decision would be forthcoming.

"It won't be forthcoming," the judge said, "until I have some assurances first."

"What assurances, Judge Johnson?"

"I want the assurance that when I issue this order for the plaintiffs — and they rightly deserve this order — that it will be backed by the government of the United States."

"Backed?" The attorney general was puzzled. "Well, I think we can back it."

"I don't care what you think," Johnson said. "When I say I want assurances, I mean I want it from the President. I don't intend to go out on a limb with an order that will not be backed up by this government. If Wallace pulls some grandstand play like he did at Tuskegee, I want to know that this government will be prepared to meet it. It won't be fair to this court and to the people to have an order that does not have support."

"All right. You've got my assurance."

"I don't want your assurance, Mr. Katzenbach. I want it from the President. I want to know before I issue this order."

"OK, I'll get back with you, Judge."

Twenty minutes later he called back. "You got it," he said.

"From the President?"

"Yes, sir. From the President. Yes, sir."

"Good enough," he said, "I'll issue the order."

It came out that afternoon; some newspaper editors in the South denounced it. So did Wallace.

THE ORDER

The plaintiffs, as Negro citizens and the members of the class they represent, filed with this court on March 8, 1965, their complaint... (which) seeks relief from the denial of the equal protection of the law under the 14th Amendment of the Constitution... and seeks redress of the deprivation of rights and privileges ... guaranteed by the first, 14th and 15th Amendments.

The evidence in this case reflects that, particularly in Selma, an almost continuous pattern of conduct has existed on the part of the defendant Sheriff James Clark, his deputies, and his auxiliary deputies known as 'possemen' of harassment, intimidation, coercion, threatening conduct, and sometimes, brutal mistreatment toward these plaintiffs and other members of their class who were engaged in their demonstrations for the encouragement of Negroes to attempt to register to vote and to protest discriminatory voter registration practices in Alabama.

The State Troopers have participated and have extended the harassment and intimidating activities into Perry County where, on Feb. 18, approximately 300 Negroes ... were pushed, prodded, struck, beaten and knocked down ... and one was shot and subsequently died.

In Dallas County, the harassment and brutal treatment on the part of the defendants Lingo and Clark, together with their troopers, deputies and 'possemen' reached a climax on Sunday, March 7. Upon this occasion approximately 650 Negroes left the Brown Chapel in Selma for the purpose of walking to Montgomery, to present to the defendant Gov.

Wallace their grievances concerning the voter registration processes in these central Alabama counties. The state troopers, the deputies and the 'possemen' attacked the Negroes with clubs and used tear gas . . . resulting in injury to nearly 80 Negroes . . . . The attempted march alongside U.S. Highway 80 involved nothing more than a peaceful effort on the part of Negro citizens to exercise a classic constitutional right; that is, the right to peaceful assembly and to petition one's government for the redress of grievances. The acts and conduct of these defendants . . . have not been directed to enforcing any valid law of the state of Alabama . . . . The law is clear that the right to petition one's government for the redress of grievances may be exercised in large groups. Indeed, where, as here, minorities have been harassed, coerced, and intimidated, group association may be the only realistic way of exercising such rights. These rights may also be exercised by marching, even along public highways, as long as it is done in an orderly and peaceful manner. And these rights to assemble, demonstrate and march are not to be abridged by arrest or other interference. There must be in cases like this one now presented, a 'constitutional boundary line.' In doing so, it seems basic to our constitutional principles that the extent of the right to assemble, demonstrate and march peaceably along the highways and streets in an orderly manner should be commensurate with the enormity of the wrongs that are being protested and petitioned against.

In this case, the wrongs are enormous. The proclamation as issued by the governor of Alabama on March 6 banning any march by any manner — regardless of how conducted — constituted an unreasonable interference with the right of Negro citizens . . . to use U.S. Highway 80. Such a proclamation by the governor as enforced by the state troopers and deputies stepped across the 'constitutional boundary line' . . . This court finds the plaintiffs proposed plan to march . . . to be a reasonable one (they will march 300 people two abreast along the left side of the highway). It is recognized that the plan as proposed and as allowed reaches, under the particular circumstances of this case, to the outer limits of what is constitutionally allowed. However, the wrongs and injustices inflicted upon these plaintiffs and the members of the class they represent have clearly exceeded — and continue to exceed — the outer limits of what is constitutionally permissible. It must never be forgotten that our Constitution is intended to endure for ages to come, and consequently, to be adapted to the various crises of human affairs. With an application of these principles to the facts of this case, plaintiffs proposed plan to march from Selma to Montgomery, Alabama, for its intended purposes, is clearly a reasonable exercise of a right guaranteed by the Constitution of the United States, provided the march commences not earlier than March 19, and not later than March 22, 1965. The defendants' contention that there is some hostility to this march will not justify its denial. Nor will the threat of violence constitute an excuse for its denial. It is also appropriate to note that neither the defendant Governor Wallace nor the defendant Sheriff Clark testified in this case. The state has had ample time to present their arguments. Their only argument is the threat of white violence. These plaintiffs . . . are entitled to police protection in the exercise of this constitutional right to march along U. S. 80. This court recognizes . . . there will be a considerable burden imposed upon the law enforcement agencies of the State of Alabama. This court has been informed . . . that the United States Government stands ready, if requested by the governor of the State of Alabama, to assist in providing protection for this march. This offer on the part of the United States to assist if requested is not — whether the offer is accepted or refused — to be construed as lessening the duty on the part of the State of Alabama law enforcement agencies to afford this protection. The defendants are enjoined from arresting, harassing, thwarting or in any interfering with the effort to march from Selma to Montgomery.

JOHNSON

After the Selma-to-Montgomery march decision, attorneys for the State of Alabama informed me on the spot that they were going to appeal.

So I called the U.S. Fifth Circuit Court of Appeals in

New Orleans and told the judges it was coming and reminded them of the need for speed. Sometimes an appeal can take months to even be heard, but since the march was to begin within a few days, the Fifth Circuit agreed to an expedited session to consider the state's appeal.

To further expedite the proceedings, I called the Montgomery airport to find out when the next plane would be leaving for New Orleans.

Returning to the conference room where the attorneys were waiting, I told them, "You can get a plane in about an hour."

They looked perplexed. Finally one of them says, "Well, Judge, did you make reservations for us, too?"

I didn't, to be sure. But I assured them there would be plenty of room on the plane.

When the state attorneys failed to get a reprieve of my order in New Orleans, they returned to Montgomery, apparently convinced there was no need to go to the U.S. Supreme Court. They felt, I suppose, that since many of my past orders had been upheld, this one would be, too. So they didn't bother going to Washington to ask for a stay on the march. But by noon Sunday, March 21, it was all academic. The march was beginning at Selma.

While the blacks had been preparing to march, Wallace was urging the Alabama Legislature to take steps to prohibit the use of the state National Guard to protect the marchers because, he said, the cost would be too steep. The lawmakers, quite predictably, complied with his request.

George argued — and the press gave him front page coverage, of course — that the people of Alabama could not afford to call out National Guard troops and put on extra state troopers to provide security for the march from Selma to Montgomery. But it just pointed out how inconsistent he was.

He didn't have any problem calling out troopers and hundreds of guardsmen in June, 1963, when two blacks, Vivian Malone and James Hood, were trying to enroll at

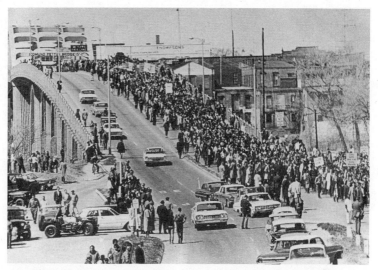

Following Judge Johnson's order, nearly 4,000 demonstrators crossed the bridge at Selma on March 21, 1965, to begin the fifty-mile march to Montgomery.

the University of Alabama. He didn't say anything about costs when he put guardsmen and troopers at Tuskegee to keep blacks from entering Tuskegee Public High School. I didn't hear him talking about costs when he sent hundreds of troopers to Selma to halt the first attempted march from that city to the state capitol.

In George's mind, I suppose, he could do what he wanted when it came to thwarting a court order and never mind the costs; but when it came to obeying a lawful order to provide protection for citizens involved in a constitutional right, he couldn't pay for the costs of using his manpower.

It's my personal opinion that George Wallace never hated or even disliked blacks. Growing up in rural Barbour County, he was close to them; even shared the same poverty with them. George did what he did as governor, I think, because he felt that's what the majority of the white people wanted. And white people held the votes. The George Wallace I knew in college was not a hateful person. That's what was so sad about all the hate-mongering he did with his racial rhetoric. There have been stories that George was upset when the state troopers slammed into the blacks at Selma and beat them and used tear gas on them. I believe he probably was upset. But still, when push came to shove, George stood up and fired off wrathful statements about the march order I had issued and said he couldn't pay for the protection of the marchers going to Montgomery.

I had never agonized over the Selma march decision as some have said. I felt the plaintiffs deserved the injunction, but I wanted the assurances from the President of the United States that it would be backed. If a judge issues an order and there is no backing, then it's perceived that the government does not put much faith in his order. It also encourages those who disagree with the findings to challenge them in the streets, and takes away whatever clout the judge has. I had seen what George Wallace would do when he sent the two hundred state troopers to Tuskegee; I had seen what the Ku Klux Klan would try to do when the Freedom Riders came through Alabama.

I felt the Selma case would come to me, because there was no question that some of the lawyers who worked in the civil rights field deliberately aimed at my court. There's no doubt of that, no big secret. They came to me because I gave fair rulings, and they knew it. In a way it seemed I was being penalized for giving fair decisions. I didn't ask for the cases; in fact, there were times when I wished I didn't have to hear them. The Freedom Riders case was one of them, but this Selma-to-Montgomery march case was even more so. The emotional fever in Alabama at the time was unbelievable. On the one hand, blacks in Selma felt they had to make the march to dramatize the denial of voting rights there and in other Black Belt counties; on the other, the whites were hysterical about a group of people marching along a major federal highway. I wanted very much for the State of Alabama and the Southern Christian Leadership Conference to work out some kind of agreement on the march.

And more than that, I wished the State of Alabama and in particular, George Wallace, the governor, could have moved forward in opening the voter registration process. I hoped that the SCLC people might back down a little on the demand to march. But there was not to be a compromise; there was only the rhetoric and the fiery oratory from both sides. I was the man in the middle in the final analysis, and in the end it would be up to me to make a ruling which I knew would create an emotional outburst. I didn't know any other way of doing it, but to do it.

I didn't like demonstrations, even though I understood the reason blacks felt they needed to employ them. I feel now, and certainly felt during the Civil Rights Movement in the South, that there is no place for anything that stirs up trouble or strife. All the boycotts and sit-ins and marches in themselves did not cure the illness of discrimination. It was the court decisions that did it. In the long run, the discrimination that existed by law in Alabama and Mississippi and the other Deep South states could have been remedied without the demonstrations,

In a cool March drizzle, the demonstrators stride along U.S. Highway 80 toward Montgomery.

230

although they did serve to focus public attention to the problem. I've always felt that the whites from the North who came South to join in demonstrations did not use good judgment. Certainly, they had a legal right to come here . . . but there's a world of difference between legal rights and good judgment.

32

WHEN THE THOUSANDS of marchers reached downtown Montgomery, Johnson, who in the past had assiduously avoided demonstrations, stood on the upper floor of the federal building to watch. Multitudes trudged through the morning drizzle; walking two abreast, they clapped their hands and sang freedom songs. It took them two hours to pass the Jeff Davis Hotel.

JOHNSON

If I had been a black person, I might have been there. If I had been black and been subjected to some of the laws they'd been subjected to, I might have had some serious questions about this democracy being the best political system.

From the moment I issued the order permitting that march, I had been certain that I had done what was right according to the laws of this nation. As I watched those people — and some were mere children — I was absolutely convinced I had been right. I had never watched a march or demonstration before, but there was something special about the Selma-to-Montgomery march. I think the people demonstrated something about democracy: that it can never be taken for granted; they also showed

On March 25, 1965, thousands of citizens from Alabama and throughout the U.S. marched up Montgomery's Dexter Avenue.

that there is a way in this system to gain human rights. They had followed the channel prescribed within the framework of the law. I think the march decision also showed some black people that valid complaints can be addressed within the system, according to the Constitution, and can be addressed without resorting to violence.

As Johnson watched the marchers parade below him, he felt someone at his elbow and turned to see Judge Rives standing there.

"Well, Frank," Rives said, "you were right about one thing."

"What's that, Judge?" Johnson asked.

Rives grinned and his eyes twinkled. "This clearly stretches the Constitution to the outer limits. It surely does."

Estimates of the crowd size varied from 25,000 to 50,000, but it was something that a Southern Capital had never seen before. The crowd gathered in front of the Alabama Capitol, massing on Dexter Avenue, ironically at the spot where, 104 years earlier, Jefferson Davis had been sworn in as the President of the Confederacy.

Governor Wallace watched from his office window and heard King shouting, "Glory, glory, hallelujah." The crowd roared, the sound echoing over the downtown.

Johnson, meanwhile, returned to his office and got a look at some of the mail that was coming in on the heels of his order.

A professor from Florida State University wrote:

This is the first fan letter I've ever written. But I know of no one to whom I want to write and hand a bouquet of roses more than you. I can't tell you how inordinately proud I have been of you since you have been a judge. I can just hear Dean Farrah (one of Johnson's law school professors) now as he sits in Heaven surrounded by open law books, burned matches and smelly old pipes, chuckling and saying, "That's one of my boys."

A man named Will Shafroth from Chevy Chase, Maryland, wrote:

Your decision on the Selma march was the judgment of Solomon. I'm sorry you have to go through this ordeal, but glad for the country that we have you there to handle it.

Another one read:

Dear Mr. Johnson: I think you are a vary (sic) good judge,

Johnson's decision allowing the Selma march was not universally approved. This counter-demonstration in Montgomery called for his impeachment.

because you were right about puting (sic) that news in the newspapers. Please don't turn against us. I am not Negro, but I do believe the Negros (sic) deserve freedom. Here is my picture and here is my address. I am 8 years old and I appreciate what you are doing for our great country.

Love, Dawn Bennett,
San Diego, Calif.

But there were others, too. One man wrote:
  Dear Sir: I would like to know why federal officials jump
every time Martin Luther King says "jump." The Negro had
equality after the Civil War, but abused it. They controlled the
Southern states and about bankrupted them. If it hadn't been for
the Ku Klux Klan they would still control it and, by God, that
isn't going to happen.

A man in Concord, New Hampshire, warned the judge:
  We are making a list of all the low-down traitors. The
vigilantes are forming. When the fight is over, not one single
Negro will be on this side of the Atlantic. They will be back in
Africa. Or dead. In the process, thousands of white people, like
yourself, will not be with us. If you recall the Apache Indians and
what they did to their enemies may be something for you to think
about.

In August 1965, less than five months after Judge Johnson
heard the Selma-to-Montgomery march case, Congress passed
the Voting Rights Act, which opened the way for thousands of
blacks in rural sections of the South to gain the right to the ballot
box, the right to have some say in their political destiny, a
destiny which would also impact their social and economic
status. The heart of the bill was based in large measure on the
decree Johnson had written in the 1961 voting case in Macon
County. It required registrars in states of the Old Confederacy
to pass black applicants if they were on a par with the least-
qualified white applicant. It was known as the "freezing" principle. The law also prohibited the arbitrary "testing" and difficult
exams that had been so prevalent in some states, especially
sections of Alabama, Mississippi, Georgia and Louisiana.

JOHNSON

In my opinion, President Lyndon Johnson rose to
the occasion with regards to civil rights, even when it was
against his earlier stands. He was a pragmatic politician,

but he left that behind when he became President, and his was a key role in getting passage of the Voting Rights Act, the most effective piece of legislation this century as far as blacks are concerned.

I've always felt that the answer to the South's racial problem was simple — just give the black people the right to vote. To me, the Voting Rights Act of 1965 was a far more important piece of legislation than was the Civil Rights Act of 1964.

All the Civil Rights Act did was codify the Fourteenth Amendment, which said that all citizens of the United States are entitled to the equal protection of the law. The Civil Rights Act of 1964 merely re-worded the intent and spirit of the Amendment.

And any judge could reach a conclusion as to whether a person's right to equal protection had been violated.

But the Voting Rights Act of 1965 was quite a different matter. It carried some new law with it. The Fifteenth Amendment had said that a person's right to vote could not be abridged because of race, color or creed or because of a person's history of having been a slave. That's all it said. But it did not spell out the requirements for a person to be a voter; it left that up to the individual states. Thus, you had Southern states like Alabama applying tests and grandfather clauses and so on to thwart the rights of blacks to vote. But the Voting Rights Act brought the process of voting registration to a uniform style and made it abundantly clear that there were to be no literacy tests and poll taxes and so forth to abridge the right of blacks and poor whites to be a part of the election process. The Voting Rights Act, therefore, was some new law.

Part VII

'Rabbit tracks in the snow'

The KKK trial
1965

33

THERE WAS A SENSE of relief when the mass rally concluded in a driving rain at St. Jude that night of March 25. The historic march had been accomplished without violence. A shot had not been fired ... not even a stone thrown. There had been some shouts and jeers from white spectators, but the closest thing to disorder came when Gillis Morgan, a reporter for the *Birmingham News*, took a near-miss from a white man who spat at him. That the massive demonstration had been carried out without violence was attributable, in large measure, to Johnson's stringent order which directed the state to provide protection. State troopers and national guardsmen, backed by a force of regular army units, including paratroopers, had patrolled the entire march. Then, too, it had all taken place during the daylight hours.

The effectiveness of this force — awesome by peacetime standards — diminished considerably at the conclusion of the rally; the marchers' return to Selma was undertaken in piecemeal fashion in cars and buses during the hours of darkness.

One of those handling the shuttle service was Mrs. Viola Gregg Liuzzo, thirty-eight, a white housewife from Detroit, Michigan, who had felt compelled to come to Alabama after the March 7 episode at the Edmund Pettus Bridge.

Ironically, she almost missed her self-appointed duty; someone had borrowed her car earlier that day and she was unable to

locate it. Just prior to the rally, she was beginning to look for a
ride back to Selma for herself . . . until the other civil rights
workers appeared in the crowd and one of them handed her the
keys. It was to cost her her life.

Accompanied by a young black, Leroy Moton, she drove
one carload to Selma, deposited them at Brown Chapel, then
swung around and headed back to Montgomery. Crossing over
the Pettus bridge, a car began to pursue her. It stayed behind as
she sped by Craig AFB, and on into Lowndes County . . . hung
close as she hurried through the night, through those forbidding swamps. Then it swung around her. Shots rang out, exploding the window and striking her in the head. She slumped to her
right. Her car veered off the road, coming to a halt in a swampy
defile.

Within hours of the murder, the FBI was on the move,
centering its investigation in Birmingham; by early afternoon of
March 26, President Lyndon Johnson announced from the White
House that four klansmen had been arrested in connection with
the night-rider slaying. Charged with murder by the State of
Alabama and with violation of another's civil rights by the
federal government were Eugene Thomas, William Orville Eaton,
Collie Leroy Wilkins and Gary Thomas Rowe, all of the Birmingham area.

They had, the FBI said, driven to Montgomery the morning
of the 25th, loitered around the Capitol, and when the civil rights
marchers held their rally, had shouted insults at blacks. After
drinking several beers, they had then gone to Selma looking for
some blacks to intimidate, they had spotted the car with the
white woman and black man in it, followed, then sped around,
firing the fatal shots. Matt Murphy, the attorney for the klansmen,
took the case, charging it was a frame-up.

Wilkins faced the first murder count in Hayneville in May;
the setting was the magnificent Lowndes County Courthouse,
which overlooked a lush town square. In the heat, blacks clus-
tered on one side of the second-floor courtroom, whites on the
other. Wilkins appeared at the scene wearing a cowboy hat, and
added to the spectacle as he once angrily kicked at newsmen as
he strode across the lawn. His cocksure manner left many
wondering whether an all-white jury could find a klansman

guilty, regardless of what evidence might be presented.

Rowe, it turned out, had been working undercover for the FBI. Granted immunity, he gave a vivid commentary on the slaying. He was called a liar and a traitor by Murphy, who raged through a closing argument in which he appeared in the open window for the benefit of television and news photographers. After the eight-day trial, the jury could not reach a unanimous verdict; ten men voted guilty, but two held out for acquittal. A mistrial was declared. A second trial, held in October, saw Wilkins turned loose, a free man. But still ahead was the federal trial on conspiracy charges; the state's murder cases against Thomas and Eaton were postponed pending the federal charges.

Trial was set for the last week of November. Johnson would preside. First Deputy Attorney General John Doar would head the prosecution. Attorney Murphy, meanwhile, had been killed in an auto accident as he returned home from a KKK rally that summer. Named to replace him was Arthur Hanes Sr., a former Birmingham mayor, and his son, Art Hanes Jr.

From the first, the elder Hanes was confident of an acquittal; even though it would be before a federal jury, that jury would still be comprised of Alabamians and Alabamians in Lowndes County had not found the evidence strong enough to convict. It was not likely, he surmised, that the government could present a stronger case. The trial was set for November 29.

"I drove down to Montgomery that morning," Hanes remembered later, "thinking it wouldn't last even a day. Why, I didn't even take an extra shirt with me, 'cause I figured I'd be back home for supper. After all, it was just a little old case . . . or so I thought. But, Good God, I got down there and saw these government attorneys . . . and they had a command post set up across the street from the federal building. And television crews and newspaper people all over the place — shoot, it was a major production. But I still didn't think it would take long to wrap up."

As it turned out, he would have to buy a couple of shirts. A jury of twelve white men and a white woman alternate was selected. As in the state murder trial, the key witness was Gary Thomas Rowe Jr., the FBI informant.

FBI agent Neil Shanahan was the first major witness to appear and testified that he was the "control" agent assigned to oversee Rowe's activities and follow up on his reports.

"How long has he been doing that?" Doar asked.

"Since 1960."

"And what did you find," Doar inquired, "with respect to the regularity of the information which was being furnished, or—"

"I found that the information," Shanahan volunteered, "previously furnished by him was accurate as best as we were able to corroborate."

"Your honor," Hanes intoned, "we object."

Johnson nodded. "I sustain that. That last statement will be excluded."

Doar examined his notes. "Now, can you tell me whether or not on March twenty-fifth, in the morning of that day, you received a call from Tommy Rowe?"

"I talked to him on the telephone," the agent replied. "I received a call from my office advising me that he had called, so I called him back."

"And on that morning, did he furnish you certain information?"

"Yes, sir."

"What morning?" the judge asked.

Doar glanced at him. "The morning of March twenty-fifth."

"All right. Go ahead."

"And what did you do with the information?" Doar asked.

Shanahan's reply was matter of fact: "Relayed it to Montgomery on the teletype."

"Can you tell me," Doar went on, "whether or not you received another call that day from Tommy Rowe?"

"Yes, sir, I did."

"And what time was that, Agent Shanahan?"

"I received a call from my office at eleven-thirty that evening, and they left me a number to call Tommy Rowe, and I called him back immediately at that number."

"Subsequent to that call, did you meet with Tommy Rowe?"

"Yes, sir," the agent said, nodding. "I met him personally."

"And where did you meet him?"

"I met him initially at the parking lot of the West End Baptist Hospital in Birmingham."

"Now at that time," Doar said, speaking with deliberation,

"did Tommy Rowe give you a gun?"

"Yes, sir, he did."

"Do you recall about how long you were . . . conferred with Tommy Rowe on the night of March twenty-fifth?"

"From about twelve-thirty until . . . from about twelve midnight until two a.m. in the morning of the twenty-sixth. Maybe a little longer."

That concluded Doar's questioning of Shanahan. Earlier, Montgomery Police Lieutenant Paul J. Dumas had testified that he had received a teletype message from the FBI office in Birmingham on March 25 to be on the lookout for a certain car which contained four men who were armed.

Art Hanes Sr., approached to cross-examine Shanahan. "Was Rowe an agent?" he asked.

"No, sir."

"A special employee?"

"No, sir. He was an informer."

Hanes lifted his hands in a gesture of surprise. "Then he was an informant, is that correct?" Before he could receive a reply, he went on: "Or what do you call them now? Confidential sources? Or what do you call them by now . . . he was an informant, is that correct?"

The agent shrugged slightly. "Yes, sir."

"All right, sir. Now the basis on which Rowe was paid was on the basis of information delivered. Is that correct?"

"Yes, sir."

"That was his product," Hanes probed, "selling information?"

Shanahan nodded, testifying that informers were paid based on the value of the information they provided the agency.

On redirect questioning by Doar, he testified that Rowe had called him on the night of March 24. "He told me that Gene Thomas (one of the defendants) had asked him to go to Montgomery on the twenty-fifth."

"And did you tell him to go ahead?" Doar asked.

"Yes, sir. I told him to let me know when he got back."

By 4:45 p.m. the government had completed laying its groundwork for the appearance of its star witness, Gary Thomas Rowe. Ever since it had been revealed that he was an FBI informer who had infiltrated the KKK, agents had surrounded his home in Birmingham; a task force of agents and marshals had maintained that guard in Montgomery; security at the federal building had been doubled. As the judge recessed trial that first day, Hanes still doubted that there was going to be any new evidence to convict his clients.

Rowe was called to the stand on the second day of the trial. He was escorted by three FBI agents. He was a rather large man, not overly tall but huskily built, with close-cropped reddish hair; his nose was short and straight, his eyebrows heavy. He faced the court bailiff, raised his hand and took the oath. Then he sat down. Doar approached to begin the questioning.

"Would you state your name, please?"

"Gary Thomas Rowe Jr." The voice was slightly high-pitched.

"Speak up in a loud, clear voice," Doar said, "so everyone in the courtroom can hear you."

"Gary Thomas Rowe Jr.," he repeated.

"How old are you, Mr. Rowe?"

"I'm thirty-two."

"Where did you live in March . . . in the month of March of this year?"

"Birmingham."

"Mr. Rowe, were you ever contacted by agent . . . by an agent of the FBI with respect to furnishing information to them?"

"Yes, sir, I was—"

"—with respect to racial activities in and around Birmingham?"

He nodded briskly. "Yes, sir."

"When did that first occur?"

"In 1961, sir."

"Could you tell us how that . . . how that came about?"

"The Federal Bureau of Investigation sent an agent . . . an agent came to my home and had several meetings with me."

"At that time, were you a member of any organization such as the Klan in Mississippi? I mean in Alabama?"

"No, sir."

"On the basis of those meetings, what did you do?"

A brief pause. "Eventually, I joined the Klan organization for the FBI."

"And how did you happen to join the Klan?"

Rowe shrugged and gestured with a hand. "Because the FBI asked me . . . requested that I do so."

"Did you join a particular branch, or klavern, of the organization?"

"I joined the Eastview Thirteen Chapter of the Knights of the Ku Klux Klan at that time."

"And you have been a member," Doar continued, "of that chapter since that time . . . through March twenty-fifth, 1965?"

"Yes, sir," came the reply. "But it has changed to the United Klans of America since I have been a member of it."

Doar nodded. "But it was the same organization?"

"Same people, same meeting place," Rowe answered. "Yes, sir."

"And who is the head of the . . . that Klan?"

"Robert Shelton."

"Now let me ask you this: Do you know any of the persons sitting at the counsel table on my left? To your right?"

Rowe shifted his eyes to them; Wilkins, Eaton and Thomas stared straight ahead. "Yes, sir," came the reply.

Doar turned to the defense table. "This is . . . could you just point out to the jury the people that you know there?"

Rowe nodded his head toward them. "Gene Thomas on the first, Wilkins in the center, and Eaton."

"And when did you first know these . . . these gentlemen, approximately?"

"What . . . well, I have known Thomas about five years, and Eaton within two years — I mean, Wilkins approximately two years — and Eaton within a year or so."

"Can you tell me whether or not these men are members of the United Klans, Knights of the Ku Klux Klan?"

"Yes, sir, they are.

"Mr. Rowe, did you come to Montgomery on the day of March twenty-first, 1965?"

"Yes, sir."

"And . . . and who were with you on that day?"

Brow furrowed, Rowe paused, thinking. "I was with Leroy Rutherford, Robert Thomas and Jack Crawford."

"Who are they?"

"They are other klansmen."

"What was the purpose in coming?" Doar asked.

"Came down for a parade and motorcade."

"Let me show you this photograph," Doar said, moving beside the witness. "Do you recognize this?"

He studied the print for several seconds. "Yes, sir. It's the rally at Cramton Bowl on the twenty-first."

Leaning closer, Doar asked. "Recognize anyone in the picture?"

Again a pause, while he looked it over. "Yes, sir. I see Eaton and Wilkins in this (picture marked number) eighteen."

"You see Mr. Thomas?"

"I can't say that I do," Rowe said hesitantly, frowning at the photo. "I don't recognize him as such — yes, I do, too!" And he pointed to it as Doar bent near. "He is over to the left. You can see just about a half-head shot of him . . . from his nose up."

"Would you mind marking that with a circle, please?" Doar handed him a crayon and Rowe marked the photo. "Now when did you return to Montgomery again?"

"On the twenty-fifth of March."

"Well, how did you happen to return on that day . . . to Montgomery?"

"I was instructed to go to Montgomery."

"And who instructed you?"

"Gene Thomas and Robert Thomas," came the quick reply. "Gene Thomas called me at home."

Doar turned with the marked picture and tossed it back on the table. Over his shoulder he asked, "And what did he say?"

Rowe's eyes lifted for a moment. "He said, 'Babe Brother,' he said, 'You going down the road with us, right?' Or words to that effect. And I says, 'No, I am not.' And he said, 'Aren't you dressed?' It was about seven in the morning when he called. And I said, 'As a matter of fact, you got me out of bed.' And he said, 'Well, you are going down to Montgomery today,' and I says, 'No, that has been called off,' and he informed me it wasn't called off, that I was to go."

Doar raised a hand. "Now, he used the words 'baby brother' or 'babe brother.' What is that term?"

A shrug. "That is what several of them used to call me."

"To call you?"

"Yes, sir."

"What was your job in the KKK?"

"I was a klan investigator."

"And Robert Thomas?

"He was the titan," Rowe replied.

"The titan?" Doar asked. "What is the titan?"

"The titan," he said, "is the head of a province embracing about six or eight different units."

"Did it include Klavern Thirteen?"

"Yes, sir."

"And what klavern was Gene Thomas in?" Doar asked.

"Klavern Twenty."

"And these other men at the table?" Doar asked, pointing at them. "Mr. Eaton and Mr. Wilkins . . . what chapter were they in?"

"They were in Twenty."

"Your honor, we'll object to that," Hanes said, almost amiably. "The Klan organization is not on trial here. Robert Thomas is not here."

"I assume it will be material and related to the issues of this case," Johnson said. "Overruled."

"Now, Mr. Rowe," Doar continued, "when you went to Montgomery on March twenty-fifth, how did you go?"

"In Gene Thomas's car."

"What kind of car?"

"I believe it is a '62 Chevrolet."

"Did you have a purpose in going there?"

"We were going to Montgomery to observe the march that was to take place," he said. "When we arrived, we rode around for a few minutes and then we went to a parking lot and parked and walked down toward the capitol."

"Now, can you tell me who, if any, of the men was armed?"

"Eaton and Thomas was armed."

"How long were you in Montgomery?"

Rowe studied for a moment. "I guess about four or five hours."

"What did you do in all that time?"

"We stood around . . . we talked . . . and we harassed the

marchers, hollered at them, booed them, got in an argument with some of the colored spectators." Rowe shrugged. "Things of that nature."

"What then?"

"Well, later on we decided to go to Selma. Gene Thomas stated, 'We are going to Selma,' and Eaton asked why and he (Thomas) says, 'Well, you know why. We got things to do and we are going to get them done, and we might even get down some of the entertainment from Shelly Winters. She is a real pig, anyway,' or words to that effect. And we proceeded to Selma."

"Was there some discussion then, after you left and got something ... well, did you stop anywhere first?"

"We were going to eat and go to Selma."

"And why were you going to Selma?"

"Your honor," Hanes said, "we are going to object to that."

"I sustain it to the question," Johnson said.

"That calls for a—"

"You can ask what was said," the judge said, addressing Doar.

"What was said?" Doar asked Rowe.

"Gene Thomas said we were going to Selma, and I think—"

"Object to what he thought, your honor," Hanes said.

Johnson nodded. He looked at Rowe. "Just . . . the question, Mr. Rowe, calls for what was stated. The substance of it—"

"Gene Thomas—"

"—and by whom," the judge added.

"All right, sir," Rowe said. He collected his thoughts, then: "Gene Thomas stated, 'We are going to Selma.' Eaton asked why and he says, 'You know why. We got things to do and we are going to get them done'—"

"All right," said Doar, cutting off the repeat of an earlier answer. "When you got to Selma, what happened?"

Rowe blinked. "We got flagged down by a state highway patrolman . . . a trooper."

"I see. And what happened then? When you got flagged down?"

The trooper, Rowe said, was operating a radar check. He had told Thomas, who was driving, that he was barely within the acceptable speed limit, but was being stopped because another trooper had noted his improper muffler. Doar asked if a ticket was issued to Thomas. Rowe said there was. He had seen it, he said.

"All right. What did you do then?" Doar asked. "I mean, did you drive on?"

"Went into Selma."

"After you got into Selma," Doar pressed, "where did you go?"

"The first stop we made after we got into Selma," Rowe answered, "was the Silver Moon Cafe."

(It was near that cafe on March 9, 1965, that several white men had attacked and fatally beaten the Rev. James Reeb).

"And what did you do, when you got to the Silver Moon?"

"We ordered a beer."

"Had you had anything to drink before then?" Doar inquired.

"Yes, sir."

"Where?"

"At Jack's Beverages in Montgomery," Rowe replied. "We had two beers."

"Is that yourself?" Doar asked. "Or the four of you?"

"The four of us. Two beers each."

"Now, how long did you stay at the Silver Moon?"

"About thirty minutes or so."

"Was there a discussion?"

Rowe testified that another man, allegedly involved in the Reeb beating, came to the booth and talked to them, putting his hands on Thomas's shoulders and saying, "God bless you, boys. I did my job. Now you go and do yours."

Then, he testified, the four of them left the cafe and drove to Brown Chapel AME Church where a crowd of blacks had gathered. Rowe also said there were Army trucks with troops on them riding about. That, he said, alarmed the four and later they left, driving to the downtown, where they stopped at a traffic light near the Edmund Pettus Bridge.

Rowe continued the story: "Sir, we was approximately two or three blocks from the steel bridge, we had just stopped for a red light, and just as we stopped there was an automobile pulled up on our left; there was a white woman and a Negro in the automobile and Wilkins says, 'Looka here. I will be damned. Looka there, Babe Brother, looka there.' And I looked . . . it was a white woman driving the automobile and a Negro sitting in the front with her."

Rowe paused, and after a moment Doar told him to continue. "Yes, sir," he said. "Gene Thomas says, 'Wonder . . . wonder where they are going? Let's follow them, we are going to see where they are going. I think they are going out to the woods on a dirt road and park somewhere together.'"

"And what . . ." Doar gestured with a hand. "Was anything further said?"

"The . . . at this point we had left the light and proceeded and Gene Thomas says, 'Get down back there,' said, 'below the window level. Don't let them see you . . . we are going to follow them and take them.'"

"Was anything said about who the people were?"

Hanes objected. "He is leading the witness."

"I sustain it," Johnson said. "Just ask him what else, if anything, was said, Mr. Doar."

"What else, if anything was said?" Doar repeated.

"At this point we got down below the window level and GeneThomas made the statement, 'I believe we got some of the brass.'"

"And what else was said?"

Rowe's eyes focused at a point above the spectators.

"He says, 'They are going out on the highway and make love.' He says, 'We are going to get them tonight,' he says. 'We are going to get them tonight.'"

"Did you . . . did you observe what kind of car it was?"

"Just at a glance," Rowe replied. "It was a light-colored Oldsmobile."

"Did . . . did you observe the license plate."

"It was a Michigan plate on it."

He then described the start of the chase as they followed the car south then east on U.S. 80, headed toward Montgomery. "This automobile started going extremely fast, Gene Thomas was going extremely fast, with speeds ranging from . . . say, ten miles an hour, up to ninety and one-hundred miles an hour. Gene Thomas was trying to catch up with the automobile and it was over in the left hand side of the lane, and we were in the right and Gene says, 'Baby Brother,' says, 'get ready, we are going to get them on our side,' and I said, 'We are?' He said, 'Yeah,' and he started to get up even with them and I looked over to the right and it was Craig Air Force Base and I said, 'Gene, you better get back.' She had moved over to the right, and I said, 'Good God! That woman is going in the Air Force base,' and he said, 'Nope,' he said, 'we are going to get them tonight.' The automobile veered to the right like it was going to turn into the gate of Craig Air Force Base and just veered out, not real sharply . . . whipped in and veered, then really stepped on the gas and went on down the highway. We kept following . . . at speeds eighty, ninety miles an hour. Gene says, 'Well, this is a good place, we'll take them now.'"

As he related the high speed chase in the night, Rowe's voice had risen in pitch, the delivery became more rapid; he sat with his shoulders slightly hunched, his hands clenched tightly on his lap; every spectator in the packed courtroom strained forward to catch every word.

"Gene Thomas started to overtake the automobile and Wilkins says, 'Gene, you better be careful up there,' said, 'the radar is right up there a little piece,' and Gene said, 'No.' Wilkins said, 'Yes, it is, Gene. It is right up there a little piece.' And I said, 'Yes, it is, Gene.' Gene said, 'It damn sure is.' He slowed down to . . . he observed at this point the radar over on the left on the far hand side of the freeway." Rowe testified that Thomas slowed down because of the Alabama State Trooper radar unit that had been posted on the highway earlier. He testified that they saw a trooper car with the dome light on, stopped behind a vehicle which had apparently been stopped for speeding. Then, he said, the chase resumed. "He sped up again to overtake this automobile . . . he got close to it again," he said.

"All right," Doar said, "what happened then?" Rowe's eyes shifted from Doar to a point above the crowd.

"We started to catch up with the automobile again. The highway changed from a four-lane to a two-lane. Gene asked, he said, 'How you want me to stop them? You want me to bump it from the back, run it off, get up beside of it and run it off the road? Or how do you want me to stop it?' Wilkins says, 'No, brother,' says, 'you can't stop it like that. If you get one speck of paint on this (car) we will be caught, you just get up beside of it and we will stop it.' We started to catch up again but there was a building . . . what appeared to be a . . . a . . . to me a two-story building . . . old graying, wood building, with kind of floodlights and several automobiles around it. I said, 'Gene, for God's sake, let's go back to town. We can find somebody else back there if you just want to see somebody. We are going to get caught. We are going to get in trouble.' She was weaving this time, she was kind of going real fast and kind of. . . the car was kind of weaving a little. And I said, 'I am afraid she is going to turn it over.' And he says, 'By God, we can't . . . we got to get them before much longer; they will be in Montgomery the rate we are going.' And I said, 'Gene, let's go back to town.' He said, 'Baby Brother, you are in the big time now. We are going all the way tonight. You are just shook up. You are going to be all right.' We kept following. He began to get up pretty close and it was kind of a hill like and just over the hill you could see headlights . . . he slowed down as two big trucks passed by . . . then the next thing that happened was ... was in a kind of a swamp area like, and he says, 'This is it. We are going to take them now.' He started around this automobile, and just as he started he handed Wilkins his pistol."

"What kind of a pistol was it?" Doar injected.

"Sir, it was a thirty-eight caliber." Doar nodded, and Rowe continued, his face intent, the eyes still fixed on some point above the crowd.

"And he says, 'Get your guns out, we are going to take them.' So we got our weapons out. He got to passing and the automobile was on the right hand, and we were going around it, and just as our back got just about even with her front,Wilkins stuck his arm out of the window just about nearly at the elbow length with Gene Thomas's pistol in his hand. And at this point the woman turned her head and kind of looked over toward the automobile . . . into the front window—" and Rowe snapped his fingers twice. "—and Gene Thomas said, 'Shoot the hell out of them! Everybody shoot the hell out of them!' And Wilkins told Gene to give it some gas, and Gene gave it some gas to speed on around it. At that point Eaton started firing, and he said, 'Here,

brother, put your hand out the window,' Wilkins told me, and I
put my hand up pretty close to the side of his head and held it . . .
and as Gene passed the automobile, Wilkins continued firing,
and whenever he was still completely past, Eaton was leaning
back out the automobile with his arm out trying to fire."

"And did you fire any shots?"

"No, sir," Rowe said, "I did not."

"And what happened then?"

"Gene . . . he . . . Gene sped up and I looked out the back
window, and this automobile was still coming down the highway," Rowe said, his tone reflecting awe. "This automobile was
coming down the highway just as straight as if some . . . you or
I or anyone of us was sitting up driving it, and I said: 'Good God,
you missed! They are following us now. They are chasing us
now.' And Wilkins reached over and slapped me on the leg. He
said, 'Baby Brother, don't worry. I don't miss. That bitch and
bastard are both dead and in hell.'"

There was a stir, a brief ripple of sound from the spectators,
a soft, discordant collection of "ums" as Rowe paused.

Then: "At this point, just momentarily, the automobile
began to veer off the highway, just like it was going to turn off . . .
turn up a dirt road. 'Turned up a dirt road,' is what I said, and
Wilkins said, 'It is no side road there, Baby Brother. Those
bitches are gone.' He said, 'You are just nervous and upset,' and
I said, 'Yeah.' And he said, 'How'd you like that for shooting?'
And I said, 'Yeah, you really shot hell out of them, all right.'"

35

I T WAS IN MID-AFTERNOON when defense attorney Hanes began his cross-exam of Rowe. Compared to the ridicule he had undergone in Hayneville at the hands of Matt Murphy, this questioning was mild.

"When did you first join the Klan?"

"In '61 or '60. It was '60, I think."

"All right. And did you take part in an initiation?"

"Yes."

"All right, sir. Now during the course of this initiation, this ritual or rite, did you take an oath?"

"Yes, sir."

"All right," Hanes said, his voice rising in volume. "Did you stand and raise your hand and repeat the oath that I am going to read to you?" And Hanes whipped a piece of paper from his coat pocket, holding it almost at arm's length while he adjusted his glasses.

He began reading in a monotone: "I most solemnly swear that I will forever keep sacredly secret the signs, words and . . . any and all other matters and knowledge of the Klan regarding which a most rigid secrecy must be maintained which may at any time be communicated to me and will never divulge same nor ever cause same to be divulged to any person in the whole world . . . I most sacredly vow and most positively swear that I will never yield to bribe, flattery, threats, passion, punishment, persecution, persuasion, nor any enticements whatever . . . for the purpose of obtaining from me a secret or secret information of the Klan. I will die rather than divulge same, so help me God."

He folded the paper slowly, running his fingers over the crease. "Did you take that oath?" he asked.

"That is part of the oath, sir."

"But did you take part of it?" Hanes pressed.

"Yes, sir," Rowe said.

"All right. Now . . . now you say you joined back in 1961 or so. Now during that time you took part in radical Klan activity, didn't you?" Rowe blinked quickly several times, pondering.

Hanes plunged on: "Didn't you take part in the beating of the Freedom Riders in Birmingham on Mother's Day, 1961?"

Rowe shook his head. "No. I was there, but—"

"Didn't you get in a fray," Hanes charged, "with six Negroes and get your throat cut and didn't some of your Klan buddies take you to a doctor?"

"Yes."

Hanes moved around the defense table. "And you were in some other incidents, too, I believe, weren't you. You were arrested at the University of Alabama?"

Rowe nodded. He had been there during the time of Wallace's schoolhouse door stand, he said.

"Now," Hanes continued, "about this night of March twenty-fifth, 1965. What time did you say you got to the Silver Moon Cafe? You say around six p.m.?"

"Actually, sir," Rowe said, "it was nearer to seven."

"Oh, now that you think about it?" Hanes asked, his tone mocking, "it was nearer to seven?"

"Yes, sir."

Hanes picked away at Rowe's consistency on the time element of the night of the murder, but did little to shake the story.

"How long," he asked, "did it take you to drive from the bridge where you saw this car to the point where you said the shooting took place?"

Rowe bit his lip and shook his head slowly. "Sir, it seemed . . . it seemed like a lifetime."

"Uh, huh, but just how long was it?"

"Maybe forty minutes, sir."

Rowe completed his testimony late that day; he was followed by a state toxicologist, Dr. Paul E. Shoffeitt, who had performed the autopsy on Mrs. Liuzzo at midnight on the night of the shooting. Death, he said, was caused by hemorrhage and brain damage. The fatal bullet wound, he said, "penetrated the left side of the head. It struck forward of the lower part of the left ear, it ranged to the right, slightly upward to the rear to a point at the base of the brain where the cord is connected to the brain."

Until the morning of December 1, the case went about as expected; Rowe's harrowing story, which held the audience spellbound, was much the same as it had been at Wilkins's two earlier trials in Hayneville. But on this morning, the government produced a surprise witness ("They pulled her out of thin air," Hanes said later).

Until Ouida Larson turned up, there had never been any corroboration at all on any of Rowe's testimony. But the FBI found her and Doar put her on the stand. She was white. She was a waitress who had worked at the Silver Moon Cafe.

"Were you working there on March twenty-fifth," Doar asked.

"Yes."

"What hours?"

"I worked between two p.m. and midnight."

"During that time, did you remember whether or not four persons came into the cafe in the latter part of the day?"

"Yes."

"Would you speak up a little louder?"

"Yes," she repeated.

Wilkins and the others were watching her, their faces stoic.

"About what time did they come?" Doar asked.

"Between seven and eight-thirty."

"And do you recognize anyone here?" Doar asked, then added quickly, "Can you identify them?"

She turned her head to face the defense table.

"The two over there," she said, pointing.

Doar followed the direction of her hand. "And which two are you pointing at?"

"The young one," she said, nodding at Wilkins.

"And the one ...this one in the suit...the blue suit."

"May the record show," Doar announced, "that she is pointing to Leroy Wilkins. And may the record show she is pointing at Gene Thomas."

"And the one at the end of the table," Miss Larson said.

"May the record show she is pointing at Mr. Eaton." Doar faced her again. "And was there a fourth person there as well?"

"Yes."

"And is that person now in this courtroom?"

She shook her head. "I don't see him."

"And what . . . can you, in your own words," Doar said, "just tell what you observed about these people?"

"Your honor," said Hanes, "I object to the form of that question."

"Overrule," said the judge. "You can answer it."

Miss Larson shrugged. "Well, I don't really know."

Doar stared at her. "Well, did you observe where they sat?"

"Yes."

"In a table or a booth?" he prodded.

"In a booth," she replied.

"How long . . . about how long were they there?"

"I couldn't tell you," she said. "We were busy."

Hanes picked at her testimony, questioning on how sure she was that there were the men she saw and was she sure it was the night of March twenty-fifth. But she stuck to her basic testimony that she had seen Wilkins, Eaton and Thomas in the cafe that night.

Leroy Moton, the man who had been in the death car, told the jury he had not at first paid much attention to the car following them.

"But after we got out on the highway for a while," he said, "the car kept following us and I began to wonder why."

Then, he described the car passing and the shots being fired.

He had not been able to identify the car from which the shots came, he testified; he heard the glass exploding, saw Mrs. Liuzzo lurch slightly toward him, and had grabbed the steering wheel from her lifeless hands. Only for a fleeting second or two had he observed the tail lights of the speeding vehicle.

"Where were you when the shots were fired?" Doar asked.

"I was tampering with the radio," he said.

"What happened next?"

"The car ran off the road and I brought it to a stop. Then I turned off the switch and the lights. I got out and tried to stop a truck, but it wouldn't stop."

"Then what happened?"

"I got back into the car and passed out. Later I got out and tried to stop cars and ran along the highway and a rabbi driving a truck to Selma stopped and picked me up."

By noon of the third day, December 1, the government had rested its case. Defense attorney Art Hanes took little time to attempt to refute the charges; the three defendants chose not to take the stand. In midafternoon Doar and Hanes gave their closing arguments.

Johnson decided to wait until the next day to let the jury begin its deliberations. "It's been a long day," he told the attorneys. "We'll start fresh in the morning."

When court resumed the next morning at nine, Johnson turned to the jury members and said:

"You jurors give me your attention for the next few minutes, please. We have reached the point in the trial of this case where it is appropriate that I charge you as to the law that we are controlled by and that we are bound by as to this particular case. You jurors, in the performance of your duty and in the performance of your responsibility, are, in a sense, judges. And the law by operation of law casts you and me in a partnership of sorts . . . because it is our duty to see that a fair verdict is rendered in this case. I discharged my part of that duty by seeing that parties receive a fair trial. The law doesn't impose any impossible burden upon jurors, when it imposes the responsibility upon you of considering all of the evidence that has been admitted. If you can accept all of it with the truth of the matter as you determine it to exist, then accept it, and from it find your facts. And to the fact apply the law, and then as to each defendant, return a verdict."

He paused long enough to examine the notes.

"The indictment charges William Orville Eaton, Collie Leroy

Wilkins and Eugene Thomas jointly with one offense — the offense of conspiracy. The indictment charges that commencing on or about March the first, 1965, to on or about March twenty-sixth, 1965, that they conspired together with each other, and with other persons to the grand jury unknown, to injure, oppress, threaten, and intimidate citizens of the United States in the vicinity of Selma and Montgomery, Alabama, who were in the free exercise and enjoyment of certain rights and privileges secured to them by the Constitution and laws of the United States. Under the evidence in this case, you will not be concerned with whether or not the conspiracy was successful . . . if and when you find a conspiracy existed and if and when you find that one or more of the defendants became knowingly and willfully members, thereof.

"Now in determining the guilt or innocence of these defendants, there are several things that you jurors in this case and I, as judge of the court, are not concerned with. Judges are not partisans, they aren't advocates in the trial of a case like this; they, under their oath and under their duty . . . act as impartially and as fairly as they can towards . . . both sides. You are not concerned, and I am not concerned, with furthering or impeding any political or sociological causes . . . whether it be sponsored by the Southern Christian Leadership Conference, or sponsored by the United Klans of America is of no concern of mine, or concern of yours, as jurors in this case.

"We are not concerned . . . with the right of American citizens to protest in a peaceful manner, whether it be a protest or a march . . . in furtherance of some cause sponsored by the SCLC or whether it be a march or a protest . . . to further some cause sponsored by the United Klans of America . . . because it has been generally agreed by counsel, and properly so, that those that were participating in this march from Selma to Montgomery and back and lending their aid to those that were participating in the march had a legal right and a constitutional right under our American system to do that."

He reminded them that the burden of proof was on the United States government and they had to prove it beyond a reasonable doubt.

"It doesn't mean a fanciful doubt," he said. "It doesn't mean some doubt you get outside the evidence in this case."

As to the conspiracy, he instructed: "Mere similarity of conduct among various persons and the fact that they may have associated with each other . . . does not, necessarily, establish proof of a conspiracy. However, the evidence need not show that the members entered into any express or formal agreement. Intent is also a part. Intent can be supported by circumstantial evidence. And what is circumstantial evidence? Well, the best example I can think of is if you go to bed at night and it snows during the night and you get up the next morning and see rabbit tracks going by your door, you know that a rabbit went by, even though you didn't see him."

Several of the jurors responded with weak smiles.

"Intent," he continued, "can rarely be established by any other means. There can be no eyewitness accounts of the state of mind with which the acts were done or omitted; but what a defendant does or fails to do may indicate intent or lack of intent to commit the offense charged. I have a practice that I have followed through the more than ten years that I have been on the bench of never directly or indirectly commenting on the failure of a defendant to testify.

"However, when the defendants' lawyers request it, I do charge you on the law as to the effect of the failure on the part of the defendants. The defendants have not testified in their own behalf. They don't have to do that. The court charges the jury that the fact that they did not testify in this case cannot be considered in determining the defendants' guilt or innocence. You are, in returning your verdict . . . you must not, you cannot, be swayed by sympathy, prejudice, or passion for or against any defendant in this case, or for or against the government, or for or against any citizen against whom the defendants are alleged to have conspired."

At 9:58 that morning, the jury left the room, stayed out several minutes while attorneys filed motions, returned, then retired to begin their deliberations.

The time was 10:03 a.m. They recessed, returned, and in mid-afternoon sent word that they needed a dictionary.

"I can't give them a dictionary," Johnson told the marshal. "It wasn't part of the evidence or the exhibits."

At 5:35 p.m., Johnson sent them to a hotel for the night. They came back at nine on the morning of December 3 and began their deliberations again. Then, at 10:30 they came back after sending word with the marshal that they were at an impasse.

Johnson watched them come back in, prepared to give them what would be known as the "dynamite charge."

"All right," he said. "I have received word from the jury ... Mr. Kirby, are you spokesman for the jury?"

"Yes, sir. Your honor, we find that we are unable to reach a verdict and seem to be hopelessly deadlocked," the foreman said.

"All right," Johnson said. "Anything that I say now can be taken and considered along with what I charged you was the law of the case when I charged you at the conclusion of the trial. As I reminded you then, we had somewhere between forty and fifty witnesses in this case. So you haven't commenced to deliberate the case long enough to reach the conclusion that you are hopelessly deadlocked. This is an important case. This trial has been long and the trial has been expensive. Your failure to agree upon a verdict will necessitate another trial equally as expensive; expensive, that is, as far as the government is concerned. It is expensive as far as the defendants are concerned. This court is of the opinion that the case cannot again be tried better or more exhaustively than it has been on either side. It is very desirable that you jurors should agree upon a verdict."

He was not, he said, asking that any juror surrender his convictions. "You should consider that this case must at some time be decided . . . that you are selected in the same manner and from the same source from which any future jury must be. And there is no reason to suppose that the case will ever be submitted to twelve more intelligent, more impartial, or more competent to decide it." Johnson sent them back to deliberate further.

"Your honor," said Hanes, rising, "I — could I state an objection?"

"State your basis," said the judge.

"Well, your honor," he said, "I think it was prejudicial to the defendants."

Johnson made a note and stared at Hanes. "Is that your only basis?"

"Yes, sir."

"All right. You have that objection and exception."

Hanes nodded. "All right, sir."

After nearly two hours there still wasn't a verdict and at noon the jury was escorted to lunch. Johnson, meanwhile, had begun another trial. Despite all the publicity, the case was just one of a number he had to hear. While the jury was out, he proceeded with the remainder of the docket.

At 2:10 p.m. on December 3, 1965, less than forty minutes after returning from lunch, the word began flashing down the corridors of the United State Courthouse. A U.S. marshal signalled to the judge and mouthed the word "verdict."

"Verdict?" he asked.

"Yes, sir." Johnson recessed the jury on the second case he was hearing and told the marshal, "All right, get ready to bring them in." As the jurors filed in, the defendants sat grimfaced. Johnson asked the foreman if a verdict had been reached. They had, the foreman said. The judge told him to pass the paper to the court clerk. Wilkins, Eaton and Thomas rose to hear the words:

"We, the jury, find the defendant Collie Leroy Wilkins guilty—" The word sent a shock wave rushing over the courtroom. Heads turned among the spectators; there were even some faintly audible sharp intakes of breath. "—as charged in the indictment ... we, the jury, find the defendant, Eugene Thomas, guilty as charged in the indictment ... we, the jury, find the defendant, William Orville Eaton, guilty as charged in the indictment."

The defendants stood staring at Johnson in stunned disbelief.

The clerk's voice was still reading in the dull monotone:

"Signed, this the third day of December, 1965. T.H. Kirby, foreman."

"All right," said the judge. "Gentlemen, if it's worth anything to you, in my opinion that was the only verdict that you could possibly reach in this case and still reach a fair and honest and just verdict. Of course, I couldn't tell you that beforehand; it wasn't any of my business, because it was your duty and your responsibility to determine the guilt or innocence of these men."

He slapped a hand on the desk. "All right, now the marshal will escort you out. Thank you for your attention. Court is in recess."

Later, Johnson sentenced the three men to ten years each — the maximum authorized by statute; appeals were turned down by the Court of Appeals and the Supreme Court. Thomas and Wilkins served seven years and were turned out on good behavior. Eaton died in 1966 while the case was still on appeal.

The Klan case before Johnson reflected the change that was taking place in Alabama and the South: The KKK could no longer impose its will of terror without being challenged. Two years later in Mississippi, members of the Klan were brought before a federal jury on conspiracy charges arising from the deaths of three civil rights workers in 1964. A number of them were found guilty and sentenced to prison terms. Those cases and the Liuzzo case helped break the power hold of the KKK in the South.

36

AS A SEQUEL to the Selma voting story, Johnson was directed by the U.S. Fifth Circuit to go to Selma with Appeals Judge Richard Rives and U.S. District Judge Daniel Thomas of Mobile to conduct hearings on the hundreds of arrests made by Sheriff Clark during the demonstrations. He viewed it as a clean-up detail. Blacks had been charged with violating an ordinance barring rallies and demonstrations.

Many people had been hauled into jail by the sheriff for doing nothing more than exercising a constitutional right, the right to peaceful assembly. The judges stayed there for two weeks and threw almost all of the cases out, because there was no basis for them. The people had not violated any valid law of the State of Alabama, they held in a written opinion.

JOHNSON

We took up all sorts of things in those Selma hearings. Not only the unlawful arrests, but also charges of discrimination against the movie theater in Selma as well as several restaurants. They had simply declared the Civil Rights Act of 1964 to be null and void. That's one way to get around a law. But it didn't work. One of the restaurants had a sign advertising it out on U.S. Highway 80; they used nationally distributed brands of food items.

They couldn't hide from the fact that they were

engaged in interstate commerce. We had a number of cases where they just simply refused to serve blacks, and a couple where the owner called Jim Clark out and he came and arrested the Negroes. And the Willoughby Theater was just as bad. Now, they'd let Negroes in to see the picture show, but made them sit up in the chicken loft ... wouldn't let them down there where the white folks sat. Now, I couldn't hold for that. If you take a fellow's money to see a picture show, you ought to let him sit where he wants. I feel about picture shows the way I feel about churches: they should all be integrated. All of them. That business about segregated churches is hypocrisy. I could never understand it. During those hearings in Selma, we must have heard five hundred cases, and threw almost all of them out. It was then that I first became aware of the then-new Afro hair styles. Some of the people had bushy hairdos that must have reached out a half-foot in each direction from their scalps. I noted that it must have provided almost as much protection as a helmet. As Judge Rives and I sat up there one day, we noticed a young black man wearing a button on his shirt that read "GROW." I turned to Rives and said, "Well, I've heard of NAACP and SCLC, but what does GROW mean?" He grinned and replied, "Git Rid of Wallace." I laughed, then said, "I wonder how a fella' would go about joining that group?"

After his decision on the Selma-to-Montgomery March, there was a lot of mail and public comment that Johnson was the liberal judge who liked demonstrations, the "nigger judge" who would allow blacks to do as they pleased. Actually, he disliked demonstrations and would not have allowed the march had not the denial of rights against blacks in Black Belt counties of Alabama been so flagrant.

But regardless, his image was rooted in the public mind in Alabama, and nothing he might have said would have changed it. Yet, those who have been in his courtroom or have followed some of the cases he has heard, know well that his decisions have never been based on race, but rather law. Even while he was hearing the Selma march case, there were some events unfolding in Montgomery involving "sit-ins" and "lay-ins" by activists who later sought refuge in his court when they were arrested.

It began on March 11 when four members of the Student Nonviolent Coordinating Committee (SNCC) decided they wanted to present a petition to Governor George C. Wallace. When Alabama State Troopers refused to let them into Wallace's office, they left, and began walking back to Dexter Avenue Baptist Church. But Montgomery police officers stopped them and told them they had to take another route. There was, at the time, quite a lot of activity going on in the vicinity of the State Capitol. The four, led by James Forman, went limp at that moment, and fell into the street. When police ordered them to move, they refused, and lay there, impeding traffic along the street. They were arrested.

That event triggered a similar move by a hundred other persons, both whites and blacks, who went limp on the sidewalk near the church, blocking pedestrian traffic. On March 18, 19 and 22, more SNCC members sat down on streets or sidewalks, snarling the normal flow of traffic, motorized or foot.

All told, Montgomery police arrested about 167 persons and trial was set for them in Recorder's Court, City of Montgomery. The 167, led by Forman, filed suit in federal court — actually, in Johnson's court — asking that the cases be removed from city jurisdiction. In the brief, they claimed that it was unconstitutional for blacks to be tried in a court in which there were no blacks on the juries, or in a court where the judges were elected by an electorate from which blacks were systematically excluded. The demonstrators said they could not get a fair trial in Montgomery.

The defendants were represented by famed trial lawyer William M. Kunstler and others. Johnson heard the arguments, but didn't buy them. In his order, he wrote:

> The philosophy that a person may, if his cause is labeled 'civil rights' or 'states rights,' determine for himself what laws and court decisions are morally right or wrong and either obey or refuse to obey them according to his own determina-

tion, is a philosophy that is foreign to our 'rule of law' theory of government. The practice of such philosophy is untenable. Those who resort to civil disobedience such as the petitioners were engaged in prior to and at the time they were arrested and then, when arrested and prosecuted, attempt to go to a Federal court with a cry of 'civil rights' violations, cannot ... escape arrest and prosecution. Civil disobedience by 'civil rights workers' is still a violation of the law and subjects the violators to being prosecuted in the courts of the cities and states...

JOHNSON

I wasn't the black man's judge nor the white man's. I suppose that over the years I've had to call down black people more than whites. It would be a black who would be the cause of a disturbance during a case. They had a tendency to laugh out or cry when their emotions were touched. I remember this one black guy of about twenty-five or so who stood up during a trial which had racial emotions to it and held up his arm and gives the black power sign . . . stood there with his clenched fist raised up. I ordered the marshals to bring him before me. On the spot I cited him for contempt; set a hearing for him. He came in before me a couple of days later and very meekly states, "Why, Judge, I wasn't giving the black power sign. I was just looking at my watch." One of the marshals testified that the guy had a watch, all right, but it was on his left arm, not his right. I told the defendant that had he wanted to see his watch, he should have been raising his left arm. I cited him and gave him a fine.

Ever since I've been a judge, I've demanded respect in the courtroom, not for me, personally, but for the court and for what it stands. A courtroom is not a place for sideshows and fanfares ... not from whites, not from blacks. I just won't stand for it. Every case that's heard is of the utmost importance to the parties involved. It is a sign of disrespect to them to have outbursts and commotions. During the first part of the Civil Rights Movement,

Johnson demanded respect in his courtroom—and got it.

and certainly in the period before it, white attorneys often looked upon black people as inferior, as not having a worthy cause. The attitude was reflected in the questions they asked blacks who were witnesses, and in the manner in which those questions were asked.

I have never sought to embarrass an attorney in my courtroom, but I have been sharp with some of them when their conduct was unbecoming. I wouldn't hesitate to call them in line. Because in a court of law, all people are equal regardless of who they are, no matter the color of their skin. As volatile and heated as some of the civil rights cases were, the only time I've had to cite attorneys for contempt were in other types of cases; actually, only one in my courtroom, two others for something that occurred in another court in the federal building in Montgomery. The first one I had to deal with was Broward Segrest, a fine attorney from Tuskegee. Mr. Segrest just lost control of himself one day during a trial. I remember giving out some instructions on some point of law and I said to all the attorneys, "Do you understand that?" And they all nodded except Mr. Segrest who seemed preoccupied with something and so I said, "Did you understand that, Mr. Segrest?" And he shoots back, "Yeh, I heard you." Well, it was just in bad taste for a lawyer to address a judge like that. I said, "Come on up here, Mr. Segrest." I sent the jury out and I looked at him and he realized that he might have been a little out of line. So I told him, "I'm citing you for contempt. How do you plead?" "Guilty," he said meekly. "All right," I said. "I'm fining you a hundred dollars." He blinked in surprise. "A hundred dollars?" He paused for a moment, then asked, "Well, do I have to pay it right now?"

"No, not right now," I said. "But during this ten-minute recess." The problem was that he didn't have much money with him and ten minutes wasn't a lot of time to raise it. But I had to be tough with him. Contempt isn't something a judge just throws around on a whim. It's got to mean something and the fine with it has to hurt a little to make the point. So Mr. Segrest hurried around the tables and some of the opposing attorneys loaned him the money.

The second case occurred in a bankruptcy proceeding in another courtroom in the federal building. I was involved in another case myself and the bankruptcy referee came down to me during a recess and said he wanted me to issue contempt citations against two attorneys who

had gotten into a fight. The attorneys were Clarence
Atkeison, a big country-style lawyer from Prattville, and
Willie Joe Fuller. So I called them in to my courtroom and
they appeared before me, both of them disheveled, em-
barrassed and humiliated as they stood before me.

"Either of you gentlemen need a lawyer?" I asked.
"Or do you prefer to represent yourselves?" "No lawyer,"
Atkeison said. "Well, I'm in a case now," I told them, "and
don't have time to deal with this right now. So I'm putting
you in the custody of the marshal until I can hear it." I
didn't get to bring them back until five o'clock that afternoon. Between the two of them I was able to piece
together what had happened. It seems that during the
bankruptcy case there had been an angry exchange between the two and Atkeison had called Fuller a "liar *ab
initio*." It was probably the only Latin Atkeison knew.

Well, Fuller didn't take too kindly to that and during
a recess he had come up behind Atkeison and tugged at
his coat and said, "I want to see you in the hallway." So the
two of them adjourned to the hallway and, the story goes,
Fuller grabbed the larger Atkeison by the neck and
commenced to choke him.

"When he did that," Atkeison told me, "I slapped
him." "Slapped me, nothing," fumed Fuller. "He knocked
hell out of me, Judge."

I found Fuller to be responsible for the incident and
fined him a hundred dollars. Atkeison, I figured, had
already paid his dues by having been in jail all day.

One day a black man was among a group of defendants who
were to be arraigned before the judge. The man was wearing
blue jeans, an open vest with no shirt, and a chicken claw around
his neck. He was also wearing sunglasses. Johnson called the
man's attorney up to the bench, leaned forward and said softly,
"Something wrong with your client's eyes?"

"No, sir," said the attorney. "I'll have him remove the
glasses." That wasn't all, said Johnson. He told the attorney to
send the man home and come back in suitable attire — meaning
a shirt minus the chicken claw necklace.

40

JOHNSON

> I never liked the term "reverse discrimination," because it means nothing. There is no such thing as reverse discrimination, just as there is no such thing as reverse murder, or reverse robbery. It's merely something the news media conjured up to mean blacks who discriminate against whites. But there is just plain old discrimination. It can be carried out by whites, it can be carried out by blacks, or any other race or group.

The states of the Old Confederacy did not hold a patent on discrimination. In Johnson's court, not only were there cases of whites practicing it, but blacks as well. And it wasn't just the states, but even the United States government. In 1932, the U.S. Public Health Service began a long-range study on the effects of syphilis on a group of about 625 black men living in Macon County, Alabama. Some of the men had the disease and were given some treatment. Others were allowed to live without treatment to enable government doctors to study the effects of the untreated disease on human beings. For forty years, the program continued. Even when penicillin was discovered to be an effective treatment of the dreaded disease, the Tuskegee Syphilis Study, as it came to be known, went on. Then, in 1972

271

the news media heard about it and the Associated Press ran a story. It created a furor, with some critics charging that the program smacked of behavior carried out by Nazi Germany; others said it was racially motivated, that such a study would not have been undertaken with white men. In any event, Tuskegee attorney Fred Gray again filed a suit in the United States District Court in Montgomery, this time naming the United States of America as defendant. He filed on behalf of a black man from Notasulga, named Charlie Pollard, who submitted to the court a statement which said:

In 1932, I received notice of some kind of new health program in Macon County. I do not know exactly how I received notice, but I recall that it was sent out by mail and distributed to Black schools and churches in Macon County. When we were first examined some of us were told we had "bad blood." I was told that I had bad blood. I did not know then what bad blood meant and the Federal doctor did not explain it to me. Several years later I found out "Bad Blood" meant syphilis.

Pollard said he had to get a spinal tap which was painful and forced him to stay in bed for ten days. He said as the program continued he was given shots and also some white pills and green medicine. He said he did not know what the medicine was. He said he and the other men were examined once a year by a group of doctors. A local nurse coordinated the program. He said they had been promised a hot lunch and a free ride to Tuskegee on the yearly treatment day. In addition, he said, he was told his heirs would receive a "burial allowance," presumably to help pay for his funeral. Other men said they were told the same thing. In his statement, Pollard said after twenty-five years he and the others received a "Certificate of Appreciation" and twenty-five dollars from the U.S. Public Health Service. After that, he said, the examinations were held every two years. Pollard, who was in his late fifties when the suit was filed, also noted in his statement:

At one time I was to go to Birmingham to receive treatment for syphilis by the use of penicillin, but I was told by a nurse that because I was in the study I could not go. I did not know until recently that I was involved in an experiment of untreated syphilis in Negro males. I was never told by the Federal doctors who came and carried out this experimentation in Tuskegee that it was an experiment. I was led to believe by the Federal Government personnel who conducted the study that I was receiving adequate medical care and attention. I was never told by anyone conducting the study about the effects of untreated syphilis nor was I instructed as to precautions to take for syphilis.

Gray filed the suit on behalf of Pollard and others who were participants in the study, or their survivors, as some had already died. The government objected to a class-action suit, asking that Pollard's case be confined to his own complaint. Johnson decided it was clearly a case in which class action was appropriate. Later, the government asked that the case be dismissed, which the judge rejected. Attorneys for the government denied that any of the deaths were directly related to the disease, an argument that lacked conviction.

For more than a year the motions and hearings continued, and finally on May 8, 1974, the United States offered the plaintiffs free lifetime medical care. Gray and the other attorneys who had joined in the case objected, saying the care would circumvent any chances for the plaintiffs to recover any damages. Johnson allowed the free medical care, but made it clear such care would not be in lieu of any possible damage award which might arise at the conclusion of the trial. Finally, in 1975, government attorneys agreed to the obvious, that a class of black men in Macon County, had been wronged by the government; they offered to pay damages. On September 15, 1975, Johnson entered a consent order which spelled out the details of the damage assessment. It provided that living syphilitics, such as Charlie Pollard, would receive $37,000; the heirs of deceased syphilitics would be paid $15,000; living controls would be paid $16,000, and the heirs of deceased controls $5,000. In all, the government sent $8,446,000 to Montgomery which Johnson ordered deposited in three banks, each paying five-and-a-half percent interest. He felt the money should draw the best interest rate available at the time. There were hundreds and hundreds of claims made from wives, daughters, sons, brothers, sisters, great-nephews, distant cousins. Some were paid the full amount, others split the funds.

It would take Thomas Caver, the Deputy United States Clerk, years to complete the payment, as he had to verify claims. Charlie Pollard received his funds and immediately went out and bought himself a red Cadillac, according to news reports. The case file would remain open for more than thirteen years. When the principal amount of the fund was paid, the survivors and heirs then shared what there was of the amount earned by the interest payment.

Part VIII

*'I didn't want to die
without telling you...'*

**Alabama in the
post-Civil Rights era**

41

I T WAS CLEAR TO JOHNSON when he became a federal judge in 1955 that he was going to be in a social hotspot when it came to civil rights. Over the years some would idolize him, saying he was a great judge, a Godsend to the poor and oppressed, and to minorities. Others thought him to be a judicial tyrant.

JOHNSON

I've often wondered about how people rate others as far as greatness goes. Abraham Lincoln was a great president. But, in my way of thinking, Calvin Coolidge might have been a great president, too, had he been thrust into the same set of circumstances that Lincoln faced. Roosevelt was a great president, again due in large measure to the situation that developed about him as World War II erupted. Sometimes what makes one person great and another mediocre is simply happenstance, the timing of events. As for whether or not I was a "great" judge, history will have to make that determination. But chance played a part in me being where I was, when I was.

There were other judges in the Deep South who faced tough civil rights cases. Many of these judges were august, courageous men. Judges Richard Rives, Elbert

Tuttle, John Wisdom, in my opinion, were foremost among them. Judge Rives was a Montgomery native, with roots that were tied to the old plantation aristocracy. He had been born into a society bred to believe that blacks did not have the same rights as whites.

Yet, Judge Rives participated in decisions, including the one on the Montgomery Bus Boycott, that drew a terrible reaction from some of his fellow Alabamians. After the bus boycott case it was reported in one publication that he had "forfeited his right to be buried in Southern soil." He was likened to a traitor by some. And not long after that bus decision, the grave of his son was vandalized by hoodlums. Rives once sat on a voting rights case for Carroll County, Mississippi, and made judicial note of the fact that blacks were being discriminated against in their attempts to register. He wrote in his opinion:

We have called the figures startling (that no blacks were registered to vote in the county), but we do not feign surprise because we have long known that there are counties not only in Mississippi, but in the writer's own home State of Alabama, in which Negroes constitute the majority of the residents but take no part in government either as voters or as jurors. Familiarity with such a condition thus prevents shock, but it all the more increases our concern over its existence.

And the courage of U.S. District Judge Hobart Grooms of Birmingham has been documented on more than one occasion because of his forthright and even-handed manner in dispensing the law. It was he who ordered the University of Alabama in 1956 to admit a black woman, Authurine Lucy. Judge Grooms was so harassed by angry whites that he would go to bed at night with a shotgun by his side. In 1963 he issued the order for the University to admit Vivian Malone and James Hood, even as Governor Wallace ranted about standing in the schoolhouse door. Johnson does not take issue either judicially or personally with some of the other judges, whose actions did not draw the same praise from Americans at large. But the records speak for themselves. In a Mobile County, Alabama, school case, U.S.

District Judge Daniel Thomas was reversed thirteen times by
the Fifth Circuit. In a voting case from Wilcox County, Alabama,
Judge Thomas wrote in his opinion that he "saw no discrimination" in the tests given to blacks seeking to be registered, even
though there was not a single black voter in the county. He
denied the Justice Department's request to inspect voting
records, saying that the state could prohibit the federal government from so doing. Needless to say, the Fifth Circuit reversed
him as quickly as it could, rather wryly noting in its opinion that
while no blacks were able to vote, no less than 112 percent of the
whites in the county could. The judges stated further:

*We simply make the observation that in this day and age
an effort to inspect the records of a county having such a
disparity in the percentage of voters to eligible citizens as
between the races should not be frustrated by the simple expedi-
ent of the (Board of) Registrars' statement that there is nothing
wrong.*

The county officials had told Thomas during the hearing
that the reason no blacks were registered was simply because
none had attempted to do so. He apparently accepted that
reasoning as evidence that there was no discrimination. Said the
Fifth Circuit:

*"This court . . . expressly adopted the opinion of Judge
Johnson (in a case against voting officials in Montgomery
County) and affirmed his order. Thus, just as plainly as it could
be said, we have decided that the State of Alabama had no power
. . . to enjoin the acts of the Attorney General of the United
States."*

In Mississippi's Southern District, Judge Harold Cox had
been reversed numerous times on civil rights cases. In the
Northern District of that state, Judge Claude Clayton once took
four years to redirect the registrars in Bolivar County to turn
over voting records to Justice Department agents.

JOHNSON

I cannot help but feel the inaction of some judges
was a result in great measure to the social pressure they
felt. Yet, such judicial lags only added to the frustrations
Negroes felt in trying to gain the right to vote — a right
they had been seeking for more than eighty years — and
probably added to the sense of uneasiness that pervaded
the South's white citizens. Because, in the final analysis,
these white Southerners, especially the political leaders,
knew what was right, not only in voting cases, but also
those involving school desegregation. They simply
shunted the problem aside, punted it, if you will, to those
of us serving as judges in the federal district courts. Most
of them knew what the law was and merely waited for us
to make the decision. That way they could turn to their
constituents and say, "Well, we have no choice but to do
it now, because a judge has ordered us to do so." I believe
that many of them, deep down, actually wanted us to
make those decisions for them. I think any school child
could have interpreted the *Brown* decision and issued a
clear order in writing as to what it meant. White Americans in the South knew what *Brown* meant and they
understood later orders from myself and other judges.
But the social structure of the South led them to believe
that they had to resist. Now I don't doubt that some were
die-hards, ready to fight to the end to keep blacks out of
the schools and off the voting rolls, but the majority, I
believe, were prepared to follow the law. And subsequent
events have proven that assessment to be accurate.

The majority of Southern people pride themselves in
being law-abiding citizens. It hurts them to violate a law.
What thwarted putting laws into effect, by and large, was
the oral venom being spouted by some of the leaders. It
put the people in a quandary; on the one hand, a federal
judge was handing down an order saying one thing, on
the other some politician was harping about "states' rights"
or some other issue. George Wallace certainly did his
share. But if he hadn't been doing it, there would have

been someone else. What I really resented about George was that he lied to the people; led them to believe they would never have to desegregate their schools. He couldn't have believed it. He knew the laws of the land. Yet, thousands of white Alabamians did believe him. And if George wasn't lambasting me about something, somebody else would be. The thing that has always amazed me about the Supreme Court's 1954 school desegregation case is that it never once mentioned the *Plessy v. Ferguson* case, the old "separate but equal" case involving segregation on public transportation. I've never been able to figure that out. But they said nothing about the case which spelled out Southern doctrine for nearly six decades. But the *Brown* school desegregation case opened the way for the Civil Rights Movement to begin. The movement, that era of non-violent demonstrations and sit-ins and marches, lasted about sixteen or seventeen years, starting in 1955 when Rosa Parks was arrested, and it ended in late 1972 or so, with the Alabama State Troopers case. It peaked, of course, during the Selma marches. That doesn't mean to say that all discrimination by race is ended; it certainly has not. But I believe the egregious, flagrant discrimination that we knew prior to 1965 has, for all practical purposes, ended. Racial issues come up from time to time in the Deep South, and some become widespread, while others are more narrowly defined.

A case in point is the 1987 marches held in Forsyth County, Georgia, which, if they proved the interest in civil rights was still alive, also probably proved that the old tactics of the 1950s and 1960s had fallen into oblivion. What worked in Selma in 1965 and what worked in Birmingham in 1963, did not work in Cumming, Georgia, in 1987. I never liked demonstrations; I never liked anything that stirred up trouble or strife. The King followers knew what they were doing when they baited Bull Connor in Birmingham and when they baited Jim Clark and George Wallace at the bridge in Selma. They knew the reaction, knew that somebody was going to get hurt,

maybe even killed. But still, it was a sacrifice they felt
willing to make. I understood the reason blacks felt they
had to hold those demonstrations in the '50s and '60s. My
feelings were made clear on that matter in my order
allowing the march from Selma to Montgomery. Still, in
the years of the '70s and '80s, the times were changing.
And so were the social issues. But some of the old civil
rights warhorses still wanted to hold onto the power and
prestige that they found during the decade 1955-1965.
Some scholars felt there was a touch of nostalgia connected with it, but I don't think so. It was power and
prestige, and to some extent, income. The remedy for
civil rights cases remained in 1987 as it was in 1955: the
courts. The system of justice is in place. Even in Forsyth
County, Georgia, where no blacks live, the issue might
have been, not a march, but a suit filed in federal court on
the grounds of fair housing.

While Johnson refused to play name-calling games with the
governor of Alabama and other state leaders, he did, over the
years, use rare speaking engagements to fire off his own volleys
of choice words. In 1967, at nearby Prattville, there had been
racial violence, with black activist Stokely Carmichael telling
crowds "to hell with the laws of the federal government." There
had been fire-bombing and some looting.

That May, in a yearly address made at naturalization ceremonies, Johnson impressed on the new citizens the need for
respect of the law. In sparse, crisp tones, he declared:

*It is equally wrong for individuals in positions of political
leadership to threaten use of police powers of a state government
to impede, even thwart, the decree of a lawfully-constituted court
entered in a matter where jurisdiction and the governing legal
principles are basic. While one cry of defiance against our law is
couched in language that is vulgar and offensive and the other is
couched in more sophisticated terms, both are doctrines of
defiance against our laws and our government, and, for this
reason, they equally advocate anarchy.*

*The courts, in the application of our law, have served as a
beacon of hope and as a great source of law and protection of*

individual rights . . . we live in a time when one concept is that government is the embodiment of power, and the other concept is that it is the embodiment of justice. Each of us must support and defend the proposition that our law is supreme and must be obeyed. When those who frustrate the law, who undermine judicial decisions, run riot and provide uncurbed leadership for a return to medieval savagery, for the responsible American citizen to remain silent is tantamount to cowardice, and a grievous injustice to the proposition that in America the law is supreme.

Since passage of the Civil Rights Act of 1964 and the Voting Rights Act of 1965, blacks have gradually entered the social mainstream, and by the early 1980s Johnson felt they, as a group, had come to a point in their history where they must be prepared to compete on equal footing with whites in achieving scholastic standing as well as employment and fair housing, although the effects of past discrimination was a concern for him.

JOHNSON

They have tried to compete and in some cases have done so successfully. But as a people, they remain at a substantial disadvantage because of past discrimination, namely the "separate but unequal" school system. It is my belief that one generation of black children being exposed to a desegregated education has brought about a dramatic change. But even so, they come from a deprived home environment, a product of the past abuse; it may take two or three more generations before blacks can compete on an equal basis with whites. And while the law has brought about changes in schools and neighborhood patterns, I suggest that the majority of blacks are inclined — more so than whites, I believe — to maintain social contacts with other blacks instead of with whites. This is manifested in the alarm with which blacks view the demise of some of their black colleges. They want to maintain black traditions. I can understand that. But I cannot agree with it. If a college cannot attract enough students and faculty to keep itself afloat economically, then it ought to close. The problem has been that desegregation has opened the way for blacks to attend previously all-white colleges. But in return, whites have not flocked to black colleges. Black colleges had a vital role to play from Reconstruction on through the 1960s. But now, the doors of all colleges have been opened. The times have changed. If a black college can't keep going, then shut it down, put a monument on it, but don't pour mounds of federal money to keep it going just for tradition's sake.

In my own office in Montgomery, I have practiced what I have preached: equality. I hired blacks into the federal court system — law clerks, secretaries. Mrs. Marie Thurman was the first black clerk hired in the office of the U.S. Clerk. She was a teacher working in the Georgia school system, but was looking for a job in her hometown of Montgomery. She was well qualified to do the job and I hired her. In 1980, I hired Pauline Jackson in my office and she was probably the first black secretary in the U.S. Fifth Circuit. I hired her because I was mindful that blacks should have access to such jobs. But she could type like a house afire and was a computer expert. And that was the final requirement — that she could do the job.

42

W HENEVER THE MOOD in Montgomery began to get edgy over Johnson's desegregation orders, the U.S. Marshals would maintain a vigil at his house, keeping watch for hostile activity. Johnson's old friend, Pert Dodd, headed the security. FBI informants within the Ku Klux Klan had advised Johnson that on a number of occasions Klansmen had discussed the bombing of his house. So whenever such a report would come in — and they were quite regular during the mid-60s — the marshals would show up. They'd stay outside or patrol the neighborhood.

JOHNSON

So one day as the Montgomery school desegregation case was about to conclude and I was preparing to enter an order, a call came to my office. The man revealed his name and said he was employed by the State of Alabama as a meat cutter at Kilby Prison in Montgomery. "I want to tell you," he said, "if you desegregate Capitol Heights School, I'll kill you. I got a little daughter going there and I don't want any of those blacks going with her." So I said, "Mister, I'll tell you one thing: You're already in trouble for threatening me. Now you may have to get somebody else to take your little girl to school, because I'm fixing to desegregate it and you're liable to

be in the pen." Well, he was a little taken aback and I told
him to come on down to my office, that we'd talk about it.
After years of getting anonymous threats by phone or in
the mail, I wanted to see one of the persons eyeball-to-
eyeball. "I'll be right down," he said. When he arrived he
had calmed down and I gave him a little talk about the
Constitution and the rights of all people in this country.
He sat there listening. When he left, I gave him a pam-
phlet copy of the Constitution and he promised he'd read
it. I never heard from him again. He wasn't a Klansman.
At least his name wasn't on a list of KKK members that I
kept in my office. The roster gave the name, home address, the Klavern, and place of employment of each
Klansman. Many of them worked for the State of Alabama, the City of Montgomery and such reputable firms
as Southern Bell and the Alabama Power Company. I
don't mean they were executives, but rank-and-file types.
Friends have asked why I invited that man who threatened me to come to my office to talk. I suppose it's
something like when you're camping and a bear keeps
coming and getting your food. You have this desire to put
a light on him sometime and get a look at him.

Race was such a part of life in Alabama that sooner or later,
it seemed, every aspect of the state's government and lower
agencies showed up in Johnson's court. It became necessary for
him, singly or in a three-judge panel, to order reapportionment
of the state's voting districts when it was clear that black voting
strength was intentionally diluted. And the state's plan of denying welfare aid to a woman because of "immoral conduct" was
also challenged. Most of the women receiving aid to dependent
children were black, and most of the cutoffs were to women of
that race. He also had to order the desegregation of the state's
agricultural extension services.

He ordered the desegregation of the YMCA that had formed
a coalition with the city in Montgomery. Even the parks had to
be put under order. A woman named Georgia Gilmore came to
the court one day in 1963 and said her son was made to leave a
city park. Attorney Morris Dees took the case and filed it in

federal court. When Johnson ordered the City of Montgomery to cease its segregation practices, the city promptly closed the parks and covered the swimming pools. Even the zoo was closed. There's no law that says you have to have a park. But if you do, they are to be open to all, the judge said. In the 1970s, they reopened.

The Alabama State Troopers, like most other police agencies in the state, were all white. Johnson outlawed the discriminatory employment practices in the agency and directed them to hire 25 percent blacks, meaning they would hire one black for each white trooper until the 25 percent was achieved. He desegregated the state's employment ranks. In 1972 he became involved in one of the sex discrimination cases that were beginning to flower over the nation. The issue was whether a woman in military service could automatically get dependency pay for her husband the same way a male soldier received it for his wife. The Air Force said no. So First Lieutenant Sharron A. Frontiero sought a ruling on the matter in Johnson's court. She was stationed at Maxwell Air Force Base in Montgomery. Johnson sided with the lieutenant, saying in effect, that a military person is a military person, regardless of sex. The case was appealed. The Supreme Court saw things the same as Johnson.

It has been written that Johnson has never been reversed in a civil rights case. But that's not true. He lost one when blacks in Montgomery filed suit saying the local newspapers, the *Advertiser* and *Journal,* discriminated against them in their all-white society pages. Johnson held that the newspapers were private ventures not subject to the protection of civil rights laws. He ruled against the blacks. The Supreme Court reversed.

Hair also became a part of life in the late 1960s and early '70s. At Wetumpka, about fifteen miles north of Montgomery, the principal of the high school banned long hair for boys, citing a code that said they had to have short haircuts. Long hair, the official said, was a distraction in class because of the combing that was required. Students with long hair also were late for class, he said, because so much time was needed to put it in order. Johnson ruled for the students. Alabama, as a whole, was one of the states where the Vietnam War was staunchly backed. When Yale professor William Sloan Coffin, a vocal critic of the

war, was to speak at Auburn University, officials there blocked
the appearance. The American Civil Liberties Union filed a
hurried suit in Johnson's court. He heard the evidence and
promptly issued an order for the University to stand clear and
allow the man to speak.

JOHNSON

In the school cases that I heard during the years of
desegregation, the prime concern came down to the
welfare of the children. I've never believed the burden of
desegregating schools should be on them; rather, it should
be on the school officials. And while many have thought
of me as a judge who brought about "busing," nothing
could be farther from the truth.

Personally, I am against sending children long distances to achieve some racial balance. I don't think the
Constitution intended such, and I have never ordered it.
The only "busing" done in my district of Alabama was
limited distances for some students in Montgomery. Actually, it was less than had been before I ever became
involved in such cases. "Busing," is a socio-political term
that someone concocted in the 1960s. It means transport-
ing children of one race to a school where children of the
other race are in numerical superiority. In the days before *Brown*, however, many black students here in Alabama rode great distances in buses and were driven past
all-white schools. They were victims of "busing" to maintain segregation. My own feelings are that the student is
best served by attending the school nearest his home.
Most parents resent having their children sent to a re-
mote area of their school district. In my mind, busing to
achieve racial balance is simply not worth the price of the
potential disruption both to the school system and the
students themselves. In the Montgomery case, the American Friends Service Committee retained Howard Mandell
to look into what they viewed as weaknesses in my 1970
Montgomery order. Mandell, a former law clerk of mine,
filed suit in my court and I promptly turned him down. So
he filed an appeal to the U.S. Fifth Circuit. And they

upheld my decision. Mandell, a fine attorney, had a bad batting average in my court. He appealed five of my decisions by 1975, and lost them all. That should, I hope, bolster some confidence in the judicial system — that even being a former law clerk doesn't mean you'll win a case.

I had my telephone changed to an unlisted number for two reasons: One, to avoid the crank phone calls that were so common during the early years in the Civil Rights Movement; secondly, to keep attorneys from calling me at all hours. I felt it necessary to be careful about who I socialized with. On occasion, I will go fishing with an attorney, but there is a rule that we don't talk about litigation pending in my court. Mandell went fishing with me once, and he did real good for a while . . . kept the talk to the weather, the bugs, the kind of bait we were using, real fisherman's lingo. But somewhere along about the second or third hour or so, I noticed him edging the conversation toward a case that he had before me. So I started questioning about where he bought his fishing gear. Or I'd ask him if he wanted a chew of tobacco. He soon got the message. We might be friends, but a case is a case, and it's going to be heard in the courtroom.

43

THERE HAVE BEEN stories and personal testimonials to Johnson's harsh courtroom manner. Some probably have been true. He did not like and would not permit spectators to be coming and going during testimony. It was simply too much of a disturbance, he said. He expected attorneys to be on time.

JOHNSON

An attorney named Bo Torbert (who later became chief justice of the Alabama Supreme Court) once represented a client in a civil case in my court. The opposing attorney, Bob Wilson, had informed me that he had talked with Torbert and thought they could get together with me and reach a settlement. Well, Torbert never showed up for the conference. So we entered the courtroom and I called the jurors in. About that time Torbert comes walking in and comes up to me, says, "Judge, we think we can settle this." "We've already got the jury here ready to serve," I told him. "Tell you what. I'll give you ten minutes to reach a settlement. If you don't, we'll proceed. But either way, Mr. Torbert, you're going to pay these jurors . . . you, not the government."

Promptness was such a demand of Johnson's that one

lawyer faced a terribly embarrassing situation during a brief recess in a trial. The attorney was delayed several minutes to talk with his client. When he was able to break away, he hurried to the men's room.

While in the process of relieving his bladder, the door opened and a marshal called, "Court's back in session." The lawyer quickly tried to hold back and in doing so, managed to conspicuously wet the front of his trousers. It was such a thorough job that he agonized about remaining hidden in the rest room. But fearing something awful from the judge, he quickly removed his coat, held it folded in front of him, then boldly strode back into the courtroom. Then, to complete the charade, he made a grand show of spilling a glass of water into his lap as he sat down . . . thus covering the telltale signs of the abrupt ending. Under the circumstances, it was remarkably quick thinking, because it was his turn to stand and make his closing arguments.

Once, in Dothan, Ford Motor Company was being sued in a traffic accident case. The company attorney, James Novak, and Ford experts put a Ford engine up on a court table, a beautiful piece of mahogany furniture that had been there for several years. When they finally removed it, Johnson noticed some scratches on the table. Ford won the case, but before court adjourned, the judge told Mr. Novak: "That table has been scratched up pretty badly and I'm going to hold the Ford Motor Company responsible for refinishing it."

Novak hired a woodworker to do the job but Johnson didn't relieve the company of its obligation until he inspected the table himself.

During the Vietnam War a young man was facing trial for draft evasion. Three of the witnesses were members of the draft board from Bessemer, which lies about fifteen miles southwest of Birmingham. The court docket began on a Monday morning and Johnson began setting trial dates; the draft-evasion case was set for Wednesday morning. At that point one of the draft board members stood up and declared, "Judge, I'm a businessman in Bessemer and I have a business to run. I came to court today, but I won't be back on Wednesday. I'm a busy man."

JOHNSON

I stared at him for just a moment. He had been a little caustic in the way he had made the remark, and it was clear he wanted me to alter the entire court schedule to meet his needs. I turned to the U.S. Marshal nearby and said, "Take that man back there and show him the jail. And then make arrangements to assure that he will be here on Wednesday morning." As the marshal took the man to look over the jail, I turned my attention to the other two members of the draft board. "Now, do either of you gentlemen think you might have a problem being here on Wednesday morning?"

"No, sir, judge," they answered in unison. A few moments later the other man, the busy one, came back with the U.S. marshal and sent word up to me that he could be in court on Wednesday morning, despite his busy schedule. The story later got around that I had the man put in jail. I think telling him to go look at it got the point across well enough.

A young man pleaded guilty to a rather serious charge, one that could have landed him a visit to the federal prison. Johnson asked him if he had anything to say before pronouncing sentence on him. He very meekly asked if he could be placed on probation so he could work and support his baby. Johnson glanced back into the audience section and saw a young woman holding an infant.

"Is that your baby?" he asked.

"Yes, sir," he said.

"You married to her?"

"No, sir." The judge studied him for a moment, pondering it. Then, he said, "Tell you what: I'm going to continue your sentencing for two weeks. Then, you can come back and bring your *girlfriend* to watch me send you to the penitentiary. Or, you can come back and bring your *wife* to watch me give you probation." The young fellow nodded enthusiastically. Within the two-week span there was a wedding...

JOHNSON

Robert Kennedy, Jr., came to visit me in Montgomery in 1975 or so. He stayed over in Hayneville, in Lowndes County, for the better part of the year. One day he came by the office and told me he was writing a thesis about me; at the time he was a student at Harvard. He went back to Harvard sometime later and produced three hundred typewritten pages about my years on the bench in Alabama. So a year later he came by and said, "I turned in my paper on you." I was flattered, naturally, that anyone could write so much about me. "Well, how did you do with it?" I asked. "Did your professor like it?"

"He sent it back," Kennedy said.

"Sent it back? Why?"

"Said it was too long," he said. "Told me no southern judge is worth more than forty pages."

One of Johnson's most famous cases didn't raise any lofty or momentous issues at all. It was the so-called "peanuts case" that he presided over in the early 1960s. But scholars would recognize that it brought the light of the Fourteenth Amendment to bear on the issue of race in Alabama.

JOHNSON

It involved two black men and a white man. All three had been indicted on a charge of stealing peanuts from a federal commodity warehouse. So they came to trial and a jury was empaneled. But before we could get the thing started these two blacks get up and tell me they're both guilty. Told me the white guy had put them up to stealing peanuts for him. Well, I believed them and held off sentencing them until the trial for the white was held. The white had entered a plea of not guilty. So it turned out that the jury was all white. They heard the evidence and returned a verdict of not guilty. Something about the whole thing just seemed unfair to me. I wasn't supposed to be giving opinions, but as a judge I was expected to see that justice was done. Sometimes that involves balancing the scales of justice, you might say. When the jury turned that white man loose, I just told them to remain in their seats for a while and I had the marshals bring in the two black men who had already pleaded guilty. Now, in my mind, if they were guilty, so was the white man. And if he was not guilty, neither were they. But I couldn't undo the fact that they had already said they were guilty. So right in front of the jury I imposed sentence on them. I remember them standing in front of me and the jury was there watching and I said in a solemn voice, "I'm sentencing each of you two defendants to a total of thirty minutes in the custody of the U.S. Marshal. Court is adjourned."

Well, one of the marshals comes up and asks what's to be done with the two men for thirty minutes, and I says, "Go get them a cup of coffee or something." I felt it was the fair thing to do. I suppose if the white guy had been found guilty then I would have probably been a little heavier on them.

44

I N AUGUST 1977, PRESIDENT Jimmy Carter nominated
Johnson to be the director of the FBI. The judge had some
ideas about the agency, and crime in general. He wanted to
bring agents from the Alcohol, Tobacco, and Firearms bureau
and throw them into the fight against drugs. He felt those agents
were spending too much time looking for moonshine stills,
when the major problem was drugs. But after the Johnsons had
sold their house, their plans to go to Washington were jarred
when a routine medical checkup revealed a blood vessel in the
judge's stomach had swollen, and was in danger of bursting.
The resulting surgery and recovery took more time than he had
anticipated, and before the end of the year, he notified Carter
that he was withdrawing his name from consideration.

By early 1979 Johnson's health improved and he began
taking long walks again, wearing combat boots. While he did
not especially want to leave Montgomery, he was receptive to a
change in status. In the springtime President Jimmy Carter
once again brought Johnson's name forth in nomination, this
time as a member of the U.S. Fifth Circuit Court of Appeals.
While the Fifth was based in New Orleans, Johnson could
maintain his residence in Montgomery. His confirmation was
little more than a formality, and in July, 1979, after twenty-four
years as a federal district trial judge, he took his oath as a
member of the Fifth Circuit. The Alabama Bar Association

noted that the change was "like the old infantry soldier who knows it's time to pull back off the line."

When President Eisenhower nominated him to be United States Attorney in 1953 and two years later to be the United States District Judge in Montgomery, Johnson was required to pass muster before the United States Senate, first before the Judiciary Committee and later the full Senate. But it was always done by long distance and he did not have to go to Washington and undergo lengthy questioning. But in 1979, when President Carter nominated him to the U.S. Fifth Circuit Court of Appeals, he was asked to go to Washington and appear before the Judiciary Committee, chaired by Senator Edward M. Kennedy. A visit to Washington in May seemed inviting enough. Ruth and he were going to Boston where he was to speak at Boston University and receive an honorary degree; stopping by to see Washington fit into the plans. The hearing was to be held May 16 at 9:30 a.m. at the Dirksen Senate Office Building. Another nominee, Delores K. Sloviter, was present; she was named to the Third Circuit Court of Appeals in Philadelphia. Kennedy started out by saying some nice things about both of them, then yielded to Senator Donald Stewart of Alabama, a Democrat, who began with: "I must say, Mr. Chairman, that this is the first time that I ever supported a Republican. It may well be the last." There was laughter.

Stewart continued his kind remarks:

"Frank Johnson, I respectfully submit, merits the support of both Republicans and Democrats. I am sure that Judge Johnson, as you said, is no stranger to the members of this committee, or to you. You are aware of his reputation. You know that he was nominated to the Director of the FBI. I am certain you are aware of the many landmark decisions that he has authored during his time on the court, in Alabama. With your permission, Mr. Chairman, members of the committee, I would like to talk very briefly about Frank Johnson from another point of view, as seen by an Alabamian and an attorney. I practiced law in the northern district of Alabama, so I never had the opportunity or the privilege to appear before Judge Johnson. Having talked many, many times with attorneys who have appeared before Judge Johnson, I have heard two words mentioned about him more than any others.

"Those are 'fairness' and 'courage.' Every attorney knows that he will be treated fairly in Judge Johnson's courtroom, for Frank Johnson has no favorites. He demands equal amounts from counsel on both sides. The lawyer and his client get a fair hearing with every opportunity to present their case and to prove their case. After all the evidence has been heard, the opinion handed down from Judge Johnson will be fair. I have heard many lawyers who disagreed, as lawyers do from time to time with judge's opinions, about Judge Johnson's opinions. They use many words to describe him, as lawyers have a habit of doing from time to time, but never have I heard a lawyer describe Judge Johnson's opinion as being unfair. The other word used to describe Judge Johnson is 'courageous.' He has handled the most difficult, the most controversial and the most explosive cases to be heard in Alabama during the last twenty years. During this time, Judge Johnson has never backed away from a case. After hearing a case, the judge handed down what he believed to be the correct decision, no matter the consequences for him or his family as a result of that decision. Many people might have disagreed with some of his decisions. There are few Alabamians who do not respect Judge Johnson for his courage. Many people talk of justice. Judge Frank Johnson, as a judge, has practiced that throughout his life on the bench. It is my privilege and honor and pleasure to join with my colleague in presenting him to the committee, this morning."

Senator Kennedy nodded. "Thank you very much, Senator Stewart."

Kennedy then turned to Senator Howell Heflin, a big man with thick brown hair and bushy eyebrows. "Senator Heflin."

Heflin, who had been Chief Justice of the Alabama Supreme Court, had been a friend of Johnson's for years and spoke of him with great eloquence, telling of the stock from which Johnson had sprung in the "Free State of Winston," his family, his military record, his marriage to Ruth Jenkins, and his years as a judge.

"Judge Johnson's career as a jurist is well known and well

documented," said Heflin. "He was appointed to the federal bench on November 7, 1955, by President Eisenhower, and at the age of thirty-seven, he was the country's youngest federal judge. He has been described, accurately I believe, as the most influential, innovative, and controversial trial judge in the United States." When he concluded, Senator Kennedy beamed and shook his head. "Judge Johnson, that was quite a sendoff," he said. There was laughter and then Kennedy asked the judge if he had any comments he would like to make.

Johnson grinned. "Senator Kennedy," he said, "I would be perfectly willing to stand on the statements made by our two senators from Alabama." There was laughter again. Later he said, "I should make one correction, Senator Kennedy. Mrs. Johnson and I have not been married as long as the Senator indicated." He thought that should be on the record. Kennedy and Heflin laughed, and Ruth chuckled. Even before any questioning began, Johnson was told by Kennedy that his nomination was a near certainty. Johnson knew he had his support, as well as that of Heflin and Stewart, but he did not know about some of the more conservative senators, such as Orrin Hatch of Utah, Strom Thurmond of South Carolina, or Alan Simpson of Wyoming. Simpson was on the panel that day, representing the conservative side of the committee, and the judge waited for his questions or statements. They were surprisingly mild.

"Judge Johnson, your reputation precedes you here," Simpson said.

He continued: "Obviously, you are a man of rare judicial temperament. I have watched you from afar, and Wyoming is certainly from afar in connection with your activity. You have certainly had a very active role in the judiciary and in the life and times of Alabama and the nation also. I think you are extremely well-qualified. I think I would say that from what has become a very serious review at the instruction of our good chairman, Senator Kennedy, and those of us on the committee and Senator Thurmond, the ranking minority member. I would have to say that of all the judicial appointees, your qualifications seem to outshine them all in my mind. I think that I have some questions that have been submitted by other members of the minority, and if I might, I would submit those to you. They are in writing and you might just respond to them in writing at your earliest convenience. As for myself, Judge, I think the only possible question I have — and it comes with mixed admiration and interest — is your role or your view of the role of what we refer to in the trade as 'judicial policy making.' Would you just review that in your own words? I have read your very interesting comments. They are very, very deft and very appropriate and very understandable, but if you would just please review that role as you define that role."

Johnson nodded. "Well, with regards to policy making as such and in the popular sense of the term, federal judges have no business being in the policy making business. As a fallout from decisions that courts find it necessary to make once a case and controversial question is established, once standing is established . . . as a fallout from that, it would be less than candid for me to say, and I think any judge to say, that important judicial decisions do not have some basis for forming policy. That goes back from the time that *Marbury* against *Madison* was decided in 1803, and *McCullouch* against *Maryland* in 1819 and *Gibbons* against *Ogden*.

"All of those cases formed policy: *Brown* against *Board of Education*, *Dred Scott* decision . . . . All of them formed some public policy, but that was a fallout and that wasn't the reason for the decision of the court. If any of the cases I decided had the effect of forming policy in any sense, then it was a fallout from the decisions that the lawsuit required. That wasn't the business of the court in making the decision."

Simpson nodded. "I appreciate that very much. I think we do think of those things as policy making, and perhaps there are things that are long overdue that get labeled that and that may be one of the definition problems. I commend you, sir. It is a pleasure to see you here. It is a pleasure to see a man of your caliber present himself."

Before the hearing concluded, Senator Heflin made note of the presence of one of Johnson's former law clerks, Edward Ashworth, who had heard that Johnson was coming to Washington and had telephoned earlier to invite Judge and Mrs. Johnson to his wedding. In fact, he asked if Johnson would officiate. Only a few states and the District of Columbia authorize federal judges to preside at a wedding. Said Senator Heflin of Ashworth, "He is going to be perhaps a victim of Judge Johnson, if I could describe it. Federal judges do not have the opportunity very often to marry individuals. I think—"

"Perform the ceremony," Johnson injected.

Heflin looked at him. Then he grinned and repeated, "Perform the ceremony." Kennedy and Simpson broke into laughter. Heflin, nodding emphatically, said, "Yes."

Kennedy, still laughing, glanced at Heflin, saying, "I see the clarity of wisdom of words."

Heflin concluded with, "So today he will perform the marriage ceremony of Mr. Ashworth. I thought it was a little unusual. I would bring it to your attention."

"Well, now our record is complete for the day," said Kennedy. That evening, Johnson did perform the ceremony for Eddie and his fiancee, Priscilla Parish. After the hearing, Simpson came down to Johnson and shook hands. Then, his voice low, he confided, "Judge, I'm not going to bother you with any written questions. I just said that. Everything is fine."

Johnson was confirmed as a Judge of the U.S. Fifth Circuit Court of Appeals.

45

I N 1979, THE U.S. FIFTH Circuit was reorganized and the
Eleventh Circuit was created, which was composed of Alabama, Georgia, and Florida. While it narrowed the territory,
it did little to ease the huge number of death sentence appeals
that were before the court. There were more such cases in the
Eleventh Circuit than any other circuit in the nation.

JOHNSON

My personal view of the death sentence tells me that
the taking of a human life for retribution, or for a deter-
rent effect, or any other deliberate reason, is contrary to
my basic moral concepts. I have always believed that. But
moral concepts are not the last word when a judge does
his duty. There is nothing in the Constitution, as it has
consistently been interpreted, that opposes capital punishment as such. It would prohibit it if it was to be carried
out in an arbitrary or cruel and inhuman manner, which
would violate the provisions of the Eighth Amendment or
the due process clause of the Fourteenth Amendment.
Thus, in cases where a state court has imposed a death
penalty, the role of federal judges has been to ensure that
the penalty was not being applied in violation of the
constitutional principles that have been evolved through
the years. If it did not violate these constitutional prin-

ciples, then it fell on the federal judge to decide the cases
without regards to his or her personal feelings. In that
respect, it would be like other cases that are before a
judge. During my stay on the federal bench, roughly
thirty-three years, the membership of the Supreme Court
changed, and so did the Court's interpretation of law. The
decision I made in 1965, allowing the march from Selma
to Montgomery, might not have been favorably received
by the justices in 1980. I believe that had I made that
decision in 1980, I would not have relaxed with the same
confidence I felt in 1965 under the Court which was then
headed by Chief Justice Earl Warren. The Supreme Court
of the 1970s and early 1980s, under the leadership of
Chief Justice Warren Burger, tightened up on some issues with which I did not personally agree. I was even
more at odds with the Court's decisions on pornography,
some of which I felt were ridiculous. In my opinion, they
violate my concept of the First Amendment. I believe any
mature adult should have an unfettered constitutional
right to see, read or view any book or paper or magazine
he chooses. I do not think that local police, or state police
or federal police, or any judiciary officer or school board
member, have a right to tell a mature, consenting adult
what he or she can and cannot read.

But that is not the status of the law, which states that
any work that appeals to the prurient interests and has no
redeeming social values when measured by the standards of the community, can be censored. That ruling is
about as ambiguous as I have seen. In earlier years, in the
1960s for instance, the Supreme Court's view on such
matters was more liberal and I ruled on some cases. An
example was a ninth-grade teacher in the Montgomery
County School System who was fired because she let her
students read Kurt Vonnegut's *Monkey House*, which I
think is a contemporary classic. I ordered her reinstated.
Another time the Montgomery city police went on a
censorship jag and stalked about book stores and news-
stands looking at the magazines to see if they saw any
pictures of naked women. Well, they did and confiscated

books and magazines from a man named Poullas who owned one such store. He came to court and I enjoined the police. But I did order Mr. Poullas to agree to put up a partition where the oglers could view the books, but the customers of a tender age would be excluded.

In 1986, as a member of the U.S. 11th Circuit Court ofAppeals, Johnson sat on a panel with Judge Lanier Anderson of Macon, Georgia, and Judge Tom Clark of Atlanta, Georgia, in one of the most brutal murder cases in Southern history. It involved the killings of five members of the Ned Alday family near the town of Donaldsonville, Georgia. The men arrested in the case were escapees from the Maryland prison system; the leader of the group was Carl Isaac. All were tried in Donaldsonville, even though the defense attorneys had wanted the trials moved. The men were convicted and sentenced to death.

JOHNSON

On appeal, our panel agreed that defendants are entitled to a fair trial. We ordered the State of Georgia to retry them at other locales in Georgia, away from Donaldsonville, where there had been so much emotion surrounding the trials. Our decision drew the greatest outpouring of anger I have encountered from any case, including some of the explosive racial hearings in Montgomery. People in Georgia wanted us impeached, and some wished the same fate on us as had befallen the Alday family. It was a heinous crime and even though I was personally (but not judicially) opposed to the death penalty, I felt that if you are going to have capital punishment, this was the case that would have justified it. Yet, even in such a shocking and brutal crime, I believed the defendants should be entitled to a fair trial. The other two judges agreed with me that the defendants had not received a fair trial because of the publicity in the area around Donaldsonville, Georgia. But when the men had been tried in Donaldsonville it was later revealed that one of the jurors in one of the cases had been a distant relative of one of the victims. In our system, you can't have that. As long as I can read and understand the Constitution, I'll have to rule as I did. And if a judge can't follow the Constitution, he had better quit. We sent it back for the State of Georgia to change the location of the trials. Carl Isaac was later convicted again and sentenced to death, but the other two were given sentences of life without parole. In another death penalty case which had above-average public interest, I was on a panel with Judges Phyllis Kravitch and Robert Vance of Birmingham, and we received another outburst as we stayed an execution.

That was the case of Theodore R. Bundy, convicted of three murders in Florida. Bundy had filed an appeal asking that his 1978 conviction be set aside because he was not competent to stand trial in 1980. Bundy had been charged in the death of twelve-year-old Kimberly Leach of Lake City, Florida. We stayed the 1986 execution pending our review of his claim that he had not been competent to stand trial. He and his attorneys submitted a fifteen-point argument, all of which we rejected in 1986. Bundy's own actions proved his undoing. While advancing the argument that he was incompetent, his own words showed just the reverse. A tape of him during the original trial showed him making an argument before the trial judge. In the tape, Bundy delivers a cogent, well-reasoned argument. He could be seen flipping pages of a legal pad as he went through his argument. The tapes made by Bundy while awaiting the verdict and shortly after the verdict demonstrated that he had a rational understanding of the proceedings. If I had been a law-maker instead of a judge, I would have worked to end the death penalty, because I feel it is morally reprehensible. In both the Alday and Bundy murder cases, I had voted to stay the planned executions because I believed strongly that you cannot make a mistake in a death penalty case. A judge cannot afford to make a mistake. If the execution goes forth and a mistake is later found, you don't have a chance to rectify it. You can't bring a dead man back. If you're going to make a mistake, a legal mistake, you should make it on the side of granting a stay. That way, the person lives until the air can be cleared. If a legal mistake is made by that procedure, then no harm is done. The convicted murderer is still alive and the death sentence can be carried out.

Johnson later authored the opinion that resulted in Bundy being executed.

46

I N TWENTY-FOUR YEARS as a district court judge, Johnson heard literally thousands of cases and thought he had
come across just about every possible complaint that could
be filed under law. But then, in August 1982, as a member of the
Eleventh Circuit Court of Appeals, he heard the case of Blackie
the Talking Cat.

Blackie's owners, Carl and Elaine Miles, filed suit in federal
district court challenging the City of Augusta's right to force
them to buy a city license. The Mileses had been obtaining
"contributions" from persons on the streets of that Georgia city
who stopped to hear Blackie say a few words, such as "I love
you." The gist of their argument was that they were not really
selling anything, and that donations were not the same as a sale
of an item.

Further, they contended that to force them to purchase a
business license for fifty dollars violated Blackie's right to free
speech under the Bill of Rights. Also, the Mileses argued that
the city ordinance did not cover talking animals. The legal
argument was not at all novel, but the idea of a talking cat was a
change of pace.

At no time was Blackie's unusual ability at issue before the
court. U.S. District Judge Dudley H. Bowen Jr., in fact, in his
opinion, declared that he, himself, had heard Blackie purr, "I
love you" as he had encountered the cat one day in downtown

Augusta. But the judge, nonetheless, felt the city had a right to doggedly insist that the Mileses buy a city license.

JOHNSON

They appealed to the Eleventh Circuit and that's how the case came to me. I studied the testimony and related evidence along with Circuit Judges Tjoflat and Hatchett. We agreed on our findings and the matter of writing the opinion fell to me. But in doing so, I first had to make some background notes on the case. Blackie, it seemed, had been purchased by Mr. Miles in South Carolina, and, according to his testimony, the kitten was talking by the time it was six months old. Such a talent could not be contained and soon Blackie was appearing on local television shows and ultimately was a guest on a national TV show called, "That's Incredible." The public's affection for Blackie was the catalyst for his fame.

In the written opinion, I noted: "Sadly, Blackie's cataclysmic rise to fame crested and began to subside." That's when the Mileses moved to Augusta and put Blackie on display in the streets. Then came the police warning to buy a license. The couple paid the fifty-dollar fee, but filed suit. We judges had no choice but to categorically rule for the city. The contributions were clearly payment to hear the cat speak. When money was not paid, the evidence showed, Blackie would become catatonic and not utter a word. As to the claim of a violation of Blackie's right to free speech, the opinion declared: "This Court will not hear a claim that Blackie's right to free speech has been infringed. First, although Blackie arguably possesses a very unusual ability, he cannot be considered a 'person' and is therefore not protected by the Bill of Rights. Second, even if Blackie had such a right, we see no need for (the Mileses) to assert his rights *jus tertii*. Blackie can clearly speak for himself."

While it was the civil rights cases heard by Johnson that captured most of the attention of the press in the early sixties,

there were occasionally other legal matters before the federal
courts that sometimes earned some reportorial ink. One was
known as the "Ha-Ha" case that Johnson heard on November
13, 1962. Mrs. Peggy Grau had filed the complaint against the
Proctor & Gamble Company, charging that its toothpaste, Crest,
had caused her lips to be irritated and swell. This unfortunate
development, she contended, occurred as she and her new
husband left for their honeymoon. The company hired Montgomery attorney James Garrett to defend it and during the
course of the trial Garrett made known his derision by occasionally emitting a "ha" sound from the corner of his mouth.

JOHNSON

A shrewd lawyer, Garrett was polished in the way he
did it, sort of shift about in his chair, turn his head to one
side and give the "ha" or the "ha-ha" so as to make it
appear he might have been trying to clear his throat. It
wasn't outright laughter, something that I could have
called him down for, but it was being done so effectively
that at one point one of the jurors even rejoined with a
"ha" of his own. Well, all the while the court reporter,
Glynn Henderson, was taking down every word, including Garrett's "ha-has." As the case progressed, it became
clear that Mrs. Grau's complaint did not have much teeth
in it, and at the request of Garrett, I directed the jury to
enter a ruling in favor of the defendants, Proctor & Gamble.

So ended the case. But Mrs. Grau decided to enter an
appeal to the U.S. Fifth Circuit so court reporter Henderson had
the transcript of the trial typed up and copies made, which were
sent to the parties and to the Fifth Circuit on January 8, 1963. In
typing the transcript, Henderson included Garrett's "ha-ha"
sounds. Garrett read it and quickly filed a motion to have those
portions of the transcript struck from the record.

The exact portion of the document he wanted struck was as
follows: Page 24: MR. GARRETT: "Ha, ha, ha, ha." Page 42: MR.
GARRETT: "Ha, ha, ha." Page 74: MR. GARRETT: "Ha, ha."
Page 82: MR. GARRETT: "Ha, ha, ha." Page 106: MR. GARRETT:
"Ha, ha, ha, ha." JUROR: "Ha, ha, ha." In his motion, Garrett

wrote that although he and the juror may have made some sound at such times, that it was an inadvertent mannerism, such as a person coughing, clearing his throat or otherwise "making a sound." He said including the "ha-ha" sounds would clutter the record. Johnson studied the matter and on February 1, 1963, mirthfully entered an order which read in part:

> Those who know the Honorable James Garrett, Attorney at Law, who was, according to the record, doing all of the "ha, haing," would hesitate long and deliberate seriously before suggesting that he is not a highly competent practitioner of the law. As is generally true in the case of successful trial lawyers, Mr. Garrett is a past master in the art of suggestive psychology. His long and active experience in trial work enables him to practice with proficiency this art of suggesting through the use of auditory stimulation. He undeniably demonstrated this art of using the hypnotoxin of laughter in the trial of this civil action. When this art is practiced as Mr. Garrett practices it, it is with finesse and without reflecting a lack of respect for the witness, for the opposing counsel, or for the Court. The proficiency of Mr. Garrett in the use of this art is vividly demonstrated by at least one juror (page 105) joining him in his "ha, ha, has." (T)his Court recognizes that the reporter has, in this instance, taken the liberty of interpreting the noises made by the parties to whom they are attributed. There is question but that these parties were, on the occasions indicated, showing some mirth, satisfaction, or derision by a peculiar movement of the facial muscles and, further, were emitting some explosive or chuckling sounds by the exercise of the vocal cords. The interpretation of these sounds whether they be considered in the courtroom or to the appellate court as amusing, humorous, merry, facetious, waggish or sportive is not the appellant's or the appellees' prejudice. For the reasons herein expressed, it is ordered that the motion of the defendant appellees filed herein on January 22, 1963, seeking to have this Court strike and eliminate certain portions of the record as made and filed by the official court reporter herein on January 8, 1963, be and the same is hereby denied.

47

I N THE MID-1970S THE FBI agents and U.S. Marshals who
had guarded Johnson's house were withdrawn, a certain
sign that racial feelings in Alabama had subsided. But he
still had some inhouse protection in his dogs. He always had a
dog around. The first ones were Great Danes, which grew to be
close to two hundred pounds each. He named them Angus,
Hannibal, Shalamar. In 1982 he purchased a Doberman pin-
scher and named him Nebuchadnezzer, or Neb, for short. He
only weighed eighty-six pounds, but he seemed as good as the
others, and even more alert.

JOHNSON

When we got Neb I'd bring him in to the house at
night and he'd lay there on the den floor by Ruth's chair.
If he heard a sound that seemed the least bit unusual, his
ears would come up and he'd sit up and listen. If he heard
it again, he'd go into the kitchen to the back door and go
outside and check things out. Then, he'd come back in,
things being all well outside, and sit there looking at me.
I guess if it was after nine o'clock at night he'd wonder if
I was going to go to bed or sit there and fall asleep in my
chair. Neb is not only an alert dog, but a dedicated one as
well, and once put his life on the line for me. Ruth and I
had bought a house at Lake Martin and one hot day in

June, 1984, we went up there to clear some of the brush around the place. There were a lot of vines hanging down from the big oak and persimmon trees, and the brambles along the shore was heavy and laced with poison ivy. I was walking down near the boat pier with Neb when all of a sudden he started whining and running in front of me. He had spotted something and whatever it was, it had him alarmed. I stopped and looked but didn't see what it was. But suddenly Neb let out a yelp and I saw him backing up a few inches, then lunge forward again.

That's when I saw the snake, a thick, ugly water moccasin that appeared to be about as long as a coffee table, five-feet or so. I called for Neb to get back, but he wouldn't listen. He kept making short lunges, barking and yelping at the same time. The snake was coiled with its head held high in the attack position. I called again for Neb to back away. Then the snake lashed out and Neb let out an anguished whine. I saw blood on his nose. But he kept ignoring my shouts and kept after the snake. I was afraid that the dog might die, as it was plain he had been bitten. I had a .22 caliber rifle for the express purpose of shooting snakes, but it was back at the house. All I had with me was a spray can of WD-40. I held it up and sent a shot of spray which missed the snake but hit Neb in the face. That got him backed away from the snake. He must have wondered whose side I was on. But he backed up enough so that I could get hold of him and drag him back. Then I ran him to the house where I got the rifle. I ran back to the place but the moccasin was gone. Ruth and I got Neb into the car and sped back to Montgomery. He was glassy-eyed and I feared for his life. A moccasin can kill a man with one bite and Neb had suffered several it seemed. We took him to an emergency animal clinic and the veterinarian gave him a shot. Then he told us to take him home and let him rest.

Neb slept the rest of the day then laid around for part of the following week. Then, along about the following Wednesday or so, he got up and was suddenly his old self. He had escaped and was in remarkably good shape,

The Johnsons enjoyed relaxing at their cabin on Lake Martin, about forty-five minutes north of Montgomery. Their Doberman, Neb, was a constant companion from 1982 on. The Judge seldom took his work home with him, and learned to relax by fishing or working in his wood craft shop.

none the worse for the experience.

A few weeks later, I went back up to the lake and took Neb with me. I had my twelve-gauge Remington shotgun and a can of gasoline. The idea was to find a snake hole and pour the gas into it, then back off and wait for the moccasins to come out and then catch them with a volley, blowing them to kingdom come. But after trying a couple of holes it was clear the snakes were not at home, but probably out in the water cooling off. About that time I glanced out into the water and there, about five yards from shore, was a big snake curled up around a log that protruded above the surface.

I could tell that it wasn't the big varmint that had bitten Neb. It wasn't quite as long, but it was still a big one, all right, about as thick as the other one and just as ugly. He had spotted me, too, and his head was raised a few inches off the log. I put the gasoline can down, raised the shotgun, took aim and squeezed the trigger. Neb jumped from the sound. The blast took part of the log with it, knocking pieces into the air. And the snake flew up, too. "There you go, Neb," I said. "There's one snake that's not going to bite you." I found a long pole, snared the carcass and brought it to shore, holding it up for the dog to see. But Neb wouldn't even look at it; he just turned away. I guess he wanted another live one to tangle with.

In the mid-1960s, Mrs. Johnson, who was busy during the day teaching school, decided she wanted to earn her masters degree. She enrolled at Alabama State, one of the state's black colleges. When she told her husband she had signed up there, he shrugged and said he thought it was a fine idea.

JOHNSON

Ruth just wanted to be another student, but Levi Watkins Sr., the president, heard about it and came over to her on one of the first nights and rolled out the red carpet. As it is at any college, parking is a problem, but President Watkins took the issue by the horns, telling

Ruth, "When you come here and can't find a parking place, you can use my personal one if I'm not in it." One night later she drove onto the campus and, sure enough, there wasn't a parking place within a mile. So she spotted Watkins' private parking lot and pulled in there.

While she was at class, the campus police cruised by and saw the car in the space reserved for Watkins. They towed it away. When Ruth got out of class about nine o'clock she saw that her car was gone and went to the campus police station. When she told them her car was gone, the officer told her what had happened. Then he informed her: "It'll cost you twenty-five dollars to get it out." Her Irish temper hit the roof. "I'm not paying twenty-five dollars," she said. "President Watkins told me I could park anywhere on campus." "He didn't mean his private parking space," the officer said. "He said I could park there if it was empty," she shot back, then proceeded to give him a good tongue lashing. About that time the poor officer got on the telephone and called Watkins at home. Soon, he was nodding his head and saying, "Yes sir, yes sir." Then he handed the phone to Ruth. On the other end was Watkins, who apologized profusely. Meanwhile the officer was hurrying out the door, saying to my wife, "I'm getting your car, ma'am. I'm getting your car."

Once while in Florida, Ruth and some friends wanted to show me the high fashion shopping section of West Palm Beach. Since I was in the market for a new belt, I decided to go with them. We went to Worth Avenue, the most affluent collection of shops in the world. Fifth Avenue in New York can't compare. You saw Rolls-Royces and Cadillacs double-parked with chauffeurs waiting. I just wasn't impressed. The most pretentious of all was a place called Gucci's. They had a garden with fountains gushing water, manicured shrubs, automatic perfume emitters and all sorts of things. There was a gold-colored Rolls-Royce parked in this little garden. Inside the decor was flawless; the carpeting was thick and you couldn't tell a sales person from a mannequin. I told Ruth I didn't care for the place at all but she told me it was the ultimate store to shop. "All I need is a belt to hold up my britches," I said. So she found a revolving rack that must have had a thousand belts on it and I started looking at them. Two things got me: The least expensive I found was sixty dollars, and all of them had the letter "G" on the buckle.

So I went over to one of the mannequins and asked, "Don't you have any belts cheaper than sixty dollars?" He raised his eyebrows and stared at me as though I had intruded into sacred space. "Also I want one without the letter 'G' stamped on it," I added. "Perhaps you can find a cheaper belt down the street somewhere," he said, speaking in a nasally tone. Then he turned and walked away. Well, I just can't stand being snubbed and talked down to by a phony aristocrat. I followed him across the store and when he got to where there was a little crowd of customers, I reached out and tapped him on the shoulder. He turned around, an expression of snobby surprise on his face. "Yes," he said. In my loudest, most hillbillyish voice, I asked, "Hey, y'all got a spittoon around this place?" The frozen expression on his face didn't change. I grinned at him a moment, then turned and walked out.

He has been called a "tobacco-chewing, whisky-drinking iconoclast."

48

FRANK JOHNSON'S LONE battle on the civil rights firing line did not go without due note from the press, the American academic community, or, most importantly, from his peers. In 1967, he became the first federal judge to make the cover of *Time* Magazine, a drawing which he said resembled "a mule chewing on a mouthful of briars." By then, most major newspapers had carried stories about him, the majority zeroing in on the Selma-to-Montgomery march case. He avoided reporters and was never seen in a television interview. But he kept abreast of what the press was saying. Once, a bemused Johnson read an account in the *Atlanta Constitution* which described him as a "tobacco-chewing, whisky-drinking iconoclast." The judge gazed at the article for a moment then asked an office visitor, "What's an iconoclast?" When the visitor expresssed ignorance, Johnson began thumbing through a dictionary. After a few seconds of study, he read aloud that iconclast meant "one who breaks sacred images." He chuckled, then said, "Well, they got that part right."

Johnson's honors were extensive. Just about every spring some major university was presenting him an honorary doctorate or special award. Notre Dame was first in 1973, followed by Princeton, St. Michael's College, of Winooski, Vermont, the University of Alabama, Mississippi State University, Boston University, Yale, Tuskegee Institute and New York University.

But perhaps the most rewarding honor came in November, 1984, when Johnson was selected as the recipient of the Devitt Distinguished Service to Justice Award. Scores of nominations had poured in to the selection committee, headed by U.S. Supreme Court Justice Lewis F. Powell Jr. A young attorney from Birmingham, Dayle Powell, no kin to Justice Powell, took the lead in mounting the drive to nominate Johnson. "He's my hero," she said simply.

It would appear he was a hero to others as well: U.S. Circuit Judge Irving Goldberg of the Fifth Circuit wrote, "Judge Johnson has not only been a great jurist, he has also been a watchman of our judicial conscience." He later added, "It is rare when one leaves Frank Johnson's presence without being cleansed of error and purged of any judicial sin that he was about to commit. He is an idealist, but at the same time, a man of practical ways. He upholds his moral code without sanctimony. He epitomizes dignity without pretense." And still later in the nomination letter, Goldberg wrote: "Judge Johnson never surrendered to consensus in order to achieve a majority. He stood his ground as a soldier would. Judge Johnson demonstrates that a great judge is more than a scholar, a student, a writer. He is fearless in his defiance of injustice. He cabins no prejudices, but he is brigaded with convictions."

John C. Godbold, the chief judge of the U.S. Eleventh Circuit, wrote in nomination, "No judge in America stood on a hotter firing line than did Judge Johnson as a district judge. But never ducking, never flinching or faltering, he quietly carried out what the Constitution and laws of the United States require of all of us, without counting heads to see who approved and who did not." "No more courageous judge ever lived," wrote U.S. District Judge Foy Guin Jr., of Birmingham. "His strong resolution and clear-eyed navigation using the Constitution as his pole star led him to sail through the roughest of seas but without ever veering off course. He stayed the course, no matter what. In my judgment, to honor Frank Johnson is to honor the entire federal judiciary, for he exemplifies its ideals."

A former law clerk of Johnson's, Walter Turner, also wrote a nominating letter. Then Chief Assistant Attorney General of Alabama, he recalled seeing Martin Luther King, Jr., in the hallway of the federal courthouse in Montgomery during a break in the Selma-to-Montgomery hearing. Speaking of the judge, King had said, "He is one man who gives true meaning to the word 'justice.'"

And perhaps the most touching of all the nominations came from another former law clerk of the judge's, Sonia Jarvis, managing attorney for the Center for National Policy Review in Washington. "As a young black girl growing up in the South during the early '60s," she wrote, "I needed a role model such as the Judge to help me sustain my belief that someday our government would become more responsive to the needs of all members of society. Because Judge Johnson was able to demonstrate through his impeccable legal scholarship that the Constitution did indeed include women, minorities, the poor and handicapped within its protection, he has helped to transform that belief into reality." She then concluded, "If it is possible, I left my clerkship with even more respect for Judge Johnson than when I began."

49

DURING THE EMOTIONAL tumult of the Civil Rights Movement, Johnson shunned the press and never used it as a means of responding to the salvos fired at him by George Wallace. He would not grant interviews and seldom even talked to reporters.The main reason for that, he said, was simply that judges are not to discuss active cases with the press. But there was another reason.

JOHNSON

In the days of the Civil Rights Movement the press in Alabama was to a large extent anti-federal government and very much pro-segregation. And to a great extent I feel the Alabama news media was responsible for the hysteria and passion that flared among the white people. Some were nothing but race-baiters. They were reactionary and I would not grant an interview to a reporter who would go back to the newspaper and turn around what I might have said. I'm not the smartest person in the world, but I knew better than that. I saw the biased, prejudiced reporting. I think this reactionary feeling among the newspapers of the state was at its peak from about 1961, when the Freedom Riders were in the news, to 1965, when the voting rights drive was on in Selma and other Black Belt counties. But it was interesting to see how the press — not to mention the politicians — became more objective once blacks got the right to vote. Then, they held blacks and their demonstrations in a somewhat different light. After all, blacks were now political equals. After the Selma-to-Montgomery march and passage of the Voting Rights Act of 1965, the media became more fair and I did on occasion grant interviews. But even before that period there were some notable reporters in the state, among them Ray Jenkins of the *Alabama Journal* in Montgomery, who was an exceptionally fair and impartial observer of events that took place. But others were easy to turn down. And they were not all Alabama reporters, either. In the late 1970s, CBS sent its *60 Minutes* crew to Montgomery to interview me, but when I learned it was Mike Wallace who wanted the interview, I rejected the request. I just do not have any respect for his brand of reporting. On the other hand, Bill Moyers of National Public Television was a man I respected and I did grant him an extensive interview for a two-hour televised program.

By the mid-1980s, Johnson was beginning to take a look back at his years on the federal bench and someone asked if he missed being a trial judge, hearing cases on the first level of the federal judiciary. He missed it, he said. Then, he was asked if he missed hearing the civil rights cases, the ones that created such a clamor, so much hate and anger. Johnson laughed. "I miss them the way a kid misses having the mumps," he said. But even so, there was just a touch of nostalgia as he looked back on those days.

JOHNSON

I have good feelings about it all. And I think it was expressed the best by a man who had been one of my strongest critics, Sam Engelhart. Sam had been in the administration of Governor John Patterson during the early 1960s, the days of the sit-ins and the freedom rides. He was a big man in the White Citizens Council. But one day when it was all over, when blacks could vote, when the "white only" signs were gone, when the schools were desegregated, when blacks worked beside whites in the halls of the State of Alabama, one day I met Sam Engelhart on the downtown streets of Montgomery. He called to me, "Hey, Judge. Judge Johnson, sir." I stopped and waited. And Sam says, "Judge, I just wanted you to know that you were right, and we were wrong." I stared at him. "I appreciate that," I said. And Sam nodded. He said, "Well, I didn't want to die without telling you that, Judge."

50

J OHNSON CONSIDERS HIMSELF a religious person; as a boy in Winston County, he was raised by parents who believed church on Sunday was an essential part of life.

JOHNSON

Religion with me is not demonstrative, but personal. Its basic precept is that I have the intelligence to determine right from wrong, and have the courage to accept the right and reject the wrong. There is no room for emotion in it, and this basic precept applies to everything I do and every decision I face.

I come from a region of the country where there are a lot of religious fundamentalists, a lot of "foot-washers." But I prefer to pray quietly in my own way. I have been asked if I have prayed before handing down a court decision. And the answer is no, I have not. I've never been a judge who says, "God, help me decide if I have jurisdiction in this case." I don't think God has time to be a judge or put shoes on a horse or draw plans for an architect. My idea is that if I did ask Him for help in a ruling, and there was a way for Him to respond, He'd probably say something like, "Why, man, you're the one drawing the judge's salary. You make the decision." I believe He gives us the ability and the wisdom to make decisions and choose right from wrong. In my earlier years I was a little more outward with my religious feelings and once Ruth and I attended a sacred harp concert [singing the notes instead of the words]. I was impressed with the way they were able to perform the songs. I got up and asked permission to lead the choir in a number. Granted permission, I took my place in front of them and led them in *Amazing Grace*.

By the mid-1980s there was a new concern in America about the activity of some church groups that not only espoused racists views, but mixed it with religion. But such a mixture must have been in existence for a long time, Johnson believed.

JOHNSON

I think it was manifested in the Deep South, and possibly all over America, by the song-singing, Bible-toting fundamentalists who were not willing to worship in a desegregated setting. And in order to enforce this refusal, you had in many of the larger, more "respectable" churches, including some Baptist and Methodist, male members who were posted at the entrances to see that blacks did not try to enter. That was a manifestation of a strong racial bias and it is not a great step from that practice to using religion to commend your social, political and economic views on people. It can be, and is, a bad mixture. It was wrong when John Brown did it, it's wrong when Jerry Falwell does it. It pits race against race, politics against politics, economic status against economic status, all in the name of religion.

Martin Luther King, Jr., was a religious man who used his beliefs as he led marches and demonstrations. King got up there and said, in effect, that he believed his cause was just, and therefore it was all right for him to violate some laws to make his point. That bothered me because it was the same thing the other side was saying. Wallace and Jim Clark and Bull Connor all felt their cause was just (that being to preserve "our way of life") and they felt they could bend or break some laws, too. I didn't buy either argument. To me, breaking the law is breaking the

law, whether you have a Bible in your hand or whether
you have a sheet over your head and burn a cross. There
is nothing in the Constitution that gives anyone a right to
violate a law. There is much in the Constitution that
prohibits the violation of the law.

I'm neither a segregationist nor an integrationist; I
simply apply the law to the facts. I have always felt that
blacks should have equal constitutional rights the same
as whites — or any other color. It is my belief that one of
the greatest hypocrisies of this country is in the segregation of churches. If people really believe in God and
believe what the Bible says about Him, then they could in
no way justify keeping a person out of their church
because of the color of his skin.

On the other hand, I have a different view on interracial marriage. My opinion is that such marriages are bad.
I feel that way because marriage is in some part designed
to produce children. But the feeling that prevails in this
country at this time, and for the foreseeable future, is that
children of a mixed marriage have a definite stigma by
reason of that and in many instances it develops into a
psychological impairment. I don't think people have that
right to deliberately do that to their offspring.

The United States is made up of many races and
ethnic backgrounds. Personally, I'm proud of my race.
Most responsible blacks are proud of their race and their
heritage. I'd like to see it maintained. There is no reason
under our government and our Constitution that it cannot be maintained with all being accorded their constitutional and legal rights.

But just because I believe that way personally does
not mean I would rule with disfavor in a case involving the
question of interracial marriage. For instance, if the state
of Alabama had a law that said blacks couldn't marry
whites and it came to my court, I'd have to see some
pretty convincing law to support the state's position. And
right now I don't know of any. In fact, I have ruled on one
case in which the police in one city picked up some
children and the only reason they did was because the

white woman who was their mother was married to a
black man. That wasn't enough reason to say they weren't
providing a proper home and I ruled against the city
police.

51

I T WAS SHORTLY AFTER the Supreme Court upheld the
bus boycott decision that white officials in Alabama began
taking precautions against the changes they felt certain
were coming. And, if the issue had not been so serious, these
efforts to deny voting rights for blacks would have been almost
comical.

In Tuskegee, for instance, where blacks made up roughly
eighty percent of the population, white leaders feared the day
when the Negro might sweep them from office. To avert that
situation, the Alabama Legislature in early 1957 passed a bill
that allowed Tuskegee to change its boundaries. At the time, the
shape of the city was roughly a square. After the change, the
town lines resembled an erector-set model of a sea horse, with
no less than twenty-eight sides. The new look affected not one of
the six hundred white voters but excluded all but ten of the four
hundred blacks who had been registered. (While blacks were
denied the right to vote across most of the Black Belt counties,
in the college town of Tuskegee their race had managed some
voting strength, although always kept a safe margin below the
number of white voters.)

To further ensure that a black political victory should not
occur in Macon County, the Legislature approved a referendum
for state voters which called for Macon County to be abolished
as a political entity. In December, 1957, it passed. But it was

never taken beyond that ludicrous step. Meanwhile, in the new city limits with twenty-eight sides, Dr. Charles Gomillion, chairman of Tuskegee Institute's division of social sciences, filed suit in Johnson's court, charging the city was gerrymandering the limits on racial grounds.

JOHNSON

I received the case and decided that the central issue was the right of the town to alter its boundaries. Volumes of cases over the years supported that right, and I ruled along those lines. The Fifth Circuit upheld, despite a marvelous dissent penned by Judge John Brown. He said that while he was hesitant to see federal judges do the work of state legislatures or local governments, there were exceptions, and Tuskegee was one of them.

The U.S. Supreme Court saw it his way and overturned, saying the Tuskegee case was clearly one of "fencing out Negro citizens."

JOHNSON

Scholars have asked me from time to time if, as a Southern judge, I could have made different decisions in those civil rights cases, and still have been within the law. I might have. I would have been on safe ground legally in both the bus boycott case and the Selma march case by ruling against the plaintiffs. But my posture in those matters wasn't the social change that loomed, but merely applying the law as it was intended to be applied. It meant bringing relief from unjust and illegal state laws for black people who couldn't ride in the front of the bus, who couldn't vote, and those children who could not attend public schools with white children.

And it wasn't enough to merely issue an opinion. You had to back it up with effective orders if it took that to bring the relief sought. There have been judges who have issued rulings and then sat back when those rulings were not obeyed. A judge should not do that; he should not sit back and throw up his hands and say, "Oh, well, I issued the opinion. That's all I can do." It means nothing if the wrong isn't corrected.. A judge cannot be a judicial abdicator. That is why, when I issued my orders in some of the civil rights cases, I made it clear that they were going to be backed . . . and backed effectively if necessary by the United States government.

If I had been a practicing lawyer in those times, I could have taken up the cause for or against blacks in those cases. I'm not a crusader, I've often said before. But if that Colvin girl or Rosa Parks had come to me back in those times, I would have been their advocate. That's a lawyer's job. I would have been in there arguing for their legal right to sit in the front of a bus. I would have battled for blacks to have voting rights and rights to sit at a lunch counter. But, by the same token, I might have represented Claude Henley, too. I might have been his advocate. But there is no doubt that, as a judge, I was sensitive to the plight of the black people in the South and some other areas in the United States. I was sensitive not only as a federal judge but also as a human being. They were in this area actually second-class citizens. They had been denied full rights for decade after decade. And when a few of them did manage to break out of the constraints of this southern society, and managed to earn a decent education and enough money to buy a house, they had to buy it in a segregated section. They were the underclass.

Now when blacks became voters, George Wallace began to change. He hired black secretaries and kissed black homecoming queens at colleges. But George really didn't change. The political situation changed and he reacted to it. Blacks could vote. As for me, even though I was sensitive to the injustices to blacks, I attempted to issue rulings without personal feelings.

I deliberately weighed things on merit and evidence, not my gut reaction. By 1984, I felt that blacks in education should have to compete with whites on an even keel. The time had come when there had to be one set of standards that would be fair to everyone, black or white. In no case that I had decided, had I ever compromised quality. I admit that past discrimination had a terrible impact on blacks and the children of those blacks who suffered from it, but sooner or later blacks must be able to compete on the same level as whites. By 1984 an entire generation of blacks had grown up in a desegregated school system and society.

The Civil Rights Movement lasted ten years, from 1955 to 1965. In terms of history, it was a short span in which a remarkable stride forward was made in the South by blacks. It began in Montgomery with the bus boycott; it ended with the Selma-to-Montgomery march. In the following years, Johnson was convinced the gains attained were not so much the result of boycotts and marches, but rather the product of court orders entered by federal judges. Of all those judges, he had been at the front.

JOHNSON

In Montgomery, the boycott did not bring an end to segregation on the buses. The court order Judges Rives and I entered did. If we hadn't ruled as we did, I'm certain blacks would still be boycotting and walking. The white power structure would never have yielded. The same thing could be said of voting rights; the Selma marches didn't bring them, court orders and the U.S. Congress did. As to my role, I would say the decisions stand and speak for themselves. I have never thought of myself as a trailblazer or one who sets landmarks. I merely followed the law. I applied the facts to the law and made a decision. I have a paperweight on my desk that serves as a source of inspiration from time to time. It is made of glass and inside are some words of Abraham Lincoln. The words say: "I do the very best I know how; the very best I can, and mean to keep doing so until the end. If the end brings me out all right, what is said against me won't amount to anything. If the end brings me out wrong, ten angels swearing I was right would make no difference." To me, what makes a good judge is intellectual honesty, which encompasses such things as being fair. It is measured in that way you decide a case, the time it takes to decide, and the manner in which you decide it.

I have a deep and abiding devotion to the American flag and what it stands for, much the same as I do for the Constitution. When I was sworn in as a federal district judge in 1955, there was a well-used American flag in the courtroom. It was one of those made of pure silk; it would probably now cost more than five-hundred dollars. Later, the flags were made of nylon and polyester and other such material. But I kept that original flag from my courtroom. It had forty-eight stars on it. In later years, about the early 1970s, the government furnished me a new one. I had the staff put it up in the courtroom, but I kept the original one. I kept it covered with paper and placed it folded over a clothes hanger in my office closet.

With it I have my original robe I got in 1955 when I was sworn in. Over the years it began to wear in places and I would patch it up, sometimes using black electrical tape to keep a tear or worn spot from showing. I kept that robe in the closet hanging beside my American flag.

Judge Johnson in his office in the Montgomery federal court house which now bears his name.

PENNY WEAVER

*In 1988, Ruth and Frank Johnson celebrated their
Fiftieth Wedding Anniversary.*

Afterword

When I go fishing I don't take the problems of the job with me, and I seldom contemplate deep legal issues when I'm out there. But I do think about things: I think about where the fish are biting the best; what kind of lure I should be using, and sometimes I wonder whether to have a can of pork and beans for lunch, red-rind cheese, or some vienna sausage. When I fish, I fish. I don't agonize over court cases. I sometime agonize over a bad catch and there have been times in the Gulf of Mexico when the big yellow flies that come from the swamps made the trip an agony. The flies would get on the boat when we were near shore and go with us. Bite the fire out of you. But one day out there about fifty or a hundred of them were on the boat and all of a sudden there came three or four big yellow-and-black bumble bees. You could stand and watch the bees grab the flies and carry them off. Before long all the flies were gone . . . the bees had run them off.

I think one of the most awesome sights I've ever beheld was one bright October afternoon when I was fishing with Pat Sims, a former law clerk, near the Chandeleur Islands off the Mississippi Coast. We had been there all day, in green Gulf water so shallow you could see the sea grass growing on the bottom. Suddenly I looked up and saw ducks and wild geese of every description and color, flying in formation, honking and squawking as they sailed above me, their wings rising and falling in a measured rhythm. There were hundreds of thousands of them that day; they covered the sky from horizon to horizon. I stopped fishing and stood there on the deck of the boat, just watching. It was a magnificent sight . . . .

Index

W
Wade, John 81
Walker, Wyatt T. 145
Wallace, George and
    Lurleen 57
Wallace, George C. 87–94,
    163, 189
  Judge Johnson's perceptions
    of 227
Wallace, Lurleen 181
Wallace, Mike 320
Ward, T.J. 5
Warren, Chief Justice
    Earl 302
Watkins, Levi 313
White, Byron 109
Whitesell, Calvin 112
Wilkins, Collie Leroy 240
Williams, Hosea 203
Williams, James (Ace) 131
Wisdom, Judge John 278
Wyatt v. Stickney xiv
Wyatt, Willie 170, 174

Y
Young, Andrew 153

Z
Zwerg, James 120, 136